Published Books
We Are More than Conquerors in the Mind of a Poet

Work Published in the Following Books:
Windows of Perception
The Lightness of Being
The Best Poems & Poets of 2001
A Sublime Remembrance
The Best Poems & Poets of 2002
Collecting Memories

Divine
Interventions

Henrietta Trotter

authorHOUSE®

AuthorHouse™
1663 Liberty Drive
Bloomington, IN 47403
www.authorhouse.com
Phone: 1-800-839-8640

First published by AuthorHouse 10/7/2010

ISBN: 978-1-4520-6815-2 (hc)
ISBN: 978-1-4520-6816-9 (sc)
ISBN: 978-1-4520-6817-6 (e)

Library of Congress Control Number: 2010912610

Printed in the United States of America

When I tell my life story it will be somewhere between hell and glory

"For it was not an enemy that reproached me: then I could have borne it; neither was it he that hated me that did magnify himself against me: then I would have hid myself from him. But it was thou, a man mine equal, my guide, and mine acquaintance" (Psalm 55:12–13)

Setting the Captives Free from Domestic Violence!

The Seventh Commandment (Broken Wedding Vows) Thou shalt not commit adultery

This Book Is Dedicated to
Bishop Clyde Harris, Sr.
Bishop Willie Basnight

Special Tribute
My Family
Rodolfo Trotter, Husband
My Children with Love
Virginia Britton, Sister

Henry Boston, Jr. (twin brother)
Born December **28**, 1953

In Loving Memory
Henry Boston, Sr.
March **28**, 1914–February **28**, 1988

Grace Britton Boston
November **28**, 1918–December **28**,1953

Contents

Preface

"Thou shalt not commit adultery." (Exodus 20:14) (The KJV is used throughout this book.)

This book tells about my quest for justice; chapter after chapter relates how I was attacked in different areas, but learned how to withstand the storm that comes without warning; this contributes to my success. The secret to Job's happy ending was not his struggle; we all struggle. It was his endurance. In some books before, some ministers accepted their calling; you never saw their history behind their deliverance, looking as if they were blessed with perfection out of their mother's womb. We all have a past that God has delivered us from. I have written my life story as an open book; it tells how the enemy tried to attack my marriage, my home, my job, and my children. As disasters and tragedy struck, God's voice interceded with divine protection way beyond any security system. His miracles showed how I was blessed supernaturally; only the hand of God could have given me the strength to overcome. I took my orders from the Master as He disarmed my enemies. Yes, I was born with a gift; throughout this book, you will gain more understanding about how God used me to comfort others and myself.

God's voice motivated me to write. When God spoke, I couldn't help myself; that's why I named this book *Divine Interventions*. The voice overwhelmed me and wouldn't let me rest. I would write in the middle of the night, riding down the street, in the shower, anywhere at any time. I felt compelled to rush and write what the voice instructed. If I disobeyed, I always lost the words since they were not my thoughts.

This book includes the breaking of the Seventh Commandment and setting the captives free from domestic violence. It is based on true and undisputed facts. According to abuse Web site statistics, 4 million American women experience a serious assault by a partner during an average twelve-month period! One out of three women around the world has been beaten, coerced into sex, or otherwise abused during her lifetime. Some estimates say almost 1 million incidents of violence occur against a current or former spouse, boyfriend, or girlfriend per year. 74 percent of all murder-suicides involved an intimate partner; of these, 96 percent were females killed by their intimate partners, and their stories were never told.

Remember what Jesus went through until the prophecy was fulfilled. Changing your thought process, you can reshape your destiny. I'm hoping to help others by reliving a tortured past. I went through hell but it didn't define who I was or what I would become. Afterwards, I went on a personal crusade against suffering from being hit by someone who had the keys to my heart and my home. I did not know when or how I would come under attack after the demonic spirits cast a spell of rage in my home, which became a prison with no bars. Our forefathers founded this country with the right to speak freely, and they fought and died for religious freedom. I love this great country; promise me you will never allow the enemy to bring down our religious rights with the twisted illusion that somehow love is based on hating others and bringing them down. If we get rid of religion then the ships need to sail back to England with the devils on them.

Everybody has a story; the difference in my story is, between every line, pain began talking and deliverance took form. At the end of the day, it gives God the Glory. Even if you never believed in God, by the time you get to the final chapter, you will ask how did I escape while still keeping my right mind? I started writing just weeks after my brutal attack on October 20, 1991, but when

I came to myself and got it together to write, my writings looked like those of a mad man; I couldn't understand anything that was written, the handwriting was clearly that of a disrupted and battered woman. Years later the land of milk and honey unfolded. This book introduces God's power and favor as it reveals His Glory! It confirms the promises made to Abraham that the seed would be blessed.

I spent ten years overseas as a military wife, where most of the attacks took place; there were no news reports or TV coverage of what happened. All my tragedies went unnoticed. I was alone with no family; my ex even had me committed to the hospital overnight after I almost had a nervous breakdown. I was able to tell my side of the story to a doctor and he set me free the next day. When I returned to the United States, I was brutally attacked and almost lost my life at the hands of my ex's new lover. Yes, it's my season; I'm ready to reveal and uncover the full details I almost took to my grave. It was like a slow death living in violence, it was so embarrassing and humiliating. It is an undesirable pain only a victim can tell.

Most people think of a victim as being a certain race or from a certain financial background. I was at a GS-7 level, a well-respected manager overseas, and an account manager at a well-known bank as well. My children's father held prestigious jobs and was well respected among his peers at work; however, he hid a dark secret from others. You see, many victims endure the pain to keep their homes together and to support their children. My story confirms what the news media says: Domestic violence has no status; it attacks any home, at any time, without warning. It divided and destroyed my family.

I have tried to bring some closure to past hurts and learned how to let go. You will read about my struggle and how I wanted to give up, until I witnessed tears in the eyes of some of my fans. They told me how they had to endure when others had given up on them. Just like me, many of you have a story. Your stories motivate me to keep writing. I will always be sympathetic to your fight for survival. This book doesn't praise the weapons used against me but glorifies the fact the weapons never prospered! His divine power intervened and rescued me and restored my blessings; it regenerated my spirit and gave me more than I had.

My therapist said in order to live with myself, after each attack I would blank out the details in my mind as too horrifying and devastating to remember. I endured the suffering and pain that an average woman could not bear or comprehend. Years ago there was no support system for victims like me. Once a police officer came by after I called him. He then saw my legs and arms all bruised up, and he saw my ex at a distance, after he had just taken the keys to my new sports car and drove fast around the corner past him as he stood at the door; he asked, "Why do you stay?"

At the time, I couldn't answer; however, years later, I'm writing about it. My situation escalated when I was away from my family; I was attacked in a foreign country and was put through unimaginable situations that were almost too painful for me to even write about; for years, I would not talk about them. The enemy thought I would turn my back on God, which I almost did, but instead my spirit connected closer to His Divine spirit, which empowered me to go on in my darkest hours when I was attacked.

My past allowed me to press on to the mark of a higher calling! God anointed and empowered me as a servant; man licensed me to preach. I realize now I was chosen to go through to see His Glory after overcoming adversity. When I first undertook this mission, I was reminded God gave His first instructions to women at the tomb. God decided to use a wounded, hurt, abused soldier like me to become a warrior for justice. He ordered my footsteps for an assignment that was much greater than myself; if I had it my way, I would have said, "No way, I'm not going to tell the world of my failure." On my journey through life instead of losing my mind, I learned to trust in God and His delivering power.

If walls could talk, they would reveal there is an unseen guest with us at all times that sees all our pain. At times, I was blessed and didn't know it until it was revealed years later. He was a lawyer in the courtroom, a doctor in the hospital; this book will reveal such power! There were times I questioned why God allowed the enemy to attack me so violently and with so much force! I was given a warrior's mentality not to be defeated. I believe some things were preordained so I could tell others how I was delivered! God's voice gave me divine instructions to write each line and chapter of this book. After reading this book, you will see how God used me for His Glory. He gave me a sound mind and empowered me to go into the enemy's camp and take back what was mine. "When I tell my life story, it would be somewhere between hell and Glory." The enemy received his eviction notice after he tried to curse my entire family. Yes, God shut him down; this book focuses more on the deliverance not just the attacks. I became the Christian the devil was warned about, after God intervened time after time on my behalf.

God's gift to me was giving me *Divine Interventions* to disarm Satan of all of the tools. This gift allowed me to outthink and overthrow my enemies with wisdom and knowledge. When I was positioned in the right place to take full control of the attack, I defeated my adversaries. Most books tell you how to go into the enemy's camp but leave out what to do once you get there. Your enemy secretly plots and schemes to destroy you. Make their attempts null and void when you overpower their next move. Everyone wants a bailout. You must have the power to bail yourself out. If your enemy wants to destroy you, don't make it easy for them. *Divine Interventions* allows you to study the essential quality, the nature of the beast. You get defeated after your enemy judges your reaction to their attacks; they just laugh, thinking you are easy prey. They win by just saying and doing the same things over and over again to upset you and getting the same reaction; they have studied your every movement and know just what button to push to get your attention. They push the same button when they return to shut you up; they make you feel it's your fault they left and you should be grateful they returned.

Sound familiar? If you know it upsets you, why not get a

different approach, a counterattack, and be ready the next time by not allowing evil words to come out of your mouth, which gives them a reason to treat you bad and blame their behavior on you. When faced with a life-threatening and dangerous situation, have a plan; don't just lie there, you must put your war clothes on and declare war! You can have power; however, if you perceive yourself to be weak, you will be. You win if you begin to act totally different than what is expected. The enemy should never know your next move; your thoughts are your secret weapon. Another one of my fans asked me at a book signing, "How could you have been so strong?" I told her one-day I made up my mind after hearing God's voice clearly saying to me, "Never give in to a lesser power!" From that day until now, while going through darkness, I began to have tunnel vision.

My father-in-law, whom I respected very dearly, said, "You control life; never let life control you." Since birth, God's voice has guided me to safety and gave me a way of escape. Doors that seemed to be closed for others, I could walk through easily. In situations the enemy tried to curse, God made them my footstools. He revealed His Glory while I was in bondage, and all chains of captivity began to fall off. I even saw the chains fall off my brother's legs while he was still a juvenile after he was falsely accused.

The devil is supposed to tremble when he sees you, not when you see him; always know the joy of the Lord is your strength! In my book, defeat is not an option! My life crusade is being an activist for nonviolence. For years, my own family didn't know I was a victim until I returned to the United States. My enemies were sent to destroy me. After longsuffering I realized the enemy mission was to rob me of my inheritance. I was a captive; I was fed lies and lived in denial. Unfortunately, I had to go through the fire before I could encourage you. In my weakest moment, I still gathered strength. Yes, after reading my survival story, I'm hoping it will make a difference in your life. Yes, there is a story behind my Glory. I had to take a stand; I could no longer stay silent anymore!

Hupernikao (Greek for "Super Victorious")

About the Author

In 2001, I began my ministry and published my first book with a company called Watermark Press; in 2003, another company began publishing my writings. My books are on all major Web sites, bookstores, and libraries. My work has attracted media attention from newspapers. For years I've had TV commercials on the *Lifetime for Women* network. I'm proud of my nursing homes and radio ministry as well. After I accepted my calling, I began sharing the lost and hidden pages of the chapters of my life experiences with you. Three years ago, after signing the contract for *Divine Intervention*, I chose to abandon my assignment until now. I just couldn't write about the tragic events, which were too painful to remember. I refused to write again; I chose to just forget and go on with my life, until I saw Chris Brown on *Larry King Live* saying he didn't mean to hurt his girlfriend, saying there weren't any books out there to help him. I thought he was talking to me; I remembered this book *Divine Intervention*. God dealt with me; there are many books, but the one he needed I had publishing rights to but had abandoned the assignment; a voice came to me just like Moses: "You must tell the enemy to let my people go!" When an abused victim says you just don't know what I've been through, I can say with clarity, "Yes, I do!" I admit some of my downfall was bad choices. Studies have showed every fifteen minutes, someone somewhere is a victim of abuse. The cries reminded me of my promise to serve God. I began to write day and night on my way to work early in the morning and in the midnight hours.

I'm trying to stop the stereotyping of what an abuse victim looks like. I'm writing for the ones who were like me, focusing more on their image, too ashamed to come forward. I worked every day for thirty-four years, nonstop, except for vacations. As a manager both in Germany and the United States, I wore fine suits and dresses; I became a professional woman at her best. In today's world, the face of a battered woman might surprise you. Unfortunately at that time, if I was asked, I would not have been able to appear on TV or magazines covers, or photo shoots, right after any attacks because both my eyes were blackened, my legs and arms swollen to the size of two on different occasions, my face damaged from cups and glass plates that were thrown at my head, I was punched in the chest and head, sometimes with his fist, sometimes with objects, he cut and tore my clothes (some he took with him so I would have nothing to wear). I finally decided enough was enough; I will never underplay what happens to someone else. Abuse is abuse; however, I'm just saying the "Face of a Battered Woman" would not be available for interviews. Did I seek police protection? Yes. Did I seek help from a therapist? Yes. Is there evidence, pictures in court, and hospital records? Yes. Did I get restraining orders? Yes. This tell-all book gives victims of domestic violence a glimmer of hope and brings the devil and his imps to open shame.

Rite, Write, Right!
C. Boston

I write and cry.
I cry and write and
I write till the ink runs out,
Change pens
Change color and I'm writing again
When I don't write I become confused
because it's too many,
Way too many thoughts to be diffused
But as I start to do that dance the
pen and my fingers love
It's the legible tango and
My heartbeat is the tempo
The rhythm is my music
Like deaf Beethoven's was
As I write I start to hear my thoughts to song
And the pages are clear
My thought processes prioritizes and then away go my fears
Thank you for finger, eyes, and ears
Thank you, for patience learned over the years
Write, little child
Write!
Write yourself from wrong
Write yourself strong
Write through your pain
Through your disdain
Write for justice, your truth, and your life
Write yourself from struggle
Write yourself high

Write till you get where you need to be
To dispel the curses of the less seeking
You are the light you are above
Never take for granted for which you have advantage
Rite, Write, Right!

Teardrop Falling from Eyes

C. Kim Horold

I felt a teardrop falling from my eyes, as I
looked back on the events of my Life.
The wasted time and efforts I had made
seemed so far and yet so near.
My heart still aches from the hurt it had to endure,
and it will get better of that I am sure.
To start anew at the time I should be able to look
back at a life almost fulfilled, instead I look back
at a life of wrong choices I have made.
I am asking in this sphere is there what we
call the good life waiting out here?
Did I miss it? Did I not see? Was I so wrong
to trust in thee, the human being?

I realize it does not matter now; I need to
start over and with the grace of God
I will know how!
I am convinced in what I know now and I really can see,
it may still hurt and God will take the hurt from me.
The faith in God I most certainly will keep, because mankind will
hurt you and like a sharp knife it will cut you oh so very deep.
My heart still cries, though not for long, because God took
the reins and His will be done. Yes, I will learn and go beyond
and God will watch and His deeds be done. As He prepares
for me to take the next step, I will walk tall and straight as
an arrow on the road of God's will, which is so very narrow!
His light will engulf me and make me shine
to be an example to all mankind.

Chapter 1

Death Angel Took My Mother

1953–1958
"Early Years"

Life began for me on December 28, 1953. Life ended for my mother on that same day. On that day, divine intervention first took form, saving my life for the first time—but not the last. This was my first encounter with Divine intervention. I always felt alone since I had no mother to raise me. My twin and I stayed in the hospital months after the birth until a decision was made what to do with us. It was years later before we met any family from either side and knew who they were. We were born on the twenty-eighth of December. It was something about that day I always knew was a blessing to me, or a curse! No one could ever explain to me how both my mother and father were born on the twenty-eighth and they both passed away on the twenty-eighth (in different years). Signs and wonders, or mere coincidence, mere encounters?

When I was sixteen, my father talked about my mother's death to me in his living room in Norfolk, Virginia. Before then he never spoke of it, and I never asked again since it was so painful for him to talk about. (He was a man of few words unless he got angry.) Whenever my father told the story, tears always filled his eyes as he struggled to hold back his emotions; it seemed to me like nothing but sorrow as his wife—my mother—died the same day I was born. My dad said tragedy struck and life for him ended that day. He said they always wanted another child, since they had waited five years to have children. My father said my mom did see us that day for only a few minutes since she was very ill; she was happy to hold her twins in her arms, and my dad was a proud father. My mother was alive when my father brought my sister to the hospital to see my mom. My sister got her wish when she saw us, she had asked for a sister or brother and she got both; she was so excited. At the time, my sister was eleven years old. After my one and only sister Virginia combed my mom's hair, Dad took her home and she never saw her alive again. Upon my father's return with my mom's nightgown in his arms, what seemed all so right went so wrong. The doctor had my mom's wedding rings in his hands with the bad news.

My dad said later that day he went to pick up some things that Mother had requested, not knowing that would be the last time he would see her again. He recalled a stormy day; he would never forget walking into the hospital room and seeing the doctor walk toward him; he could hear the thunder and lightning as the doctor approached him. He said the doctor held out his hand, which held my mother's wedding ring. My father said a sense of coldness and stillness came over his body; as the thunder sounded louder, he looked up at the doctor and said, "You don't have to say a word, she never took off her wedding rings; she must be gone."

The doctor told my father she had hemorrhaged inside and they couldn't stop the bleeding. That day the grace of God and divine intervention saved Henry, my twin brother, and me in the delivery room; it was all because of His Glory that we survived. What a high price to pay. I had to carry the guilt, knowing it was because of us that a loved one was taken away, to bring us into this world. In that short time, the lives of my father and my sister were turned upside down; their lives were never the same.

My story reminded me of the story of Jabez in the Bible, how he was born in pain. It was somewhat of a sign of amazement how my grandmother, who I never met, named my mother Grace, and peace came over me as I quietly thought to myself, *Mercy took over as God showed His Grace over my life time and time again*. It was all I had to hold on to, since all our grandparents on both sides of the family had passed away before we were born, and I've never seen a picture of them. Twelve years later, I saw a picture of my mom when we found our sister again. After my brother and I were born, our father was too grief-stricken and overworked to care for us, so he paid a lady from the church to take care of us.

My mother's oldest brother took my sister away from my father, and my father said he was too upset at the time to fight him. But he vowed to keep Henry and I together when his sisters wanted to separate us; that's why two ladies (women of God) raised us. In later years, my sister Virginia told me that a neighbor told her of my mother's death before my dad arrived back from the hospital; to this day, it bothers her. That's why I said what seemed so right went so wrong. My sister then said at birth, I was born with a veil over my face to have visions and dreams.

During the months we stayed in the hospital, my father had to work but always dropped by the hospital to see us. I was told a nurse took us to North Carolina to live with her distant cousin. We called her Momma Carry; that's all I know about the connection. I could remember a man who looked like he was white (I later discovered he was mixed but looked white) coming from Virginia to see us on the weekends before we were five years old. He would take pictures with us; I have them hanging on my bedroom wall. He drove a pretty black shiny car; one thing I always remembered, he always had a suit on, and his car was always shiny, and he always had something good to eat with him up until we were grown: a bag of apples, a bag of oranges, and some strawberry ice cream. I guess I always knew he was my father; it's just that from birth to five years old, it just didn't click since we only saw him on weekends because he had to travel so far to see us. My father always delivered food and gifts.

My second encounter with divine intervention, I was playing a game of hide and seek, and my cousin hid me in an old icebox and closed the door. I couldn't open it from the inside at age five; it really frightened me, until my twin brother found me. He had gotten upset because he didn't see me; we are still close today.

My brother would get in many fights to protect me. When I wasn't playing with my brother, I was a one-girl show, reading the Bible to the group of children who were circling around me to hear me speak by the time I was four years old. I will always remember a little girl saying, "One day you will be a great preacher." It was not until after 2001 that I accepted my calling.

My dad took us from the hospital to live in North Carolina from five months to five years old. My father lived in Virginia; he had moved there after fighting in World War II; he really looked good in his uniform from the pictures I have of him. That well-dressed visitor with that shiny car was my dad; he brought us a white goat as a pet. We loved and played with that goat until one day, I was riding my small bike around the clothesline, and I began to scream at the top of my voice. Everyone came running, saying, "What's wrong? What's wrong?"

It was a while before I could talk. When I finally got my voice, I said, "Who killed my goat and hung the skin on the clothesline to dry?" My brother was more upset than me. When my father came down from Virginia, they told him what had happened and asked him to take the meat with him since I was so upset and would not let anyone eat it. The husband of the lady who kept us in North Carolina butchered the goat. What I saw was the entire goatskin hanging on the line with clothespins. It frightened me; however, that's what some country people did in those days. My father then brought my brother a small black goat; we played with it until he ran away. My sister told me in later years the goat was not bought as a pet; I just made it my pet like someone would have a dog; that's why I got so upset.

I also remember we had to go to out-houses with no electricity; we had to use lanterns. I was always afraid, so I would go to bed early and sleep all night. Now that I think about it, my beginnings represented who I was, because all through life I never really faced darkness. Somehow I could find a hiding place. Back in the fifties, life was hard for everyone; I was living in the country, all I saw were old houses with no running water, bathrooms were known as outhouses, we had to raise animals for food and grow vegetables. If you wanted milk, you had to milk the cow yourself. (There was no government assistance in the sixties.) My dad was a very proud man, and he didn't ask for or take anything from anybody. He just could not work and keep us in Virginia at the same time, so he would only come on weekends; he had a government job in Virginia.

One day, the nice man didn't come by anymore. I know my readers are saying, "Why do you keep acting like he was a stranger?" Just for a moment, you have to put yourself in my shoes: age four, no mom, no real family (didn't meet them until years later). The nurse and her husband were old, and all they did was feed us and put us to bed; no one talked to us about anything, living a sheltered life. I was young; all I knew was he was a nice man who came to see us, stayed a few hours, and left to go back to Virginia, but when I realized he was my dad, I kept wondering, where was my dad? I hadn't seen him in a while. I was told he had a bad car accident while he was driving alone from Virginia to North Carolina. I cried so much that they had to drive me to Virginia, where he was. When I saw him, I cried even more; he was in a cast from his head to his stomach and had to eat out of a straw. I still have the pictures, which I will always keep to remind me how God brought him out! For months he stayed in that cast. It was heartbreaking to see the only one who seemed as if they really cared in that condition; it was just too much for me to bear at that time. It would be months before I saw him again. I found out later, Momma Carry said she could not take me again until he got well, since I acted up so badly. When he got better, he came down the same as before. Since we had not seen his side of the family, yet he began making plans.

Before we were five, my father got into two car accidents coming to see us. My brother and I were with him in the second accident; a kind man rescued us. It was a Sunday afternoon, about a year later; my mother's brother, who I rarely saw, told him not to drive home; it was raining too hard. My dad took off with us to Virginia to see his sister, driving like the speed of lightning in that pretty black car. The car turned upside down; we were four years old. The reason I will always remember was my brother and myself were on our knees, looking up at the sky, singing; we were very happy that we finally got to leave the country and go to the city for a while with that man in that shiny black car, but in a matter of minutes it went from the blue sky to the green grass in the air, upside down in a ditch. The cars were made out of steel back in the day. As we lay there upside down, I began to scream. A man came by on that dark, lonely road and pulled us out. I remember how he took us to his house; my pretty pink dress had blood all over it, and my brother was a mess also. The man and his wife washed us up and gave us some of his children's clothes and something to eat; they even drove my dad back to Virginia, where we saw our Aunt Dell for the first time. My dad then gave him some money and thanked him, because he was a stranger who came out of nowhere to help us; we never saw him again. Another escape from the brush of death: my third divine intervention.

In this book, you will see many more. After that day, I could see the worry on my dad's face; he wasn't happy after two near-fatal accidents, having to drive so far (two hours every weekend) just to see his children. He had sisters and brothers but they wanted to separate us, and Dad told me he had promised himself he would never separate us, no matter what. Months later I met the lady who raised my brother and myself from five years to sixteen years. It would be years later before we met the rest of Dad's family; my brother and I stayed together until we grew up. My dad and me might have been living in different houses but our hearts had the same beat. Thanks to my loving father, who was always there for us. After he fought in World War II as a military policeman, he returned to Virginia to live. He was a hard worker who retired at the naval base after forty years of working for the government. Yes, he was my hero.

Henrietta Trotter

Chapter 2

Trying to Fit In

1959–1970

"Moving to the City"

When we were five years old, we moved to the city, where we met the lady who raised us to the age of sixteen years old. She was a kind, soft-spoken lady who had one common goal: to raise us in a Christian home. She was no blood kin to us; however, we loved her just the same.

One day, Dad noticed a pretty lady standing at the bus stop in front of his house. He had admired her from afar for sometime but never had the right opportunity to talk to her. Dad was a gentleman and always respected a lady. It was raining hard; he gave her a ride home; she had just gotten off from work; she worked at the high school not far from our house. They became lifetime friends. Now that I think about it, the Bible mentions the later rain, meaning the next rain would be better than the first; my father was a farmer before he went into the military; that's where he got his grass roots of wisdom. I learned early in life some divine principles that guided my footsteps on a journey to the unknown. If you plant your seed in moist and fertile ground, the harvest will be great!

The lady, who would later be my foster mother, was named Ms. Evelyn; she said I could call her Ms. Evelyna, which I did. Now that I look back, we had moved several times around the world and back, and my son PJ graduated from Booker T. Washington, which was the same high school where the lady who made a great impact on my life worked before my dad asked her to quit her job forever and raise his children. Is that divine intervention a sign or what? Meeting her was my fourth divine intervention. She was the best example of a Christian woman I've ever known; my dad and she had one common goal and purpose: to raise us in a Christian home. After dedicating herself to helping us, she later married one of the deacons in our church. I always told other people if there was an angel, she was one.

Just like in the Bible how David admired a lady from afar, that was how my dad met Ms. Evelyn. We moved to Virginia, which was the foundation of living in a Christian home. Dad only lived down the street but he wanted us to go to school and church, and live at Ms. Evelyn's house; he felt it was better for us since his sisters—Aunt Dell, Aunt Mary, and Aunt Adel—wanted to separate us; they also had other issues (our color was one of them); we stayed with him on the weekends and his off days; he visited us whenever he could. Separate houses, loving heart. He told me because of religious reasons; he didn't want to live with a woman if he wasn't married to her because he respected her that much. That's why he paid for live-in day care at someone else's home.

I never met my birth mother but others said I looked just like her; she was the kindest lady they ever knew; even some of my bad cousins had good things to say about my mom, and God blessed me to have a foster mom who fit in her shoes.

Divine intervention has always been present in my life, as this book composes stories of God's vast miracles and grace.

We met my dad's entire family for the first time on a summer vacation, while I was still living with my foster mother, visiting my country cousins on my dad's side in Plymouth, North Carolina, the ones with the color issues. One of my girl cousins was upset with me for no reason at all; she told me to stay outside of the store. That day it was hot, and I had gotten weary from standing outside the store, all alone in a strange town. I began to call her by name loudly from the outside. She said, "Now those boys know I have black in my family."

Moments later, after coming out of the store, the same cousin and her two sisters were running with me on a hill that they were very familiar with; they knew it had gaps in the middle; as I ran behind them, just as planned, my foot fell into one of the gaps. The miracle of the day: there was a small tree just at the top of the hole; a voice said, "Grab it fast"; when I looked down, the hill was as tall as a building.

I cried out for my cousins; they kept running. But one of them, who walked with a limp, came back and pulled me up: my fifth encounter with divine intervention at an early age. As soon as I returned, I told my aunt (my dad's sister), and it was years before the girls got along with me again; however, my boy cousins and I have always gotten along. To the boys, I was just their cousin; they saw no color. This chapter is the only time I speak of them. I know it was God's angels that kept me from falling down the center that hill.

A Doctor in the Hospital Protected Me Against Mental Abuse

When I was in the third grade, the enemy tried to attack my body. I began to have seizures, and at one point, I could not walk and was in the hospital for six months. I had six doctors and one specialist. At times, I would black out and find myself looking at a bright light that the doctor would use in order to bring me out of the semi-coma. Yes, God was a doctor in the hospital because God delivered me. The reason I know it was God was because the doctor told my daddy I would never live to grow up or have children. At that same age, I would recall I was different from the other children, seeing visions. I could dream and all my dreams came true; God's voice could tell me things, and it would always bring me to safety.

One of my classmates, after seeing my dad come to school for me, said, "Who is that white man that's coming to our school?" I hid under my desk so no one would find me; I hid until he left my classroom, after I got home, he asked me where I was when he came. I said, "I was there, you just didn't see me." In time I tried to get over the difference. I just didn't want to deal with the mental abuse and be rejected by my classmates because my dad's skin color wasn't the same as mine.

When I was in the third grade, until my brother stood up for me, my dad's sisters began showing signs of physical abuse; at first, I just thought they were just mean. One day when my dad wasn't home and I was visiting, my dad's sister hit me in the face with a rolled-up newspaper and knocked my glasses off for no reason. At that point, my brother starched her in the face and got in trouble, later in the year I wanted to put on some makeup; I was only around eight years old, and she smacked me in the face, again. Another time she saw me put some of her makeup on; she said I was too dark to wear her makeup (it was made for lighter skin color). What she said was right; it did make me look like a ghost, but it was not what she said, it was the way she said it (mental abuse).

Years later, after I divorced my children's father and first met my husband Trotter, I took him to meet my aunt in her nursing home; he said, "Your aunt isn't in that lobby with all the others; they are all white." I smiled and pointed to my Aunt Dell and said, "That's my aunt; my dad's sister." My family and I went to see her regularly to take her out to dinner and take her to my home on holidays until she passed at age ninety.

Since she never had any children, my daughter and I buried her after she passed away. She was family, and love don't hate. I met one of my dad's brothers; he would come over sometimes to see my dad and his sister; when Dad wasn't home, he would bring his monkey on his shoulders; he liked to play a flute and joke; he knew my brother and I were afraid of that monkey, and he would let it go just to frighten us. The monkey never caught us because we would run around the room or upstairs or under something; it was years later when I realized his brothers and sister showed signs of abuse. They only tried to scare my brother and me; they never bothered my cousins; I guess because my cousins were as mean as they were. They just liked for you to be afraid of them.

Henrietta Trotter

That next year at a family gathering in North Carolina, I put another aunt's coat on, and in front of everyone, she smacked me in the face. They were all mixed but some passed for white until they died; I understood prejudice because I took my mother's color, but in the same family, that was hard. It was bad enough my mother passed away while we were so young; family rejection was just too much. I wanted everyone to like me, so I never told, but that time the abuse just wasn't fair. I told my dad; he said if they couldn't accept his children, they couldn't accept him, and he would never come around them again. At that point they began to start treating us better. I learned early in life about discrimination, and there are good and bad in this world. I didn't have to see it on TV; I lived it.

My father tried to explain it to me one day. He said one time after coming home from the war, he went into a white rest room; some people knew he was mixed and some didn't, but one man noticed and told him to get out. He said, "I told them I just fought for my country and I have a right to use any rest room I wanted to"; he stayed until he felt like coming out. I had cousins that did pass for white; one of them lived in another country, and all of his friends were surprised when they found out after he passed away he had black in his family; my cousins took care of the funeral expenses, because they said he was still their brother. Now that I'm grown I feel the same; they are still my family and I love them very much (I forgave them because back in the day, they did what they had to do to get good jobs) and I understand. Since I took my color from my mother and my personality from my father, my foster mom, when she got upset with me, would always say, "That's Boston's child!"

In my first book I wrote a poem called "Crossing the Color Line" that was published in my local newspaper. The overall message of the poem was judging; when I spoke of grace, I wrote my story goes deeper than the color of my face. I also added, "Did you judge me on what it took to get to the top or did you look at my color and stop?"

The lady who raised me had other children; I got along with

them all except her daughter Brenda, who was three years older than me; today we get along fine. There were some issues when we were young. I didn't do anything wrong; I think that's why she didn't like me; she was always getting into trouble, and I was very close to her mom, and since I was no kin to them, she felt that I needed to stay in my place (a motherless child). At times I was just like any other small girl; I would rebel, but her mom would always put me in my place. Somehow my foster sister and me just couldn't make it as sisters. It seemed she hated me the more her brother and sisters liked me. I always knew deep down inside she cared, but she was the baby in the family, and I came along and took her place, and she just wasn't having that! When I was around eleven years old, I bought her mom a plate that had "Happy Mother's Day" on it. Ms. Evelyn was so happy, since I never called her Mother. What did I do that for, because it was on now. When Ms. Evelyn wasn't home, in front of all the other children, Brenda told me to get out of her mother's house. My father made sure that never happened again with the threat of us never returning again.

However, we got into another confrontation; this time it was physical. I got tired of her picking on me. I can't remember the reason for the fistfight; I just know we went from one side of the house to the other, breaking things and knocking everything off the walls. I was getting the best of her until she began pulling my hair, and they stopped the fight; for the life of me I don't know why no one stopped it sooner; they just watched and laughed. When it was all over, I went across the street and asked Ms. Evelyn why didn't she come home and stop the fight. She said we had been at each other for a while, and we needed to fight to get it all out. I told her if she had fought fair, I would have won. It worked, because that was the last time we got angry at each other.

Ms. Evelyn's sister told me a chilling story; she said Ms. Evelyn's husband, whom I never met, was very abusive. Her sister was very religious also; I never saw either one of them with a man; their husbands had died. She saw her brother-in-law pick up a chair, and it was coming down on her sister's head; she said she knew he was stronger than her; all she could do was pray as hard as she could. He fell and they had to take him to the hospital, and later on, he died from a heart attack in his hospital bed. It reminded me of the verse, "Touch not my anointed." Now that I think about it for the first time since her death, I believe God interceded on my foster mother's behalf to protect her from a violent attack. I had hid the thoughts in the back of my mind. Bringing up the past was too painful for me to remember, so I simply chose to forget.

We had the best of both worlds: the projects and the nice neighborhoods; my father had to work; he had a house, two government checks, and retired from the government after forty years. To outsiders we had it all but not having a birth mother was very hard, and what made it harder was all our grandparents had passed away before we were born. We didn't have a relationship with our blood family until age six; if my father hadn't brought us to them, I guess we would have never met them; even after we met, only one of his sisters, who was a preacher, ever came to visit us from the country. My sister and I are very close; however, we didn't have a real relationship until age twelve because our uncle and his wife took her after Mom's death. My dad said he didn't feel like fighting them; he just need to find someone to keep us.

Ms. Evelyn, our foster mom, lived in housing, and my dad lived in a house, but we liked housing better; all the people were very friendly like family. Dad lived in front of a college, and we hated it; the neighbors were cold, stayed to themselves, and were stuck up, but there were a few that talked to us, and the children of that neighborhood grew up to become attorneys and judges and doctors. When I was small, my best friend and her brother lived on the same street; he became an attorney also. The family that was kind enough to raise my brother and I grew up successful as well; they all grew up to have nice homes and completed college; one of my foster cousins even owns a school in North Carolina.

I guess the reason we had better times in the housing was we could be ourselves: walk around, singing out loud, just having fun.

That helped me in my management career; I believe that's why I was so successful, no matter how they tried, the enemy could never touch the jobs God gave me because "what He blessed, no man can curse"; rich or poor, I could get along with all kinds of people, because I came from and grew up with all backgrounds. God allowed my brother and I to experience the best of both worlds; to gain a relationship with people of all backgrounds is divine intervention. What some perceive to be poor, we were rich in spirit and knowledge. News reporters could only wish they had a story to share how children of underprivileged and children of plenty, middle class and upper class, connected in thoughts with real life experiences.

This intervention is a little different; it shows how a school counselor intervened and allowed me to get my wish of not standing out in my shy world of independence. I was still in high school, trying to find myself in a world I saw as bad, but my church roots said to find some good in it. Once I was student of the month; I was on the honor roll, and I got upset because the school counselor put my picture up on the wall. I asked him to take it down! The counselor said he had many children ask him to put their picture up to honor them, but never had anyone ask him to take it down. As a teenager, I never wanted to stand out. Now that I think about it, some things don't change; this is the first book I have written with my picture on the front cover.

Yes, the overall focus of this book is marriage and domestic abuse; however, it was very important to me that my readers understand that my childhood was a mixture of being hurt and being treated wrongly and how I was easily deceived. Those who have always had a mother to guide and lead them might not understand my desperate attempts to fit in. Misuse of trust and cruel treatment were the ingredients that led up to me accepting abuse at a later age, as evil behavior appeared normal to me, since my youth was a combination of many uncertainties.

When I was fifteen years old, I met my children's father on a blind date. When I first met him, he seemed nice and very sure of himself. The night I was to meet him, my dad came over to get me and my twin brother; that's what he always did: he never called, he would just show up and say let's go. We would let Ms. Evelyn know and jump in the car. You would just have to know my dad to understand. He was a man of a few words; when he spoke, you just didn't question him; he never hit me, that was Ms. Evelyn's job, not his; that's why we always had fun with him at his house; he let us do whatever we wanted to do.

When I got back from visiting my dad, they told me this boy came by to meet me and I wasn't home; I was fifteen and had bad experiences with other dates, and I really wasn't that interested at that time. Every time he came by, I wasn't there; one of the boys in our housing area had given him a picture of me, but he didn't want to meet my friends, just me. I agreed to meet him and made sure I did not go to my dad's house that time. He was my first real boyfriend, and I wasn't thinking about boys much before the blind date, because the friends I spoke to only wanted one thing that I wasn't willing to give them. However, I was getting older and boys began to start taking notice of me; I didn't have time for him at first. He was very handsome; he was only fifteen years old and very smart; he seemed to know everything; that impressed me; he was also a smooth talker. We spent hour's sitting on that porch, and it seemed like minutes. It seemed time had stopped. I guess you can say love is blind. I liked him the first time I saw him; I tried to play hard to get since he acted like he was so sure of himself. Ms. Evelyn called me to come in the house; before I went in, he asked if I would see him again. I said, "Maybe."

One night, my husband-to-be told me he had to go to the hospital because his sister Addie was having a baby; we had been dating for two years, and that was his first lie, because my cousin Tina told me she saw him at the skating rink, and my future nephew was born months later. Tina said he was so surprised she saw him with another girl, he then asked her for a ride in the same car with them to bring him home. Tina got a kick out of it; that's why she asked me if I was with him that night before she began to laugh (that was divine intervention), telling me to stay away and he was a cheater! But I blamed myself because after two years,

I had never slept with him; I thought I brought it on myself. It was divine intervention that I found out his secret. Yes, I'm glad I found out but I felt trapped because at that time, we had developed a relationship that had a bond that mistrust couldn't stop. Just because I had never slept with him (or anyone else at that time), I felt I had given him what others couldn't: my heart and all my inner thoughts. I believed I could have somehow changed him once I made a total commitment with him, which was my decision to stay in the relationship, the challenge to prevail against the odds. It later proved to be a mistake to stay, but at the moment, it all seemed right. I was only sixteen years old.

I can also remember when I was in high school, I was very good at English and math; I would get As and Bs. I would think to myself, why was I so good at those subjects and liked those the best? I would get good grades in the others also but I had a passion for those subjects. After all these years, I now know that English helped me be a great writer and math helped me be a great account manager at the bank for twenty-four years and an exchange manager for ten years; philosophy and my ministry helped me in working with people and understanding why others think the way they do. I didn't know it then but all along it was divine intervention just for a moment such as this to help others overcome adversity.

Chapter 3

Broken Marriage Vows

1971–1973

"Moving Away from Home"

Man will deceive you, which brings me to my next story. My children's father was a womanizer; what can I say? He liked women, and they liked him back. You will read about the fights I won and the fights I lost with him ... some landed me in the hospital; some caused me to wear glasses, slings, and crutches. I never hit first but he always got the best of me. It is sad but a cheater is always a cheater unless they turn their life around. We got married young. I tried to make it work but it was protocol for his agenda to cheat.

Let's try to break generational curses. We talk about domestic violence; however, it begins at home. We must teach our children to love and respect each other. You might ask what does all this have to do with broken marriage vows? Everything. Adultery is the main cause of breakups. But most Christian homes don't talk about it. Yes, God is love but He also says His people perish because of lack of knowledge. We must tell our children how to protect themselves to avoid marrying a cheater or being mistreated in a relationship. In another scenario to reflect on like destruction as a synoptic parallel, stopping street violence by not letting a gang member mislead or control by brain washing our children's mind. It seems all races are affected when our children have a lack of self-esteem.

The difference in my ministry is I never dance around the root cause of the problem. I danced with the devil once and was brought down, but I got up and declared the works of the Lord! Yes, I'm still on the chapter of broken vows; a broken home comes from broken vows that were disregarded; the trust was broken first, the major breakdown was lack of respect, which was the reason my first marriage broke up; you must get to the cause of the problem before you can find the cure. I talk about intervention after I got attacked but intercepting the attack is also important. Overcoming a wicked imagination is written in the Book of Proverbs:

"A heart that deviseth wicked imaginations, feet that be swift in running to mischief." (Proverbs 6:18) Think about it, if you knew you were going to get a divorce, would you get married? If you knew you would get fired today, would you go to work today?

When you marry an abuser, you think you are getting a gold mine. He gave me an illusion of false hope, promising a better tomorrow, and luring me with expensive gifts.

You find out soon, it was only fool's gold and came with some baggage. After they unpack some of their past issues on to you, all you want is love; instead, you receive disrespect and confusion. You must know the nature of the beast; you must study the attacker to know when and where he plans to attack, so you can get out of harm's way. I've been around long enough to know your partner only disrespects you around the people he or she is sure don't like you. The disrespect and rejection is just the beginning; it opens the door for you to get into your flesh, which is weak, and you begin to lose the anointing of your spirit; your relationship with God begins to fade out as you fight back with angry words. One example of disrespect is when they are discourteous around others. We went back to my hometown to show off our new baby; instead of a happy occasion, he ignored the child and me and made me bring my own luggage in. I planned a great party for one of his family members just to show him I cared, and he never showed up. When we were married, we would go to a party and he danced with everyone except me. At family cookouts, he acted like I was not there.

Yes, they know how to provoke you into the flesh, once you

react to the plan. Now you just gave him or her a reason to justify attacking you, which is what they wanted to do all along; however, you just fell into the trap of deception. You belong to them and the situation is out of control; you just lost it; that's what they wanted. Next time, to see if I'm right, look around before you are provoked and you will see he chose the battlefield, and he only attacks when you are alone. You gain control by out thinking your enemy, just by not responding to a deliberate attempt to provoke you with evil thoughts or unkind words; it's called a wicked imagination; read about it in Proverbs. Let it be a buzz in your ear; why entertain the devil? It's like a revolving door, he says the same thing every time, and you go off every time. He doesn't even have to change or sharpen his blades; you fall for it every time; your partner has been around you long enough to know what gets under your skin. Am I right about it?

Next time, say something short and sweet back or don't say anything at all, or develop a counterattack. He says, "You are getting fat"; just say, "You are right, I guess it's because of all that good food I prepare for you," and smile. You just confused him and took back control over your own actions. Your vows say for better or worse, as long as you are not in harm's way; if they are broken, it's your job to fix them. Yes, we can say, "Peace be still," and it has to be still, but if you rush the waves, it's your fault; you see, the devil only takes us to the fight, you give him power when you react to the fight. If he began to cheat, you can walk away; that's God's law he broke, not yours. If he is trying to make it work, do not bring it up again unless you see signs of him breaking the vows again. Remember he has already studied you and knows just when, how, and where to attack. Why do most abusers take their victims in the woods or away from family and friends? Sadly, history shows they die alone. I just gave you some sound doctrine; it's up to you to take heed and try to stay out of harm's way!

While still in high school I was faced with being a mom and a woman who was betrayed. I found a letter in our dresser addressed to Rita, my other sister-in-law, confirming a story of a past affair with a girl named Denise. It stated he was trying to get to know her better, the very girl who called my house just months before we had gotten married. It was dated before we were married. At that point my mind went back to a night Denise called my dad's house and said she was his girlfriend; he denied it. She told me he was her driving instructor at the high school. That's where he met her; he let her drive his car and she wrecked it. After reading the letter, I still had a hard time believing this girl was the same one he met when he was a driving instructor; however, the next school year, we were already married when I found out the affair was true. She had transferred to the same high school I went to; that's why we were on the same bus.

Yes, it all is very confusing; it seemed the devil had it in for me, but the knife wasn't sharp enough. Unfortunately, I had to see the blade when I went to school; instead of going off, I just put my hand up on the guardrail on the bus, high enough for her to see my wedding ring, and I received great joy in smiling at her, not because I got the cheater but the harassment would stop! That affair with her ended but years later, the affairs started up again. I thought by showing the wedding band, it gave me a sharper edge and he would change, until years later he got his zebra stripes back.

When I turned sixteen, I moved into my dad's home just to date him more. A year later, we were married, and he moved in. Our wedding vows were put to the test. The reason I decided to get married was he was thinking about going into the service. I grew up fast in my last year of high school, I was already married to him; I was having his child when another girl called and said she was dating him. Yes, I found out she was telling the truth, but it was too late, we already were married. That's why I was so hurt by him. The night of my wedding, he told me a story of how his mother passed, which is too sensitive to talk about. In later years, my children's Great-Uncle James from South Carolina told me more, and I told my children how their grandmother's children, their aunts, saw her fall to the ground and a white sheet placed over her turned red in seconds. When he first told me, I wondered why did he wait until we were married and why on our wedding night? I thought we had something in common, because my mom had died also, but I soon realized it affected him more than he would know; at times I would forgive him, thinking it was just his past that was haunting him. I later realized it would become a generational curse.

The first few months we were married, an argument took place and he got in a fight with my dad and hit him in the nose. We then had to move in with his dad; my dad said I could stay but he had to go. Since I was with child, I decided to leave my father's house and move in with his father; we just moved around the corner, and I always stayed in close contact with my dad.

Just before my ex went to war in Vietnam, he gave himself a party; before he left, I caught him talking on the phone with a girl. He was downstairs and I was upstairs with our baby girl when I picked the phone up; he told her not to say anything, and then I went downstairs and asked him whom he was talking with. He grabbed me by the hair and said it was "his ABC"; back in the day, there was a song that went, "My ABC, baby, you and me." Afterwards he began banging my head on the kitchen table while still holding me by the hair, just because I overheard him talking to a girl. That time, the pain seemed unbearable; even though his father broke it up, the mental pain lasted longer; all my friends saw him abuse me, while his newborn baby was upstairs in her crib sleeping. My father-in-law said the party was over and put everybody out. I went for a ride with my sister-in-law Addie. She said just to forget what happened since he was on his way to Vietnam the next day; that morning I took my baby girl to the babysitter, and I went back to school as if nothing happened. I know the girl didn't know what was going on since he moved in with me and she didn't see him anymore. I was still upset the way everything happened, without me knowing about his affair with the girl.

I could have stayed with my dad; however, I kept my promise to God but I had married a cheater I was with child and didn't know what to do after finding out. All I could think about was

I kept my wedding vows up until the birth of my first child and remained faithful. Just like Job, I questioned why me? I always felt two wrongs don't make a right; I just wanted some comfort and couldn't find any.

When my ex went off to war, it was hard, but I still wrote him a letter every day while he was in the war; as I said, I was young. A teacher asked me if I was getting anything from my baby daddy while he was at war; I said no. I will never forget her—that's why I say I love all races—she was white but took the time to care about me, since her husband was in the military also. After school she took me to the base to get an ID card and an allotment and start a checking account in my name. I was living with my father-in-law at the time. My teacher said I was entitled to have part of his government check. My ex wrote and said he didn't like that his check was cut. Thank the Lord for her divine intervention. I stood up for myself for the first time and said, "No, I'm going to keep it in my name for my child." He always told me when he got back from the war, he would let my daughter and me travel with him and get our own place instead of living with his dad; to my surprise, that was another lie also. As I unpacked his bags, I found some protection used when you have an affair. I was so upset; not again! I was thinking all he had on his mind was fighting for his country, while I was taking care of his child and going to school. He told another lie and said he allowed another soldier to put it in his traveling bag for safety; at that point, I knew he was full of lies and deception.

I just had to get away. I left him and told everyone I was separated. I still remembered his abuse in Virginia before he went to war. I was just tired of his lies and adulterous affairs. I just wanted to make a new start.

I called my sister in Georgia and told my family not to tell him where I was. I left with my one-year-old daughter, moved to Georgia, and told my dad not to tell also. That's why he didn't know where I was. I found a job at the drive-in, my first job at the age of nineteen years old, and I was excited about working. I was one of the first black attendants to take money at the booth, and the whites in Georgia didn't like that at all; it was back in the seventies, and they wanted me to work in the kitchen, but the assistant manager gave me the job while the manager was on leave, so I stood my ground and kept the position. After work one night, the assistant manager, who was Puerto Rican, and I went out bowling; he had a girlfriend of his own. I had met her and she was really pretty; she had white hair and blue eyes, and not once did he even try to come on to me; that's why I knew he was just trying to be nice to my small daughter and me.

I was doing fine, living with my sister and her boys; after six months, my daughter's father found me. When we got to the house one night, I noticed the lights were on; my sister always was in bed early. She told me later she was giving me a sign by standing in the kitchen with the lights on, a sign to keep driving and tell my boss to let me out at the corner so I could walk home, which I did. I wasn't all that happy because I thought I had broken away from a person who only wanted to treat me badly, whenever he wanted to.

He found me again. When I saw him, I was surprised; it had been months before he found me. He came off and on from Kentucky for two months. He must have traced the address from my allotment check to find me. Because of the abuse, it was a strange arrangement at first; I kept my distance. He was not taking no as an answer; he just kept coming to my sister's town on a plane, as if he still owned me. When he came, it was the first time my sister had seen him since I married him. He would always come in his military uniform. She saw a handsome man; I saw a hell raiser. He was a smooth talker, and he won her over at that time.

Every time he came, he said my sister's house didn't have enough room for him to stay, and he wanted me to bring his daughter to the hotel to see him. Once my sister said she would keep the baby and we could stay in the hotel for the weekend. I was so confused, because I didn't know if that meant she was tired of me staying with her or she wanted us back together.

The assistant manager had given me his picture, which I put

in our family album because I had nothing to hide. My ex was very upset by the picture; he even took me to work and had a long talk with my boss, as I watched them walking and talking; to this day, I don't know exactly what was said but I do know he told him not to take me home from work anymore; my sister would just have to pick me up. It was clear he was trying to control my every move after he saw the picture I had put in the album for all to see.

Yes, I was hopeful and thankful that my sister was trying to help me but I wanted to stand on my own; I was using her car and living in her home. I wanted a life for myself. I didn't want to put my child on someone else; I wanted to go to college and for my child to go to military schools when she got older by living on a military base. In short, I was a go-getter and wanted more opportunities. I always loved my daughter's father, I just didn't love what he had become; at times, he was big-headed, thinking he was better than me; at that time, I had just finished high school and so did he; he felt he had just gotten into the military and I hadn't accomplished much. I set out to prove him wrong by going to college and getting my children in the best schools. I always knew if given the chance, I could go high and take my child to another level living the military life. Yes, I was confused, wanting to trust someone who wasn't trustworthy, but I did hold on to optimism by playing the role of a faithful wife when we got back together. I was thinking I could change him but I know now abusers must want to change themselves. Yes, I was separated but in his mind I was still his wife. It just wasn't fun anymore trying to prove my independence. I decided to move with him to his duty station; because I didn't sign any papers, he felt he still owned me. That's why he would show up at anytime.

We were not saving any money because of his weekends visits. When he said we would have our own place and didn't have to live with family anymore, I decided to give our marriage another chance. Since I was separated but wasn't dating anyone, I decided to try and work through it for my child's sake. I decided to move with him to Kentucky. I was hoping God had intervened and softened his heart, to want to do right by his family. My small daughter and I smiled and waved to my family and friends with her little Teddy bear in her hands, as the plane took off to Kentucky.

Chapter 4

Life in a Military Family

1974

"What Went on Behind the Smile?"

When I lived overseas, I helped manage the Army and Air Force Exchange System. My children's father was in the military, and I also proudly served our service men and women in the military. One day they had all the families come to a meeting at a movie theater for a survival class. The military told us they had planned an escape route, just in case we were attacked and had to get back to the United States fast. I attended the class just before my family moved into government housing on base I listened and, afterwards, being the inquisitive, curious person I am, asked the speaker how can the people who were living among the Germans in the small towns and small villages that have no maps to even get to them could stand a chance of surviving? He laughed and said, "Are you kidding? Some of the letters we sent out to the military families in the villages were never returned; the ones that were returned had address unknown." He said, "I can't say because I represent the military but in a quick response time, what do you think?" The point I'm trying to make is whenever you go into a foreign land to fight; you are risking your life as well. Just like in domestic violence, a bullet has no name. We go into it with sound judgment and rational thoughts, but at some point when everything goes wrong just like in a bad relationship we have to get into a survival mode.

I just smiled and said to myself, yes, I was a civilian but realized for the first time I was risking my life as well for my country. My father and father-in-law both fought in World War II; years later, they said they were on the same ship going to war and didn't know each other at the time, which was amazing. My ex and my future husband Trotter were in the Vietnam War; my ex was a military policeman, and Trotter was in the Marines as a military policeman and awarded a Purple Heart. My twin brother was in the Army; he lived in Germany and met his future wife there and brought her back to our country. My grandson's older brother Eric just went in, and he will graduate this July from the same base where my son PJ was born thirty-four years ago: Fort Knox, Kentucky.

Divine Intervention at Its Best

My family grew up in a military life-style; my daughter loved the life and attended the Air Force Academy and became an officer. She later worked at the Pentagon in Washington, DC. My son PJ took the same classes as well and scored high on all the tests. He was in our local newspaper when his school sent him to boot camp on post and received an award. During my experiences as a military wife, I wanted my family to be proud of me; that's why most women of domestic violence stay in the relationships; however, there were not all smiles in my home.

I wanted to give my ex another chance; it would have been nice if he just said after he came from Vietnam he would take us with him to Kentucky; it was only after I took a stand and moved with my sister for six months and he thought he was losing me that he agreed to play the role of father and husband. At first he was so happy to see us; the first few months were great; however, after my son's first birthday, the joy of being a family man ended. How do I start? We lived in a small trailer awaiting orders for government housing; I had no job and no friends; and I wasn't driving. I stayed home and hardly ever left the house except for going to the mailbox to mail a letter. As a military wife living in Kentucky, I was a very faithful and loyal wife; just like my daughter, there's no doubt our son is his. We moved into an apartment, and one night while my ex had to work late, my daughter and I went across the hall in our apartment building to visit a neighbor; she had been asking me to visit for a while, but I knew he never wanted me to visit other people. I only stayed for an hour.

My two-year-old daughter Tonya and I were visiting the lady next door and her small child when he came home early from duty. Before that day, I had never left the house after 5 o'clock. He came home early and knocked on my neighbor's door; he asked me to come with him and said to leave my baby; he would come back and get her when we got back. I didn't think anything would happen, because he had not hit me since we lived in Virginia. He took me to those dark woods and told me to just get out, not knowing he would beat me so bad and tore my clothes off and brought me back to the apartment. He knew all along what he was going to do; that's why he told my neighbor he would pick Tonya up so she would not think anything when he came back to get her alone. I wanted to pick my daughter up myself so they could see the bruises but he said no, he would get her.

The abuse that happened that night caught me off guard. He was upset because I was next door, and that was the first and only time I had left my apartment at night. He wanted to teach me a lesson; my dad was in Virginia, my sister was in Georgia, and my brother was in Germany. That's why he did it: no one was around to tell. I just felt alone and afraid. He stopped the allotment check as soon as I moved back in with him; I know now it was all a trick so I would have no money to get back home. The next few years, I never left the house without him; I wasn't allowed to drive at that time and wasn't allowed to have a house phone or to have friends. Soon, we got orders to move into government quarters on base. After that everything seemed to be going fine; my sister came from Georgia for Christmas. When she got off the plane, I was so happy to see her I didn't tell her about the attack; I was hoping that it would never happen again, and I wanted her to be proud of me having a place of my own for the first time. I know if I had told her, she would have taken my baby and me back on that plane; I know my sister.

My son was born that April in a military hospital; my husband was so happy; it seemed every time I would become happy, something bad happened. I had a natural birth; I could hear the doctor and saw him give my husband some papers to sign just before my son was born—they were about which life he wanted to save, mine or our newborn son, because his heart was beating too fast and he would have to save one of us, because I wasn't fully dilated at that time; all I could think of was, *Not again, my mother died at childbirth!*

At that very moment when he signed the paper, God divinely intervened and saved both of us; my son's heart rate became normal. The nurses screamed for joy. The doctor canceled the emergency C-section and they did a normal surgery.

Later that day, my children's father brought my daughter to the hospital. I thought she looked so pretty with her white pants on. At three years old, Tonya's eyes seemed to light up when I told her the small baby I was holding was her brother; from that day forward, she treated him like he was a piece of gold and he belonged to her. We took him home; there were so many toys in the house, you would think a little king was going to arrive that day. My ex would come home on time every day. He seemed so happy. Writing this reminded me about years later, after Tonya graduated from the Air Force Academy and worked for the Pentagon; she became one of the highest-ranking civilians, equal to a general; she also worked for the National Guard in Washington, DC, with her own parking space with her name on it. She was given a meritorious service award; she accepted the award wearing a white two-piece suit, and the three-star admiral had a white suit on as well. The same officer who gave her that award spoke to my future husband Trotter in 2006 before the ceremony in his office.

I was just as proud of her that day as the day she came to the hospital to see her little brother with that white outfit on. She called me while I was typing this chapter and said she just saw the same officer who gave her the award. It's divine intervention at its fullest because she was three years old when her brother was born, the award was in 2006, and in 2009, I'm turning my writings into the publishing company. It's all coming together; it wasn't an accident that this book was to go out and go out with power! As I was putting the entry in this book, I couldn't help but wonder if angels weren't looking down on me.

Back to the past; our family asked us to come back to Virginia for a visit, so they could see the new baby. Everything went fine; their grandmother was so happy, and both his family and mine were so proud to see the new baby. On the way home, as the children slept, we were talking about an unrelated event; for no reason, as we crossed the West Virginia line, he turned and hit me so hard that blood came from my month. I didn't see it coming. I cried for hours until we got back home; he kept saying he was sorry.

I accepted his apology after a few days had passed and went on as if nothing happened. I could not eat for weeks because of the injuries.

A few weeks later, I went to the Exchange with his friend's wife and her children. When I showed my husband the clothes I bought for the children, he just looked at me with an angry look on his face. I was in a good mood, since for the first time I had a friend and had gone to a real store without him. I fixed us a steak dinner; he sat down and poured his drink on the entire plate, and then he hit me. I was so shocked that I walked out the house and just kept walking; remember, I was doing something unheard of: leaving the prison with no bars. He was so surprised I walked out of the house at night; he followed me, begging me to return. He found me and said again he was sorry; I came back home after about fifteen minutes of walking. I began to see a pattern. I called my sister and told her I wanted to come back to Georgia; she thought he and I just had words; I never told her what really happened until after I moved to Germany; at that time, I was too far away for anyone to get to me.

I know I could have moved back in with my sister in Georgia, but at the time, I felt that would have been moving backwards; now I had two children instead of one, and I just didn't want to put what I saw to be a burden on my family. If my brother and dad had a clue about it at that time, someone might get hurt. So I kept my secret a little longer.

I then tried something different as a social outlet to make a friend; I started to baby-sit the little girl three doors down. My children had someone to play with, and I had someone to visit me when her mother came over. I wanted to save up some money since I was living with him now and the check was cut off, and I needed witnesses if he started abusing me again. Out of the blue, we got orders to go to Germany. The divine intervention was I allowed God to lead and guide me to get a stay-at-home job so I wouldn't get attacked without anyone noticing it. I didn't have life-threatening injuries until later years. We took the children to my dad's to stay until we received our orders to be with him in Germany. We had two tours in Germany; the first time we went was a divine intervention; my twin brother was coming home from Germany the same day my ex's plane went over; their planes crossed in the air. When my brother came home, I was so happy; he saw my children for the first time. Three months later, we joined my children's dad in Germany.

My first visit to Germany was surprisingly uneventful, with no physical abuse. However, one day I was late coming home from work, and I saw first-hand some mental abuse: he cut up my favorite picture of myself. God still intervened on my behalf because just the other day, I was looking at some old pictures and saw a copy of that picture I had taken of my son's third birthday party, which means one day I could get someone to restore it from the photo. I know to others mental abuse is still bad but to me it was the absence of physical pain.

On my first tour, I was isolated a lot, and he was not home much; it was so peaceful because we lived among the German people for a while before moving into government housing. We didn't have a telephone for the first six years we lived together. My only friend was my German landlady. There were not many confrontations, and I did not see or hear of any affairs.

My landlady's kids loved my one-year-old son and three-year-old daughter, who had just started preschool. The culture and the way of life was important; I developed a relationship as I visited and learned so many things about the villages just by walking around, getting to know them and what they were all about, and more importantly, they were more friendly than some of the people I met in America; they really showed my kids and me real love. It was like living in paradise. Twice a day, I would take my son down a long hill to meet his sister's school bus. My German landlady was very nice to me; she and her family always treated my children and me very well. The United States government sent us overseas to help defend this country. In ten years, I never experienced any prejudice in their country or among their people as I traveled overseas going to different schools and events. I drove all over Germany. They said so many of them were not aware what the government was doing; they loved us and we loved them. My niece's mother is German.

One day when I came back from the bus stop, my landlady was holding an English book; her teenage son spoke English, and she wanted to practice speaking to me for herself. I bought a German book, and we began talking every day; she even invited me for breakfast with her family and watched my baby boy while I walked down that hill to the bus stop.

Years later when my children grew up, my daughter's dad was at her captain's ceremony but when she became a major, he was missing in action again with his excuses. It was good for me because I was able to help pin the bars on myself in his place; I displayed the picture of the ceremony in my last book. He loves his children but he always had commitment issues. Which brings me to a great divine intervention: when I met my friend Sarah's family years earlier and God allowed us to stay connected. Her family has always been stationed the same duty station as our family, and when my husband got out of the service, my daughter was stationed at the location to this day. God kept us together for over twenty-four years. Only God can intercede and make that happen; my daughter and her husband were stationed at the Pentagon the day of the 911 attacks.

When Tonya became a major, she allowed my friend's husband,

who was a full bird colonel at that time, to pin the bars on and help conduct the ceremony, since he had always been a role model to her. You see, if I had given up and gone back home to my family when my children were young, I would have been reaching backwards and not looking ahead.

Yes, I do talk about the hell I went through in this book, but I must end this chapter about my military experience with how I trusted in His divine power, which brought about divine order, showing God's Glory. My assignment is to encourage others and to go forward in the heat of battle and the brewing of the storm. I might have missed out; I touched on it, I will expand later on how His miracles were on their way. I feel it's important to let others know the meaning of this chapter and why I feel only those who risked going too far would ever know how far they could go!

Chapter 5

Domestic Abuse and Betrayal

1975–1984

"Coming Against Me without a Cause"

I was a professional woman in my own right, wearing business suits and expensive perfume, and I held jobs that required a master's degree. I was well respected as the wife of the manager at the Officer's Club; I was known as the wife of the vice president of the Post Office Union in my town. During that time frame, we were given recognition and won many awards; our professions were highlighted in success on our jobs; we had rental properties all over town; for eight years, I was a landlady, my ex was a landlord. We owned land as far as the eye could see: houses, cars, trucks, and a boat, on which my son enjoyed fishing with his father. We looked on the outside like the idea couple with success; the darkness of domestic violence was behind closed doors.

I never felt safe in the devil's arms. While standing in the eye of a storm and going through a war zone, there's no time to talk about it. No one wants to talk about disastrous events until they reach safety. A wounded soldier in domestic violence just wants to be left alone until they heal; they will talk about it later. I discovered you conquer first; even the news media cut all cameras off in dangerous winds. The reason it took so long to come forward was I had to study the patterns and try to analyze the traits of what makes attackers react the way they do. Most victims don't have answers; they just got hit. Hypothetically, when another car hits you after the accident, someone can tell you just what went wrong; others have to wait until the investigation is over; some never saw the car coming. I'm one of those who had to wait until I felt comfortable enough to reveal it.

My story relates to the face of a battered woman. I had all the facts; the answers were what I was struggling with. Yes, it took years; the events were much too overwhelming and caused too much pain. If victims knew what happened, there would be no problem to solve. Don't you think they would duck the punch or not be at home that night when he decided to harm or kill them? My analysis: the abuser has two personalities: one, a sweet, kind, concerned caring person to fool everyone; good-looking, intelligent, smart (or just smarter than the one they are with, because the jails are full of the ones in denial). Outer appearance is usually that of strength making you feel safe. The characteristic of a protector is that of a shepherd, but there is a dual personality; only the wife and the children know the other side, but they are afraid to tell the police; they know Daddy or Mommy (the bread winner) could be taken away.

They also know there would be consequences: they would have to get a job; some women never worked a day in their lives. You see some families and there loved ones are blinded because they are getting a piece of the pie. If the victim was really smart, she would stop listening to what he is saying and watch his actions of betrayal as he was getting amnesia, conveniently forgetting where he lives, their selfishness, sleeping in the wrong bed, while his wife and children slept alone, leaving the very ones he vowed to protect home alone on many sleepless nights, leaving a robber to steal or kill as he destroyed his own home. In this book, I speak about the nature of the beast. No matter how you slice it, cheating husbands can't be in two places at the same time; someone will feel rejected. You must walk in my shoes before you understand how it feels; how can someone who has never drank tell you how to drink? The same goes for someone who has never been abused; they can't tell you how it feels to be a victim. Sleeping with the enemy (a stranger in her bed): that's a story only a battered woman can tell.

The face of a battered woman is sometimes not seen; it's hidden waiting to be healed from all scars, cuts, wounds; they are too ashamed to show their face or tell anyone their story. They emerge from nowhere because they hid the signs of the abuse as they came up for a breath of air; unfortunately, some don't make it to tell the story, and family members make it a lifelong mission to vindicate them. Did you feel the pain? Did you experience the embarrassment, rejection, or disappointment? Do you know the fear of slow death when someone decides to instill fear only moments before the gun goes off, playing a game, or decides to let you go only moments before the final blow? Do you really know how it feels not to trust someone you thought you loved? You see, I trusted my children's father not to cheat; that's how it all started, by allowing him to go any and everywhere without asking questions, believing what he said, that he was where he said he was because he was my husband. Allowing him to take care of the bank account without any questions. He gained power by taking my trust! Then I started asking questions: Where have you been? Where is the money in our savings?

Those questions alone were enough to start a war in my house that almost took me out of this world. Divine intervention allowed the attempts by evildoers to fail. You think you know how it feels after your sister, your brother, your mom, went through it. Thanks for trying to understand but you will never fully understand how it feels, unless you received the abuse yourself and then told the story. Did you ever once talk to them about it? Before you help others, you must know something about it yourself.

Yes, I read about domestic violence and heard about it, but experiencing it wasn't the same; living in fear of anything you say or do, the abuser uses that as a way of attacking you, afraid when the phone rings, falsely accusing you of talking about them just to create an excuse to leave the house. Sound familiar? Only the ones who have been battered can answer most of the questions so many want to know. Yes, I do sympathize with those whose loved ones have been hurt, because my children and my loved ones were hurt and have the same concerns also but they have never known and will never know the extent or degree of pain or the level of suffering I felt. I honor and respect those who were never beat who came forward to help; however, I now understand why I waited and almost didn't tell my story in detail before. Seeing the laughter, watching the faces of those who conduct interviews on TV stations, not all but some were not fair, not fully understanding or comprehending why a victim stays, as if they were just crazy.

I almost abandoned the mission God set for me, after writing the instructions down and after signing the book contact three years ago and being rejected by famous prophets that came to town. I went to conventions and tried to speak to them, and I even gave some a detailed letter typed on pink paper. God gave me five names; I typed five letters for the chosen five in my vision to represent my struggle, chosen to help me in the fight to set the people free; to this day, they have not responded. I only asked them to join me in the fight for deliverance; I was already established, I just wanted help in the struggle to help others. Prophetess Juanita Bynum was the most disappointing; it seemed to me she didn't care about my story when she came to town, and a few weeks later, she went public and wanted the world to care about her story; however, I still wanted to talk to her but still no call or e-mail or letter, but she contacted the ones in the ministry and talk shows to seek media attention. Wrong answer! Having a self-righteous attitude, hypocritically observing the form but neglecting the spirit of religion. Some want you to sympathize with them when they tell their story, but yours doesn't count, just buy their books and CDs. I felt like David when God gave him instructions to bring the giants down (the abusers), and everyone thought he wasn't important enough; they called him small in stature (referring to him as "ruddy"). David would have a hard time dealing with some of today's Christians. It seems the world treats its own better.

And Samuel said unto Jesse, Are here all thy children? And he said, There remaineth yet the youngest, and, behold, he keepeth the sheep. And Samuel said unto Jesse, Send and fetch him: for we will not sit down till he come hither. And he sent, and brought him in. Now he was ruddy, and withal of a beautiful countenance, and goodly to look to. And the LORD said, Arise, anoint him: for this is he. (1 Samuel 16:11–12)

Years before I got into the ministry, I took a bottle of bills and almost died; I couldn't handle being a failure. Before my ministry, I was headed to hell for committing such a crime. That's why I can tell you firsthand, and with certainty, victims want love more than your money. Again, love and encouragement are needed more than handouts. Yes, it's easy to write a charity a check for a tax write-off, but we need books in their hands to read and send them to the ones who need them. Help the victim out when you can (hands-on) by talking to them when you give them a copy of this book and others like this one to read when they come to you for help and guidance. That would show them you are not just a big name; people are dying every day. (Show them you really care.)

Years later, I developed a relationship with God and stopped blaming Him for not being there, because afterwards I realized He was there all the time. Years ago, I had no power; bitterness consumed me, but the love for my children overpowered my fears and made me want to live. I'm hoping this book might change your way of thinking; I must carry the torch for a cause so many others have died trying to fight. Even after therapy, I still have nightmares I will live with for the rest of my life: hearing the loud sound of a jail cell slamming after a new prisoner comes in. When breakfast was served in the jail the one day I was locked up on a lie, I almost choked at the smell of thousands of eggs cooking, all because my ex-husband's lover had me arrested and thrown in jail on false charges, only to have them dismissed the next day. I could have counter-sued, but I just wanted to go on with my life. I felt overwhelming grief, knowing that his lover came into my life to beat and stalk me and destroy my marriage of twenty-four years. I'm fully aware I'm taking a chance that the woman who hurt me that day will be happy to know the hurt I was hiding inside; she may read this book and see she hurt me more than she thought or could ever imagine, both physically and mentally. The outer shell was perfect but my heart was crushed.

Unpeeling the embarrassment is worth revealing the pain to help others. When talking about the others, did you truly understand how they felt? Why did I ask these questions? You see, my strength came from them thinking I was strong. There are warning signs; whether it's only verbal or mental, abuse is abuse! Trust me, there is usually a hit or punch before the final blow that takes them out. Most married couples will never tell you if they ever got hit; they are too ashamed. The only reason they tell me is they can relate to me. That's why I say counseling is a must! My ex refused it. I had to go, because everything was just too much, and it was affecting my job (not that I was doing bad, I just wanted to give up). I always did great because the more the enemy messed with me, the more I would fight hard to achieve my goals. Before my divorce and before the attack of October 20, 1991, my therapist asked, "Where was he?" I said he just dropped me off and laughed at me as I was getting out of our truck.

The day after the beating on October 20, 1991, before I gave him the divorce papers, I shut the door as he reached for his keys; he had no idea I had the locksmith come over the day after I was beaten; he couldn't open it anymore, only after I almost lost my life and after I changed the locks on my front door. He then agreed to marriage counseling; at that point, I said, "It's too late, it's over." The judge ordered my pictures to stay in the circuit court of Virginia as a permanent record, but the pictures were never put in the media; I didn't want to advertise my near demise.

At this time, I didn't want (and would not have accepted) any media attention due to the embarrassment it would have brought me. I wasn't strong enough at that time to answer any questions; that's why it took me so long to come forward with my concerns;

however, if I were asked at that time to go on a talk show such as *Larry King Live,* it would have been default to come back home to an abuser who just watched me tell on him on national TV. If I had given him a reason, I wouldn't be talking to you. Too ashamed, too fearful of repercussions that I still faced because his lovers were stalking me. I couldn't give away my movements; I needed my children and myself to stay safe, even after the divorce. That's why many victims never come forward. Why did I stay? It was like I was on the battlefield trying to win a war; wanting my family to stay together outweighed the pain; it seemed I was losing ground. Every time I picked up ground, it seemed we were happy as a family; the enemy attacked again; I'm not going to say it was the other women's entire fault; it was mostly his, because it takes two to tango.

I was trying to change myself, taking advantage of all the schools and military advantages to support me and my children as we moved toward more favorable situations, until we almost lost it all but I still had my job, which I believe was God's mercy: Most abused women don't have the funds or resources to move out or have rich friends or a church home to support them or give them a word of encouragement or support from the Lord. They find out help isn't free; they were asked to stand in a thousand-dollar line. I know you need money to do kingdom work, and to help others, but to the others that just fatten your pockets is a curse! The needy get embarrassed and walk out of the church because they know some prophets have singled them out by allowing the people to know the last line was the ten-dollar line. Yes, they might be poor, but they still have their pride and dignity! If you are a real man and woman of God, try calling out the ones who have no money first and bless them! If you want to talk to the prophets, you shouldn't have to stand in a thousand-dollar line first. Jesus gave the word for free; show me where He took a dime for Himself. The Bible talks about the purse. Don't get upset with me. I'm still in the word: "And commanded them that they should take nothing for their journey, save a staff only; no scrip, no bread, no money in their purse." (Mark 6:8)

My God will supply all our needs. As I said, some can be on the front page while others will never get into a magazine or visit famous people's homes no matter how many times they write about the abuse. Most abusers have money; some family members saw the evil giant but he gives support to the family, which makes them turn a deaf ear and blind eye since the family was poor, until their meal ticket is cut off from supporting their relatives, not until then do they get angry.

Do the research; I have. Start with the Web site on domestic violence sponsored by the late Liz Claiborne: www.ndvh.org, or call the National Domestic Violence Hotline: 800-799-SAFE (or 7233 for the deaf).

I was trying to focus on getting my children through school and then leave but it all backfired and they almost took me to Glory and the grave that day I was brutally beaten; that's why I put on the back of my last book "O Death where is thy Sting? O Grave where is thy Victory?" (1 Corinthians 15:55)

After not wanting to go public, I decided this year after I retired to finish what I started after signing this book contact three years ago. I'm still struggling with revealing the details; however, I know it's for God's Glory and His divine purpose; it's all in His plan. Years of hidden secrets from the wounds of the past still carried scars but it's up to us how we come out. We will come out through our trust and faith that God can divinely intervene and intercede against all of our enemies' attacks against us.

It took time to heal, and I had to learn how to forgive and trust, before my deliverance was released. I know I was on a train ride bound for hell eighteen years ago, until I began listening to God's voice. The face of a battered woman: we hear about it, we read about it, but don't fully understand until it happens to us. Unfortunately, I had to hide my blood-stained face; on many occasions, I had to wear sunglasses after both eyes were blackened at the same time after he followed me to work after I refused to cook him breakfast that morning, since he was out all night. I couldn't walk on anybody's stage at a local TV station or appear on any talk shows if they had asked me to, because of the crutches and slings that I sometimes had to wear to work; my co-workers and managers witnessed the brutal effects of the battles I lost, but I lived to tell about.

My speech might have been gagged and thoughts impaired due to the sudden shock of having a loaded gun put to my head as I watched helplessly as he put one bullet in the chamber not once but twice, playing Russian roulette, and actually pulled the trigger all the way to see the fear on my face and laughed. Sorry, it would have been hard to hold my arms up after he tore my shirt off; the next day, my babysitter's husband told me my husband didn't want me and didn't want anyone else to have me. I had to agree, since that's what it looked like. I could have thrown the torn shirt in the trash as I did many times before, but I just wanted someone else to be a witness to just how evil the demonic spirits were using him. Also the same night, after being beaten by a plunger, both arms became swollen up to the size of two arms; I wore a sling to work for weeks until it healed; during the same attack, I struggled and tried to pull myself up from the floor after he hit my head repeatedly on the bathtub until the back of my neck began to swell. All because he had found a name and phone number in my pocket with the name "Dawn" on it, and he said when he called and asked for me, a man answered and knew me. I then replied, "Why shouldn't he know me?" Dawn was his wife's name, our children's babysitter. They both lived next door.

Dawn volunteered to sew my torn shirt. He then apologized and said he was sorry, but sorry can't heal the bruises. On another occasions, If someone had called to talk to me, I would have been a no show: my face, my eyes, my hands, my arms, my stomach, as he pounded me to the street as my neighbors watched while he sped off. They had no idea who he was since he was rarely home from the Officer's Club, where he was the manager. I bought him tailor-made suits, diamond rings, expensive cologne, and leather coats; I paid most of the bills, even the home that my in-laws were living in for ten years, I paid the mortgage. I came straight home from work, always stayed home with the children.

But it didn't keep my legs or my feet from getting bruised with wounds.

When I returned back to the United States on one occasion, my boss just handed me a paper with a phone number to the abuse hotline on it and the name of the bank's therapist, because it hurt her seeing me come to work with bruises on my body; she was also tired of me being a punching bag. The cost was $100 an hour, which the bank gladly paid. A decision was made, due to the severity of the abuse, that the bank would undertake a lifetime of financial help since they had never heard of a situation as bad as mine, according to my therapist.

Sorry, I might not have been able to make it to a movie premier due to being jailed overnight on false charges; his lover lied on many occasions just to get the warrants themselves in order to hinder my divorce proceedings. I was on my lunch; the jail house was across the street from where I worked; instead of just being able to sign and show up for court this time, they took my bag lunch and began taking pictures, which caused my car to be towed since I wasn't able to move it in a timely manner. His lover knew the charges were false. She got the many warrants as an attempt to embarrass and humiliate me, since the FBI bonded me on my job. The charges were dismissed the next day, but I will never forget the sounds and smells. His lover's greatest joy was having me walk out into the courtroom alone, with my husband standing beside her, not me, while he was still legally married to me. Seeing me in prison clothes must have made her day. She had a big smile on her face when the guard brought me out in prison clothes.

I had never been inside a courtroom until she began to sleep with my husband. The computer screen was blank until I met her. Once I got a speeding ticket, and the police officer said, "Who are you? The screen is blank. All I see is your name"; that was before I met her. All my vacation time was taken to defend myself on false charges without a cause. To get the warrant, she knew she had to lie; she got great pleasure in tying up the legal system; she and my ex didn't care as long as it inconvenienced me and made my life a living hell. She was hoping I would give up on life itself and uproot my way of living. After three years of going back and forth to court, having enough warrants to use as wallpaper, they were all dismissed against me. All because I used her own statements in their own words against them in a court of law, and my husband was found guilty of the charges I filed against him in our divorce hearing; the judge had pictures of the beating and their statements put in the circuit court in Norfolk, Virginia, as evidence. A police officer saw the bruises all over my body and arrested my husband and later arrested his heartless lover. My attorney Paul Lipkin decided not to file criminal charges at that time. My children's father left her a few months later; at that time, the warrants stopped. After our divorce, he dropped her like a hot potato and is now married to someone else. It took me years to fully tell the whole story, so I wrote poems and short stories.

Mentally or physically, abuse is abuse; that's why I say it's nothing you did or said. Stop blaming yourself! A victim doesn't have to do or say anything; you're just the one he or she feels they can get away with attacking because they feel you need them. He knew I wouldn't tell everything because if I brought him down, my family would go down also. That's part of the vows "I do" no one tells you about. As a victim of domestic violence and after being battered for years, I can tell you I lived in denial, having thoughts that I could always pull through no matter how hard the blow. The one who has the scars to show for the years of abuse, mentally or physically, is the face of a battered woman. This title only the brave can wear! Leaders don't quit; there are those that are just in it for the next book or immediate fame.

Where is the support when the victim needs them? All I can say is money doesn't motivate or drive my cause; helping those in need is my satisfaction. To further substantiate my claim of not wanting to rob God's people, it's not about the next book signing or who's driving the biggest bus through town; it's about caring for His people. I found pictures of affairs (and pictures don't lie) and letters on occasions he admitted to before we divorced. I could have told my story years ago but chose not to at that time. You see money can't mend a broken heart; I just wanted my readers to know I got knocked down but I didn't get knocked out!

I'm sharing with you tales of hurtful moments; one was when I questioned him on where he was, which always set him off into a rage because that's when the fights began, when he would stay out all night and when asked where he was, he would hit me so hard I almost forgot my name. I only asked if I was really upset and was willing to fight back to defend myself and would only ask when the children were asleep to spare them of the drama I knew would unfold. I first found out about his affairs and web of deception when I drove home early from work, while living at Fort Story before our second tour overseas, and saw our green sports car; I was happy, thinking I'll pick the kids up later at the babysitter's and spend some time with him. To my surprise, after the car stopped, it was a woman driving our other car; she had gotten his shirts out of the cleaners. I was so hurt, I asked her what was she doing driving my husband's car. She said to ask my husband and walked away. Flashbacks came to me as I left the Officer's Club, where both of them worked; she was a cook, he was the club manager. All I could think of was I was so dumb; many times I saw them together and didn't think anything of it because she was older and she was an employee. I can even remember one night his sister came from Ohio, and we went to the club to get some money for the movies; she was there looking at me, not saying anything, and they were all alone in the club when we drove away; he didn't come home until the next day.

That was another thing—he used his family visits as a means to disappear; it didn't matter: his sister, his dad, his brother, cookouts, his grandmother's last birthday party at my house before she passed, he didn't care. He was a no-show, missing in action. Sometimes he would step in and say hi and leave; I would be so embarrassed. We were stationed in Germany twice. This section talks about the eighteen-month break at Fort Story in between the first and second tour. His two lovers during that break, Ms. B and the lady in the red dress, both worked for him at his military job on base at Fort Story, where he started his affairs back up after years of trying to make it work since high school, without a third-party involvement. The first ten years, he attacked me but the affairs started after our first tour at Fort Story. The affair with the lady in the red dress ended at Fort Story but my husband took Ms. B with him on his second tour in Germany. When the children and I got orders to move to Germany with my husband on his second tour, the lady next door at Fort Story asked me, "What husband?" She said she thought I was in the military with my children and I was getting orders to leave alone. There were changes of events years earlier that led up to a dead end road, the final bow not to confuse these women of the night with Ms. C, the woman who had his baby years later and beat me was the reason our marriage ended for good.

Leaving a heart that could no longer be mended. One night, I asked him where he had been, and he broke two gold plates over my head. Another time, he hit me with a heavy object; the force caused my head to swell as I fell to the floor and blacked out. When he came home, he confessed to sleeping with his cook the whole time we were in Fort Story. He then asked for a transfer to the Enlisted Club and said he would change; however, he started dating another woman, a lady bartender at the Enlisted Club. She wanted me to know because my sister's two boys were still there visiting. The oldest found a letter written by her under the driver's seat and a bra with some underclothes; the letter was written on paper from the hotel they stayed at.

She wrote about how much the relationship meant to her; at that point, everything started getting crazy. I asked him where he was going, not trusting him anymore. I tried to follow him one night and lost him; the next day, I followed him to the car and he punched me in the chest as hard as he could, until I fell in the middle of the street. I told my brother about it and my brother came and talked to him; however, he didn't change. One Sunday night when I decided to go to the club just to visit him, I met the lady who put the letter in the car. He was the manager; the club was within walking distance but I never went until my world began to get crazy and I wanted answers; the trust was gone. I saw a lady in a red dress with red high heels on standing beside him as he was frying some fries; I asked him why they were the only two in the club. His answer was it was her birthday. I could tell he was lying, and she never spoke, but what puzzled me was she was a different girl from the one I had seen him with earlier, and his bottom lip began to tremble when he lied about why she was there. Now alone with another one in a club that was supposed to be closed.

Something told me to take that hot grease he was frying those fries with and put his face in it, but divine intervention stepped in and said no. I ran out of the club, went home, put my hair rollers on, and went to bed. Three hours later, there was a knock at the door; it was the lady with the red dress but she had changed into some pants and black leather gloves (later I realized she had the gloves on to hide the cuts on her bloody hands from slashing his tires before she showed up at my door). There was blood on the broken bottle next to the tires; she was driving a red sports car. I told her she couldn't come in because my children were upstairs asleep; if she had something to say, she would have to say it through the door. She looked inside and said, "The red roses on your table are beautiful; I have the same roses on my table."

I asked her what she wanted; she said she knew he wasn't home, because he was over at his other lover's house, his old cook who worked at the Officer's Club. She said he was seeing her, and that she was a new worker at the Enlisted Club, down the street from the Officer's Club, She asked me to follow her; I got a babysitter and followed her because it was a break I had been looking for; for eighteen months, he had eluded me every time I attempted to follow him. She was right: he was there.

When I drove up, my children's father and I started arguing. He was standing at a telephone booth; I asked him whom he was calling. The lady in the red dress and red sports car, the same one I followed, began to laugh and drove off; at that point, enough was just enough. I wanted to know whom he was talking to and we both fought over the phone; I let go and the phone hit him in the face. The police came and asked him how he got hurt, and he made up something.

I drove him to the hospital, where he got ten stitches (he still has the small scar). His father went to get the car the next day I went to work. I can remember one of his lovers telling me after he left her for another woman, she didn't understand why he treated me so bad; she said I was a nice-looking woman and church going and always stayed home with my children; wherever I went, the children went. She said she knew because they would ride by my government apartment at night before they would go out, and my car was always there, and the lights showed my family was sleeping peacefully, which always puzzled her, because she knew he was making my life hell and felt bad that she was part of it. One night, a man called and said he had a gun to my husband's head; he had come in and found him with his girlfriend. I was half asleep and thought he was joking and said, "Do what you have to do." Afterwards, I realized the man was telling the truth because my husband came in the next morning asking me why I told that man to do what he had to do. I really didn't know if the call was real or not but it must have been; how else would he have known about the conversation? I guess that lady in the red dress went back to the man who called. The reason I stayed was he had orders for Germany and I thought we would have a new life together as a family, a new start, but for the first time I went to the doctor; in the past, I would call the police but I never went for medical help. The bruises were too dark and severe this time.

I was in denial. Yes, most of my marriage I lived in denial, refusing to acknowledge the fact that I loved to love but love didn't love me. Disconnect occurred when the one I chose to protect me destroyed me and allowed others to destroy my home. I saw what I wanted to see and didn't see what I didn't want to see. The doctor asked me what happened. I said I fell down the stairs, still in denial, not wanting to come to grips with a rocky and unstable marriage. I walked down the hall; the doctor gave me a folder with his findings in it, which read, "Reason for injuries very questionable." That was the first time I cried tears, because my secret of not being the idea couple had been revealed. Yes, I was still living my eighteen months of hell at Fort Story between tours; a few months later, he followed me to work after staying out all night. I was still upset about the violence the months before. This time, there was no eggs and bacon on the table when he came home, no good morning as he walked in the door from who knows where. I looked at him and walked out the door. I had already taken the children to the babysitter's house next door; I told her I had to go to work early; my life was very routine. There was no breakfast that morning; the routine was about to end. I said enough was enough; he was upset because for the first time since I was hurt, others had seen my shame.

I began acting differently toward him; no smiles, no kiss, I just walked out of the door. He followed me to work and stopped me in the Navy Exchange parking lot. He asked me to roll down the car window and for no reason punched me in both eyes as hard as he could. I began to see stars, I never saw it coming; I thought he just wanted to talk or I would have never rolled the windows down. I jumped out of the car and ran into the Exchange. I was to afraid to go home; since I didn't come home, he called me at my job until my boss told him if he called again he would send the police to my house (he came on government property to hurt me). I wore sunglasses that week to work until the blackness in both eyes went away. Victims live on a bloodstained battlefield and fight private wars that are not shown on TV on a daily basis. One thing I noticed about him: when the fire got hot, he always asked for a transfer. A few days before I left to go back to Germany, I called his commanding officer and asked him about the school that my ex had said he had been attending for eighteen months (he claimed to be going to night school on Tuesday nights). His commander's answer still bothers me; he said, "What school?"

I was perplexed, hurt, betrayed, and heartbroken; all I could think of was what kind of man would put his lovers over his children and family?

When Tonya was twelve and PJ was nine years old, we went back to Germany for the second time; I remember them looking out of the window and seeing their dad trying to push me out of the car while he drove off. Another similar story: when my niece Colette, the daughter of my twin brother, was around twelve years old, she saw my children's father try with all his strength to push me down the stairs; I was helpless. She still recalls watching me hold on to the rails with all my strength; she said all she could do was scream, because he could have overpowered both of us. It worked, because after she screamed, he let me go. My ex would always say, "That's why you will never have anything: because when you get something, you give it away." You see, what I remember more than the pain was how the strength of my little ones encouraged me.

In 2001, after all of the abuse was over, I went to my friend's house in Washington, DC and told her I was writing short stories about my past abuse. She began to look at my work on the Amazon and Barnes & Noble Web sites; after a minute, she went to the Wal-Mart Web site to order. To her surprise, the cover of my first book was next to a book by former President Clinton. Yes, I'm proud that God's Glory was revealed years later; God's work was chosen to stand out. That's divine intervention!

The book is all about revealing God's power; opening doors man could have never opened. There were thousand of other books on Wal-Mart's Web site but they chose mine to display beside a very important person's book; at that point, I began to take my work more seriously. God empowered me to be an instrument of His Glory to reveal His good work and so others could see it manifested in a supernatural way. I didn't just write this book for the victims; I also wrote it for the one who does the abusing. They are reaching out for help and society has tossed them aside; that's why some move to another town and start all over again with a new family that is unaware of their past.

In my spiritual walk, when honor is given, I don't take it lightly. I must honor the God that made it possible. What better way to end this chapter on domestic abuse than a visual picture of what my work represents of showing His Glory! That's why I write my pain.

Henrietta Trotter

Chapter 6

Twists and Turns of His Affairs

1975–1980s

"His Lover Stole My Identity in Germany"

This chapter shows infidelity at its worst. As you have read, many women with a Jezebel spirit invaded my home. This chapter also tells of a direct attack to bring me down; however, I made up my mind, if my spirit is shot a hundred times, I'll still rise up from the inside because no devil in hell will break me. "Thou sufferest that woman Jezebel, which calleth herself a prophetess, to teach and to seduce my servants to commit fornication." (Revelation 2:20).

That spirit was used to destroy the marriage I had with my children's father. This morning, a voice came saying, "It's not too late"; if one of my readers with a desire to change can change, a strong man can resist a lustful spirit. Jezebel can't get to everybody.

After arriving in Germany on my second tour, the first few months after my arrival everything seemed fine; then all hell broke loose. It was an interesting twist: the same woman who said she would kill herself and who drove our green car one day in Fort Story was living in my government quarters, pretending she was me, before we had our orders cut. She had taken my identity, which was his downfall; it caused him to lose his military retirement after the CID investigated it. I did not realize he had taken his lover over there before the orders arrived for my children and me. He defrauded government housing and government schools by supporting his lover's child. The military was tired of him disrespecting me also. He only had five years to go; this time, his affair destroyed our dreams. I found out he had told me lies and was still a cheater. The sadness overtook me; betrayed again!

How do I even begin to explain such a wild story? The full details would later be my hell on earth. It was on our second tour in Germany. My son was nine years old and my daughter was twelve. My ex had brought Barbara, whom I refer to as Ms B. throughout this book, to Germany (his old cook from Fort Story), and she was living in government quarters before I arrived; she used my name to his friends and my neighbors. His affairs were all documented in military records; he lost his military retirement because of them.

My daughter was the first to find out that her dad was having an affair with the same woman from Fort Story; she had shown up in our lives again. Tonya saw Ms. B and her dad riding down the street together; I was at work and she was walking home from school in the snow; her dad didn't even offer her a ride. She said he had looked straight at her and kept driving. When I confronted him, he said she was mistaken. She stopped talking to him for one year after he lied on her. Tonya was his heart; he came and asked me to do something about her not talking to him. I said it was up to her if she wanted to be bothered with him or not. Even though my daughter told me what she saw, I guess I was still in denial. You see, a victim of abuse stays in a state of confusion because the abuser makes anyone who comes against him look bad by displaying charm and being on his best behavior. He had flowers delivered to my job, took me out to dinner, and gave me more than I asked for. I know now these were signs of an affair; it was his way of living with himself when guilt overtook him. Toward the end of our relationship, I began to recognize the pattern; when my co-workers would admire me for getting so many balloons and flowers, I would tell them that he must be up to something again and I just haven't caught him yet.

Still referring to the second tour in Germany, the lady next door told me something in the laundry room that made me drop my basket; she told me that his lover had been over there with him, living in our government quarters before my children and I came over. It was so hurting that at first I didn't want to believe her, but something about the way she was telling it made me stop and listen. She said his lover would cry many days, and they would have fights. She called herself his wife; our neighbor said she was confused when his real family came over.

I began searching for something with his lover's name on it, hoping the story that was told to me wasn't true. I asked him about it, and of course he denied it. I became really suspicious when the lady next door stopped telling me things; after that day, he gave her a job at the Officer's Club. I put myself in his lover's place; I asked myself where I would hide something if I lived in a house and wanted a man's wife to know I lived there before her. It came to me to look in the back of the master bedroom's closet on the top shelf. I searched all the way to the back and found more than I was looking for. I found a checkbook with her name on it, with a check for a million dollars made out to him as a joke. She also put other items to let me know she was there before me. I remembered that my small daughter told me she had seen a lady in his car.

I began to work at the Army and Air Force Exchange; before I got my license, I would walk to work past the Officer's Club; I wondered if it was true. I always had an eerie feeling someone was watching me when I walked past the kitchen; the curtain on a small window would always open half way. One day I went with my ex-husband to work; I walked around and introduced myself to everyone. They all seemed surprised. Now I know why he never put a family picture on his desk even after I asked him to. I asked him to at least put a picture of the children on the desk; he still refused. I just found out his lover worked there! He was living a lie before my family came over, and he was just too deep into his lies.

My strongest suspicion came true when I found a letter she

had written to her sister in his desk drawer that he had forgotten to mail. To my surprise, the return address was in Germany! At first, the letter didn't bother me, thinking she was writing to him from the States. My state of mind was defeated; I didn't want anyone writing him but I felt at least I was the one he chose to bring to Germany with him; that way I wouldn't have to worry about seeing her. After I read the letter, I found out she was over there with him all the time, which verified what the lady next door had told me.

I almost fainted and fell straight down, shaking my head and repeating, "Oh no, not again!" The letter said that he and I were still having problems and that he would be sending me back to Georgia. I thought, how could he tell this woman where my sister lived? He must be lying to her. Up until I saw that letter, we were doing fine; then the fights began again when I began asking him where he was going.

She seemed happy that I found the letter. The next day, when I was working at the Air Force Exchange, I saw her watching me when I went to get some change for the accounting clerk. I asked her, "What are you doing over here?"

She said, "The same thing you are doing here."

I then said my husband sent for me; she said he sent for her also. At that point, I said enough was enough, thinking I had been Mrs. Nice in the United States and never wanted my family and friends to know what a loser I had married. I always acted like a lady and didn't fight in public; she knew I went to church; sometimes the enemy can take advantage of you when they think you are weak. I was not yet in my ministry and didn't know about my calling. That day I was a sinner saved by grace, because after she provoked me by coming to my job and said my husband had sent for her, I began to fight her in the middle of the Exchange, showing her no mercy. They said I kicked her, pulled her hair, knocked her to the floor, and punched her until some Army soldiers pulled me off her.

One of the soldiers said, "Lady, here is your bag." He had no idea the bag was full of money; I said thanks and went back to my department and gave my accounting clerk the bag. She later said when I handed her the bag, my other hand held a lady's hat with hair in it, my face was cut from nail marks, and a small amount of blood was dripping down my face. My co-worker asked my boss not to send me for change again since I came back so messed up.

I asked if I could go home; when I called my husband, he said there was something he had to tell me. The same day, the CID called to ask about picking up her daughter from school; this revealed my husband's dark secret. I told them I didn't know who that girl was. They told me my husband had brought her and her mother over to that country as a sponsor. They said he had signed his name to papers that I was his lover's daughter's aunt and he was the uncle. My children's father had a dark secret; remember when I said Ms. B had taken my identity on my second tour and said she was me before I came over; it seems my ex had taken it a little further; he had sponsored Ms. B's daughter in military school. Again, okay, to talk about it, he was found guilty and appealed it but the military still said he would not be able to re-enlist after allowing the military to pay to send his lover's teenage daughter to high school. I only found out about his little secret when the CID called me and told me my ex and I sponsored her to come to Germany and I was her aunt. She had gotten into trouble at school and I was to pick her up. At that time I knew nothing about his lie to the government. Afterwards, Ms. B, the girl's mom, came up to my job; I was still upset about the call from a government officer. I just had to stop working and called him to ask him what was going on.

I called my office and told them I was coming back to work because I didn't want to stay in the house with him; my children were in school. They said the military police were looking for me. I then asked him to come to the MP station with me; he said no, so I went alone to turn myself in. I have always been a well-dressed professional woman; when I walked in, the police tried to pick me up, asking me for my phone number. I said, "You are looking for me."

They said no they were not, then one of them asked my name.

I said, "Mrs. Nelson" (that was my married name at the time); they then said to follow them. I went to a large room and an officer began asking why the lady and I were fighting. I told him she was my husband's lover, he brought her to Germany from the United States, she has been harassing me for a long time, and I just had enough of her bothering me. Then the officer said, "I have some good news for you, we can see you were just defending yourself, and since you have never been in trouble before, we are not going to press any charges." They said there was an old military law on the books against a soldier having an affair. It turned from me being in trouble to him being in trouble in about fifteen minutes; they went to the Officer's Club and picked him up. They took away his ID card right in front of my face; he was almost kicked out of the military that day.

I looked at him and said, "I thought you weren't coming with me," and smiled. I began to think about it; if they put him out, my children would suffer also, so I took some of my statement back, but they took the rest of my comments for their records. God intervened and I never had to go to court for fighting her because of the old military law that was still on the books about adultery. If there were an Academy Award for outstanding performance, he would get it. I asked him to go with me and confront his lover and tell her that he loved me and she needed to go back to the States where she belonged and he didn't want her anymore.

I was hoping he would use a believable facial expression with a harder voice to show her I really was the one for him. I really wanted him to tell her to leave us alone, that I was the mother of his children, but midway into the conversation I could tell it was all a show. She stood there not saying anything, showing no emotion, as if to say, is the game over yet? She then turned and walked back into the club where they both worked together, just as they did in the United States. She acted upset but I later found out they were only pretending; his major performance was supposed to deceive me. He then acted like he was sorry and said they sent her back to the United States and that he wanted to get our marriage back in order. The church was renewing our vows; I was so excited, thinking God had changed him and he would begin to be the father and husband I married. I took off from work the day I was supposed to renew my wedding vows. A lady from my job had made some flowers and a dress; my daughter was my flower girl; and my son was the ring bearer. That was to be the day I would step on the devil's foot; he came home and stood at my bedroom door. I looked up to see the beautiful wedding dress still in plastic hanging on the door; I smiled just imagining how I would look in it. To my disappointment, he looked at me and said, "I'm sorry, I can't do it."

I asked why; he said, "I'm not ready."

"Not ready?" I said; he then just turned around and walked out of the door! When I went to work, all of my co-workers asked me how it went. I was so hurt and disappointed, all I could say was, "Nothing happened," and kept on working, trying to hide the pain.

Then he started staying out all the time. It seemed my hell on earth began after he denounced our marriage; for some reason, he forgot we were still married (or it gave his girlfriend more power, because I soon found out she was still over there). He asked for a transfer to another base across town.

I thought I was losing my mind; one night I called him and the German phone lines got crossed; he put his lover on hold while he was talking to me; somehow, divine intervention, the phone lines crossed up. I am sorry I can't recall the exact words of the entire conversation; however, I heard him tell his lover he would see her after work. I recognized Ms. B's voice since I had talked to her many times at Fort Story.

Since I had overheard him talk to her, the next day when he said he was going back to work, I jumped in the car just to talk to him and get some closure. He pushed me out of the car as my children watched from the window; a few hours later, I asked my best friend's husband to take me to the club across town where my husband worked since my ex wouldn't recognize his car. The plan was great; it was like something out of a movie when I walked into his office. Ms. B was sitting in my husband's office with her legs crossed, eating a chicken dinner as if she still thought she was his wife! Remember he had transferred from the base we lived on, making it look like he no longer was seeing her. I just lost it I'm sorry. Even though I had stopped going to church a long time ago, I could not stop watching him, it was useless to try. I knew Christ before I met him but I had not yet found my calling at that time in my life. He never loved them; he played them all. My question was why was I always in the mix; let me go!

I will never forget that night; he turned around and was getting something out of the file cabinet, as if it was a normal thing; they were comfortable just being together, living a double life, while his real family was at home across town. All I could think about was how dare they pretend they were a couple; he had no shame entertaining her. While his back was still turned I went blank.

When I saw her holding that chicken dinner with her legs crossed, I knocked the dinner out of her hands. The collard greens went on the wall, and she ran down the hall. At that point, I picked up a plant and held it over his head; as it began to come down, the waitress had just walked into his office to sign out when she saw me with the plant she began to screamed; that scream could have saved me from hitting him. When he turned around, as I was holding the plant in the air, I saw the MPs coming down the hall. I came to myself after I blacked out; I was just overwhelmed to see that woman again; I realized they were still seeing each other; no matter what I said, I couldn't stop the affair.

When the military police saw me, they were running as if the club was on fire; when they turned the corner, I guess I didn't look like I was the one they were looking for because I had calmed down. They asked me if I had seen the lady who was causing trouble. I said she went that way; they ran to the left as I ran to the right, thinking thank you, Lord. I was a sinner saved by grace. I jumped into my friend Ann's husband's car and met back up with Ann at the Officer's Club. My destination that night brought me right back to the club where my children's father used to work, the base on which we lived, before he transferred to have a secret and double life on the other side of town. I should have gone back home to the United States, but why should my children suffer and another woman spend his money? I wanted to get my mind off of the spirits that were put into my life to attack me. It seemed my enemies had one mission in mind, which was to take me out and bring my family down; my husband was just a pawn in the devil's game and he was used to destroy his own home.

I went back to school at night, taking college classes in business administration since I was already a manager; I just wanted to enhance my knowledge. I began thinking I could leave him, but I needed to make sure I could take care of the children I brought into this world. Years later after my daughter received her master's degree in law, she told me she saw me doing my homework in Germany with both of them, and I made it seem like fun; it motivated her and that made her want to do well in school after I came home from work.

My ex really got mad about me trying to better myself; he tore the pages out of my books; my job paid for the college classes on the government post. He refused to leave that woman alone; even after the Army deported her, he sent for her to come back to Germany. I had to do something to show him I wasn't just going to sit back and take it. I kept going to college at night, took home-study classes, and also went to different classes all over Germany on Temporary Duty (TDY). When I went to class in another town in Germany, my job paid for the hotel and even gave me five hundred dollars to spend. I have a wall full of certificates to show for all my hard work.

One snowy night, my teacher gave me a ride home. I wanted to say no. But after looking at the weather, I said yes. My jealous husband was waiting in the parking lot and walked over to my teacher's car before he drove off. He didn't say a word to my teacher but pulled me out of his car by my hair into his van (the same van I had paid cash for him). He took me to some woods; all I could think about was how badly he beat me in Kentucky, so this time I didn't get out when he asked me to. I locked the doors and drove the van back to our house as fast as I could and locked my doors. He walked back and punched a hole in the front door, and my children began to scream when they saw his arm come through the door (they didn't know it was their dad). When the children screamed, I called the MPs. They came quickly, and I held my children to comfort them and put them back to bed. I told the military police he was crazy when he gets angry; he looked at me as if to comfort me and smiled, touched his gun, and asked, "Is he as bad as this gun?"

He didn't come back after that night. The next morning, my ex came home like nothing had happened the night before. We didn't talk as he changed clothes. I just went to work and we both began another cycle of domestic abuse.

When the Exchange sent me a check for $500 to take two more classes, he grabbed it out of my hands, tore it up, and said I was not going back to school. When I saw the movie *The Burning Bed*, it reminded me of the way he treated me, but he treated me worse. I was alone in a foreign country when I saw it. Since I couldn't go back to school, after two years, I was back wondering where he was and what he was doing.

One night I went to the Officer's Club and saw our van. I thought I would find out where he was going, so I saw him come out and asked him where he was going. He walked to the van, locked the doors, and put the key in the ignition. I stood on the front bumper, thinking he would open the door and talk to me, but instead he started driving like a mad man as fast as he could, turning the corners in the government housing area while I held onto just the windshield wipers, thinking how the insurance man had come to my job and told me he had just bought a million dollar policy and I should be careful. While he was driving fast around the corner, my legs were still on the bumper; one leg slipped off and I was still holding to the wipers. I felt death knocking at my door because one of my legs was dragging on the street; the heel on that shoe was worn down from being dragged on the street as he kept driving fast.

I could feel my other leg slip and the windshield wiper began to break, which would have been my demise; if both legs had fallen from the bumper, the van would have run over my body. That night in his rage, divine intervention stepped in; he turned a corner where the officer's quarters were, and an officer was sitting out front with his family. The office said, "Stop that van, soldier, or I'll have your rank in the morning!"

He suddenly threw on the brakes. My body fell to the street. He jumped out and began to run; I followed him; we were close to the Enlisted Club, and as he walked, I hopped behind him. My leg and foot were swollen from what had just happened; he just kept walking as if he didn't know me. A lady from the club saw him and spoke but he kept walking; at that point, I went back home. I was hurt and heartbroken; no family, no friends to call, all alone in a foreign country. I decided to go back to that parking lot to see what was so important that he wasn't coming home to his family. I never went to the club where he worked because my children were more important to me than his fly-by-night affairs. With my leg still swollen, all kinds of thoughts ran through my mind. Ms. B stayed in Germany the entire second tour. She left when he left. When I found out he was still cheating with the same woman who wrote that letter I found in his desk, it all brought back memories. Yes, I was still bothered about it.

The difference: it wasn't a letter or a confrontation with words; he was in her room in the government hotel for civilians in the middle of the night, and I was on the outside of her apartment with his commanding officer.

The story went like this: this time I had the extra keys to the van with me and got into the back of the van and went to sleep; when I woke up, I was still hurting from the pain of my leg. When I woke up, it was really dark; all I could see when I looked out of the window was a white cross with a light that was very bright. I can still remember thinking did I die? Did he really kill me this time? Am I in heaven? I then looked around and I was still in the back of the van but it had been moved. I looked over and saw the government hotel. I can remember dragging my swollen leg over to that building (remember, I had never been to that base before);

now let me tell you how divine intervention works: It was a long hall, I began hearing a voice telling me what room he and his lover were in. I knocked on the door but they would not answer.

The same voice told me to go upstairs and told me what door to knock on. I just wanted someone to help me in my desperate attempt to find some closure to my nightmare story! At first no one came. I began to knock harder, and a man came to the door. I asked him to come with me as a witness because I had no idea what I could be facing.

I said I believed my husband was in the room downstairs with his lover; to my surprise, when the man asked me what my husband's name was, he said he was my husband's commanding officer and the reason he was in the hotel was he had to go back to the States on TDY. He would talk to him if I would just stand in the waiting room; a few minutes later, I heard a loud noise as if someone had jumped out of the window. His commanding officer then told me he told him to meet him in his office in the morning. I began to hop around the building; it was just like I thought: my husband had cut a large hole in the screen and jumped out of her hotel window, trying to get away from me. After getting back in the van and arriving home, I had so many questions since I had just caught him in the room with his mistress. I know I could have gone to the military police, but I was just afraid of him losing rank, meaning the entire family would suffer. I just went to sleep, and it was just like another day as the world turns.

A few months later was his birthday; the children and I had planned the day; we waited and waited but his lover had made up her mind he would not see his family that day. He must have gone to sleep over at her apartment, and when it was almost midnight I asked the children to please go to bed, Daddy had to work late. At first, they wanted to stay up anyway. I could tell they were disappointed by the sad looks on their faces; they had made him something from school, my son had even put his handprint in some clay for him as a gift (I still have it today; I refused to give it to him since he chose to be at his lover's house).

He came home with a wrinkled white shirt too late to celebrate;

his birthday was almost over. I asked him how he let his shirt get wrinkled; he said he fell asleep on his desk (to this day, I can't see how a shirt can get wrinkled falling asleep on a desk). I was so upset; I went to get his cake; I didn't wake the children up because I knew I was upset. I said, "Here is your birthday cake." As he reached for it with a smile on his face, I dropped the plate and broke it. He went to sit down in the chair; I was tired of his disrespect, giving his lover more attention, especially since I had just caught them together a few months earlier. I was furious. I went over and pulled his white T-shirt, which caught him off guard. I then tried to frighten him with a lighter, since he always got joy in frightening me. He didn't know what I was going to do with it, since it wasn't in my nature to get angry like that. He jumped up and began to run out of the house; I ran behind him. I would have caught him but it was raining and when he turned the corner, I slipped and fell. I went back in the house. The next day, one of my co-workers said, "Did you hear that couple last night? It sounded like a woman running behind a man." She had no idea it was I.

When it was approaching time for my husband to go back to the United States, the CID made him lose three months of pay and said he could not re-enlist because of all the things he had done. He had put another woman's child in the government school and said we were her aunt and uncle; if the girl had not gotten into a fight and they had not called me at my job, I would have never known that he had sponsored his lover and her child over there. I would not have seen just how evil and deceiving he was.

He only had five years to go. I almost had a nervous breakdown after I found out his lover was still there months later. Our second tour was just a tour of drama; all I wanted to do was to hold on to his retirement, but he couldn't get that right. At that time it seemed his lovers had the last laugh after all.

Just before the military refused his re-enlistment on our second tour, my husband took me for a ride. I asked him to stop the car; he wouldn't, so at the stoplight I started to get out. He kept driving and drove me to the hospital, telling the doctors I tried to jump out of the car to kill myself. I thought that I was just going to the hospital for some rest; I was a little happy to just get away from him for a few days; a much-needed rest, I thought. At the time I wasn't aware he had told the doctors a lie to get me on the mental ward—yes, the mental ward. I went into the TV room and a lady was acting crazy so I went back into my room, where a man was acting crazy also, saying he was going to break all those windows out to get back home, since he came home and saw his wife with a man in bed.

I told myself those people were crazy but I didn't know they were. I found out that night where I was; I had slept that day, and that night when I woke up, I walked down the hall and saw two male nurses, asleep.

When they opened their eyes, I smiled and said hello. They began to scream out loud! Since their job was to watch me, they looked frightened, not knowing what I would do. I asked them what their problem was; they assured me they would tell me if I promised them to keep the secret that they fell asleep on their watch (they might get written up). I agreed and they asked my name. I told them my husband put me in the hospital for a night's rest. I just thought it was because I was having a nervous breakdown from stress.

One of them said, "You must not know where you are." He then told me I was on the mental ward, and his patients have been there for at least six months. I really began to think I must have been dreaming; I have a job; I have children to go home to. I knew I had a problem because I began thinking I had no family and my husband put me there so he could spend time with his lover and take my children away. I asked the nurses what I could do to get out; they said I sounded okay to them, just tell the doctor when he sees me tomorrow what I just told them and he could set me free!

The next day, I was thinking what to say. I knew it was my chance for freedom; when I went back into the TV room, they said they were going to the Exchange. I was happy because that's where I worked; I had already called my job and asked them to come and get me out, but they said my husband had said no one but family was to see me and he knew I had no family in Germany. My co-worker said my husband had been trying to get rid of me for a while. I told the people in there with me to wait until I changed my clothes to go with them; I thought it was my chance to break away and talk to some of my co-workers so I could go home to my children.

They said we had to wear those navy blue jumpsuits; that way they could tell the difference from the patients and the regular customers. I then said no thanks; I'll wait and talk to the doctor. I combed my hair and tried to look as good as I could since my ex hadn't been to see me since the day before. When I saw the doctor, I told my story, starting from when I first caught him with his lover and how she was living in my government quarters before I arrived and the hell on earth she had put my family through. The doctor said my husband was the one that needed to be on his ward, and he would release me that day. He said he would talk to my husband's commanding officer and make him get some counseling. He also said my husband was very abusive; he didn't know how could I tell such a horrible story and make it sound like we lived in a house with a white picket fence.

He said I was living in a house with glass walls; anything could set my husband off, and he needed help. I caught a cab home from the hospital because I didn't want my ex to know I had gotten out; he thought he was the only one that could get me out since my family was in the United States. When I walked in the house, he was in the living room. The children were at school; it seems he never told them where I was, that's why I knew I had to get out so he wouldn't lie to them. (I would have never deserted them.) He had a shocked and bewildered look, as if his plan to be with Ms. B had just unfolded and she could not move back into the government quarters she occupied before the kids and I arrived in Germany. Even though at that time I was only going to church, I received power later, but I still looked at him as if to say, "You don't know my daddy." That's why He interceded as a doctor in the hospital room. No one in my family, not even my children, knew he did that to me until now. I thought I would take that story to my grave, but I know it was divine intervention that set me free, and I had to let others know He is the same God now as He was then.

When I went back to work, I really wanted to leave him, so I began taking more management classes, home-study classes. I remember one of the ladies who worked as a supervisor at the Exchange came over to my apartment and saw I had several supervisor and manager certificates on the wall. She said she took one of those classes and had to take the test three times after studying for three months before taking it. I told her the test was easy and I only studied a few weeks and passed it. She was so impressed that she made me promise to take as many as I could since they were so easy. I will forever be grateful to her for encouraging me; my children were encouraged by the enthusiasm and my ability to multitask and become all I could be. I also took on the challenge of traveling to different parts of Germany. Yes, I set out myself on a personal journey to expand my horizon, to better myself, to show my husband and my enemies I could empower my own thoughts. God's voice, leading and guiding me, was my secret weapon. Yes, I faced twists and turns of my husband's affairs but I refused to allow the attacks of my adversaries to weigh me down. Yes, it might have been Satan's plan to rob, steal, and destroy, but I realized I had to get up from the inside, by making efforts to explore my knowledge through home-study college courses and requesting sign-offs from upper management to go and take courses in schools in other parts of Germany.

My travels included taking classes in different cities in Germany: Frankfurt, Stuggart, and Kaiserslautern; I went to manager training and on-the-job class in Wurzburg; my job paid for the hotel for six months to get my management position.

My GS-7 position in Germany required a master's degree, which I found out when I read the application on the wall just days before I was returning to the United States. To some, they are just achievements; to me, because of the struggles and unbalanced personal attacks on my home life on a regular basis, God kept me in the right state of mind to conqueror my fears; born in a motherless world, the unknown was a daily curse. I had to run on to see what the end was going to be. Because of the odds against me, I could have found many excuses and easily given up. I guess you can call it blind faith, because at the time I couldn't see the Glory.

Our first tour in Germany was uneventful; he was on his best behavior because he liked his part-time job working in the club. He didn't want to rock the boat by me asking him to quit. However, on our second tour, he had to go back to school as part of his military job. This required him to take a club management class in the United States for a few months. He wanted Club Management to be a full-time military job and not have to wear Army clothes; however, wearing suits every day gave him a big head; clubbing every night and getting paid for it took a toll on our marriage.

I was in the United States for only a couple of weeks, on vacation to see him while he was in school for his class; we all came back to Germany on the same plane, the only difference I was only a supervisor when I left and a manager in training when I got back. I put in for a position and put a card with it; I found out later the card touched the GS-15 Exchange Manager. After my college and the home-study classes I took, I decided to put in for a management position and got it. The call came in from the GS-15 Exchange Manager from Germany, offering me the GS-7 position. At the time, my husband's duty station was still in Germany but I was just visiting him in school for two weeks.

The call was divine intervention; the children, my husband, and I went back, and I made a name for myself. I received so many letters and write-ups in newspapers; I was given many titles: OSHA inspector, write-off agent, and inventory inspector. While I traveled, the children stayed with my husband. Once I wore a long, dark suede coat and tall dark leather boots with a pleated skirt to match the inside of the coat. I carried a black leather briefcase with my work papers in it. Remember, this was back in the late seventies, and seeing a successful black woman traveling alone in a foreign country in first class was unusual, and I wasn't an entertainer; that's why I never got upset when the conductor asked in German to see my tickets; I just smiled. The reason I'm stressing the way I look because it's very important that if you are a victim of abuse and your partner cheats, you should know that even though you are hurting from the inside, it should never show on the outside. You must encourage yourself.

My career was taking off; my young daughter and I were even doing fashion shows for the Military Exchange in Germany. I made another surprise visit to the Officer's Club; the same woman was there; for some reason, she jumped on the table and acted like she had a gun in her pocket to try and frighten me. I just walked away; my ex was surprised that I didn't get upset that time.

He said he was sorry. At that point, I was just tired of his lies and asked him what he was sorry for. I said, "I'm sorry that you drove me to leaving you." He asked what I meant. I said, "I just accepted a manager's position out of town and will be going into training for six months. I will be transferring two hours away and will drive home on weekends."

He said, "No, you are not going to leave me and the children."

I said, "I've already gotten power of attorney for your boss's wife to watch the children." I said if he wished, he could take me to the train station in the morning to see me off or just watch me pack.

He said again, "No, you are not."

I said, "Watch me!"

The next morning, he took me to the station and waved good-bye. I had to go and find myself, since all he did was put me down just to get out of the house. My new job was great, and I loved it, but after six months, I missed my children. They had my phone number and would call me all the time. When I first went to Wurzburg, my employees were upset that I was black; most of the previous managers were white or German. I had to put my certificates, awards, and degrees up in my office, to show them, yes, I was young, but I deserved and earned the job. I had the authority to sign my workers up for school; I signed them all up for college classes and sent them on TDY trips; the Exchange System paid for it. I won them over by showing them love instead of hate. The inspector gave my store one of the highest reports, and my picture was put in the paper with comments from many satisfied customers. I guess you can call it blind faith, because at the times I couldn't see the Glory. This was clearly divine intervention by the master's hand.

It was time for us to come back to the United States. He had the packers come and pack all our things; he was acting a little funny. He had the nerve to try and ship some of his lover's things back to the United States. I put all the German packers out; they said they had orders. I said I had orders from my government job that superseded his orders and told them to get out! My husband came home and asked me why I told the packers to only pack his things. I simply said, "I have found my own apartment and I will be using my government job to sponsor my children in school." I told him, "I have already bought new furniture and I am moving into a German apartment."

I told him good-bye and best of luck; he had played with my heart and emotions one time too many. I told him the children and I would not be going back to the United States with him.

I stayed overseas for about two years. I put my children in military school and took them shopping every week to buy whatever they wanted to ease the void of only having one parent.

My husband didn't call for a while, and I didn't call him; the kids never asked about him. One day, he came back to Germany with some red roses. I began to have flashbacks, remembering how he gave red roses to all his lovers. I told him to get back on that plane with his roses; it was a year before I heard from him again. This story ended our second and last tour.

I'm sorry the scars of rejection and betrayal went deeper than red roses. They couldn't soothe my heart. I'm jumping forward in time to compare how I was betrayed in the past and how in today's world the Seventh Commandment is still on the rise. As I was editing this book, a news flash about Tiger Woods came over the Internet. To let you know, elders have a sense of humor too; it took the spotlight off our president and our politicians. ("All eyes were on the Tiger.") On a more serious note, the media spoke of his past sins; I've always respected him but just like my ex, he was tricked; an example of getting caught up on false illusion. It wasn't in my plan to acknowledge it. But I saw a connection to my story. That's why I call this book *Divine Intervention*. This last story in this chapter temporarily closed the door to my heart.

"Everything is in God's appointed time": I'll end this chapter with the scripture: "And the Lord answered me, and said, Write the vision, and make it plain upon tables, that he may run that readeth it. For the vision is yet for an appointed time, but at the end it shall speak." (Habakkuk 2:2-3)

Chapter 7

Intervening on Behalf of the Children

1980s–1990s

"Doors Began Opening Supernaturally"

After thinking about it, I decided to give the future generation a chapter of their own. It just wouldn't be fair to place them in the middle of the battle of controversy, between lines that were lined up with hatred and deceit and uncertainty. Yes, weapons formed but they never prospered; the hand of God stopped them.

In high school my daughter always led her ROTC unit in the local parades. Tonya also led her unit on the field at her graduation ceremony at the Air Force Academy (nobody but God's favor). That very morning, I had no idea she would get so many honors at her graduation ceremony. You would have to know my daughter; she is very quiet and humble.

Children of broken homes have many demanding challenges; these disadvantages can hinder and prevent their success and growth. Once they are injured, some carry their own demons of rebellion and disobedience.

That could have easy been the case with my children; however, they march to a different beat of courage and bravery. When Tonya was in school, she was always quiet; she has always been smart as well as good looking. My son is handsome, very intelligent; he would challenge you at anything. My grandchildren have developed the same traits. That's one of the reasons we as victims must hold ourselves together: for our children; they are watching. They notice our every movement; how we deal with the attacks and the breakup can control their fate and determine how they make decisions. They may feel if Mom gives up, why should they care? I kept the affairs from them, which confused them; my son found out when his half brother's mother would call my house before the child was born. My son at age sixteen told me not to blame myself for the division in my relationship with his dad. He said the only thing I did wrong was to be too nice to his dad, and he took advantage of it. My son's statement alone turned my life around forever! My daughter was in her second year in college; both of them took the breakup very hard. I realized for the first time that my husband had taken my kindness for weakness.

I tell my children they can be whatever and whoever they want to be. The opportunities are out there; take advantage of them! Stop saying the man is keeping you down in life. Defeat is all in your mind, I'm still looking for the one the oppressor is calling the man! I'm a living witness of being alone. My mom passed away at birth; I could have used it for an excuse to not go to college and not become all I could be. They described my mom as a good-looking woman, and everyone said I looked like her; I have her picture in my last book as well. More importantly I never heard anything bad about her, nothing but praise: a hard-working, well educated, kind, and loving woman. It seems the good die young. I still had no feelings to comfort me with my missing link and lost acts of love. Writing this book gives me closure; I realize now I had to know what love was all about before I couldn't feel it. It's almost like unlocking the mystery to an unknown territory and lost pages of my life. I now know why writing has become a healing process for me to help others. My sister was a writer and a journalist in her own right; she inspired me. I did try to keep his affairs from the children; they will read about some of them for the first time in this book.

I endured the hardships and hurt from his affairs and attacks; my children's love for me kept me strong. Most of my courage came from protecting them from anyone who wanted to take their father's love away from them. I held on as long as I could but

I know if it had not been for the love from my children and the supernatural power I felt (but couldn't see), I would have been a statistic. My strength comes from the territory I defended; the war zone and the battlefield was my back yard. I'm my own person. But the innocent survivors were my children, who were too young to help when they heard and saw their mother get attacked. I had to put the smiles on their faces, in turn the funny words they said to try and make me laugh always brightened my day, in the times their father was nowhere to be found. I had the love of two little ones who helped me fix the tree, helped me cook the Christmas dinner, entertained me at school plays, and made me proud to see them get good grades and give me a reason to live when I felt like giving up.

I could always sit at the table and talk to my children, laugh with my children, and learn to grow more while teaching them to reach for their goals as I reached for mine. My children were my life. The values you establish with children at a young age will determine the course they take. I'm saying the weapon the enemy tried to use against me didn't prosper, largely because their dad forgot he gave me two little gifts of love to lean on. Now that they are older, they tell me he calls them and spends time with them. I'm happy for that, he has two children we can be proud of; it lets me know the struggle was not in vain.

Divine intervention was the source behind my strength! I'm very much aware that some who read this book don't believe in the power of God and feel there is no God; some might even say if there was a God, where was He when you got attacked time after time and when your family needed Him? I'll give you another example of strength: after you read the supernatural chain of events, you will see no one but a power not of this earth could have stepped in just in the right time to deliver my children from bondage and the hands of an evil force that wanted to destroy their future.

After seeing God's miracles, I stopped playing church and began hiding the word in my heart to Glorify Him every opportunity I had. You have already read He intervened and delivered my twin brother and myself the same day my mother passed. My brother was born first; somehow my mother held on until I was born. I know it was the grace of God that saved me (her name was Grace also). So many times a supernatural power came through and provided a way of escape.

I'll start with my first-born; Tonya was a beautiful baby, a perfect child. Yes, I mean perfect; she never gave me a reason to be upset with her about anything, her childhood was like a gift from God, born with the grace (as my mother's namesake, my mom would have been proud). I never had to help her with homework, she stayed on the Honor Society, and she always helped me out with her little brother.

Her first encounter with divine intervention was when she was a teenager. It was a hot day; I took my daughter to school to talk to her counselor to find out what subjects she needed to get into the Air Force Academy. She came back to the car crying, I asked why; she said her school counselor told her to pick another career; it was in the eighties and her counselor said it would be hard for her to get into one of the Academies because of her color.

Yes, my daughter walked into the school counselor's office with a spring in her step, mainly because I had always told both my children they could be anything they wanted to be if they applied themselves and got a proper education. My daughter had been in military schools and had learned German as a mandatory subject for years. When she entered the public school system in the ninth grade, after returning from overseas, she had been on the honor roll every year, and her grades were outstanding in all areas. Tonya was inspired by my best friend's husband, who was a captain when we lived in Germany (he just retired as a full bird colonel) After he completed Harvard University, he advised her to talk to her school about what classes to take; after seeing his accomplishments, she said she wanted to be an officer just like him.

When my daughter came back to my car with tears in her eyes, I jumped out of the car and walked into the counselor's office. I told her in a nice way I had only sent Tonya in to get the classes, not to be told to pick something else and be put down because of her color. I also told the counselor it was her job to give her the subjects she asked for, and if it was a problem, we could talk to the principal. However, it didn't get that far; she gave Tonya the subjects she asked for. Frankly, my children lived in Germany for ten years, where families of all colors got along great in the military! For fifteen years, they never experienced prejudice, saw signs of bias, or heard opinions based on emotion rather than reason—not until we came into the civilian life. The reason why it was an intervention? Not only did she get the Academy she wanted—Air Force—but she was offered full scholarships to eight major colleges, including Penn State, University of Virginia, Virginia Polytechnic Institute and State University (Virginia Tech), and Norfolk State University.

While in high school, Tonya was the highest-ranking ROTC officer in the Norfolk/Chesapeake/Virginia Beach area; she had numerous prizes, certificates, and achievement awards. She always led the parades representing her school as a member of the National Honor Society, and we attended the honor banquet at her high school every year. Tonya's science teacher was helping her get a full scholarship in the space program, which was one of her choices. That was one of the reasons our local newspaper came to our home. The reporters took a picture of our family in our own living room, while she was in high school. They wrote a full-page article on her achievements and put our entire family on a page by ourselves while her father was still living with us. I'm so thankful to God for showing His Glory on her life at that time. I was one proud mom and my son one proud brother, she was always on the Honor Society; she received numerous awards, including the cadet of the year award from the Hampton Roads Chamber of Commerce.

The Naval Academy flew her to their campus, and a West Point officer brought her to their campus after seeing her in *Jet* magazine; she stayed on their campus for two weeks to help make her decision. Tonya was in the January 30, 1989, issuing of *Jet,* the year she graduated from high school. I went out and bought a box of them and handed them out like cards because she was accepted to the Academy. Yes, I was proud. Mother and father may have; God bless the child that has its own.

Attending the Air Force Academy

Tonya received a Congressional nomination from Congressman Owen Picket; his secretary called our home to tell us she was accepted before the letter arrived. The congressman had to pick 4 out of 400 applications from four cities; the odds were against her.

Divine intervention stepped in once again. When she got accepted to the Air Force Academy, not only did she do well, she was on the dean's list. Tonya took front stage; when she graduated from the Academy, she directed the Gospel Choir and led the parade. I was so proud when they called her name out loud, saying, "Tonya Nelson from Norfolk, Virginia, is leading her battalion out on the field." It was funny because I was taking a picture of one of the Academy buses when the announcement was made; I quickly turned around and took a picture of my daughter marching on that field holding an American flag, leading her entire company.

I admired her courage back in the eighties; this was the same girl her counselor told to pick another career because of her color and said the chances of her making it as an officer were slim to none. I'm so proud of her for being one of the first blacks to open the door. When I told my tenant this story, he said, "Just show them the picture." There are only a handful of blacks among thousands. I just smiled; from that day, just like my books, I'll just show you my life, and the victory will shine through.

Her first assignment was Texas. On one of my visits, divine intervention took form; the general at Tonya's captain's award ceremony told us a story: Tonya almost got sent overseas; he had told her he would be transferring her to the Pentagon in Washington, DC. He said he went on vacation for a couple of weeks, and the next person in command re-cut some orders that were already in place; he knew nothing about it and even cut orders for all of her furniture to be moved in just two weeks. He said he knew a friend at the Pentagon that already knew about the first set of orders before they changed and asked for a special favor to reinstate the original orders that he had given her. Tonya became a major; you see God can reverse a curse through an intervention. This is a clear example you can send your children to the best schools, and the devil can still try and rob them of their inheritance.

I recently received an invitation to attend an event at the Sheraton Waterside Hotel; Senator Yvonne B. Miller will be one of the honorees. Senator Miller had a banquet in Tonya's honor when she was nominated to attend the space program; however, she chose the Air Force Academy. The senator wrote a letter to my daughter in her own handwriting, acknowledging Tonya's accomplishments. I recently met Senator Miller at a church event; I told her Tonya is now working in Washington. She was very proud.

The enemy tried to stop my son's great blessing when he was young also. His dad and I were going through a three-year divorce; my son was a teenager. I had to put our differences on the side to save our son from the fate of the system. I believe the enemy saw his future and tried to block it, but the God I serve said not so; please read how He intervened.

In the early nineties, my son was walking down the street with a boy who had just moved in our neighborhood; the boy threw a rock into a car window and ran away. We found out later the boy had mental problems; my son had nothing to do with the rock throwing. When the police picked him up, they called me. I told the officer who called he must be mistaken, because my son was in the next room. I jumped up and looked in his room, and my heart just dropped when I saw his bed was empty. I went back to the phone and began to scream at the top of my voice. The officer asked me to calm down; it was nothing to get excited about because my son was only walking beside the neighbor boy who threw the rock. Wrong place, wrong time, with the wrong person.

My son ran away from the bad boy when he threw the rock; he was almost home when the boy called his name, which put him in the area; however, in court, the boy stated my son had nothing to do with throwing the rock. My son was under age at that time and was turned over to me. My son and I really got along well. But I could tell the breakup didn't set well with him; no, he didn't like that his father was having affairs, but he still wanted his dad home with us.

God blessed us and showed favor—divine intervention—my son didn't have to serve a day in the system for that night that could have been a nightmare.

All my life, I tried to keep my children out of harm's way, and what went wrong? I was devastated; I was upset with his dad since we were going through a divorce but when it came to my child, I would break my silence toward him. I didn't call him that night but it was our son. I had my father-in-law call my husband and he came that same morning in defense of our child as if we were still together. The restraining orders I had put against my husband were still in place, but I didn't care about the rules; our child was in danger. We came together that day in peace, putting our differences aside, and the next day it was war as usual until the final decree.

My son was and has always been very obedient and well behaved. I was more in shock than anything else. So shocked that I was willing to put his dad and my disagreements away for a day, giving my son hope knowing no matter what the devil planned to steal his joy, we had his back. When he looked back to see if I was there when the judge was talking to him, it gave him hope and peace to see us both there to comfort him in his time of need. My son didn't have to say a word; my lawyer did the talking, and my son had to pay restitution just for being with that boy who had a mental problem. My son was just in the wrong place at the wrong time.

Then it was time for us to get back to trying to make it without Dad. I will be the first to admit it was hard; for years, we were a family, even the teachers at the high school would tell me it was

Henrietta Trotter

amazing my children still had the same parents, but they had no idea what I had to endure to keep it together. The glue finally fell apart when my daughter went to college and my son was in high school. In my mind, when I first married their dad in April 1971, before the devil decided to take me down, I wanted to hang on as husband and wife until PJ completed high school. The decision had to be made because of the abuse to part and live separate lives; it took time for me to stop putting an extra plate on the table. When I took my son out for dinner, it was hard because we both stared at the empty chair his father would sit in; even though he wasn't home much, I guess half of a dad was better than no dad at all.

In my first published book, *In the Mind of a Poet*, I dedicated a poem to my son called "His Eyes Are on You." The three years that I was going through the divorce, I had to run the rentals alone; the judge didn't trust him with the money. The hold-up was my ex was refusing to sign any papers my lawyer and I put in front of him. That's why I would come home from work so tired. My son was a teenager and my daughter was in college; one day, when I was very tired, a phone call came in from Rita saying my father-in-law was very ill. I found some energy from somewhere and dropped everything and started making calls to get my daughter home to see her granddad.

Tonya understood getting a military hop to Langley Air Force Base meant waiting for the next available seat to come home; it could take hours. This time was different; her grandfather had just had a heart attack and was having emergency surgery; she was still in college and needed to be here ASAP!

The general allowed my daughter to get on his plane with him; I was so surprised to see her get off that private jet! The Bible says he will make you the head and not the tail, and in this case the word was fulfilled.

Look at God; awesome! That's what I call divine intervention.

I told my son we would not be celebrating Christmas the first year we split up, because I had to pay three mortgages— two of them were rental properties—and all the utilities for the properties. I was still paying Paul for the divorce proceedings; there just wasn't enough money to go around. We separated in October and the court order for the child support was still in the making. My son gave me a Christmas to remember. He began to take over like he was the new man of the house for his sister and myself; he was determined we would have a great Christmas the first year of the separation. When I came home from work, he had the living room lit up in lights; he even had his name lit up. He looked at me and said, "Mom, you said there is not enough money to go around"; because of my income from the bank and the rental property, I didn't qualify for any government assistance, but because of my husband trying to support his lovers, money was missing. To catch up, I had more going out than coming in. It took months before the court orders kicked in. My son reminded me, "Mom, you have a credit card."

I answered yes; he then said, "Let's go shopping and buy Tonya and me some things before she gets home for her vacation." Not only did he come up with the idea for a great holiday, the laughter and singing filled the air with peace. The love of others brought us so many gifts and flowers to show their love and support.

Due to the overwhelming love from everyone, it truly became the best Christmas we ever had!

I have helped many people get back on their feet, I even had people to stay in my home or my rental property for months at a time without paying me a dime; however, at some point you must be willing to help yourself. If your child is grown and wants to give you orders, I say, sorry, no job; you can't dictate to me what to do. The Bible says if a man doesn't work, he doesn't eat. Don't tell me you are grown (my children wouldn't dare do that). You're grown? Those words alone tell me you have just outgrown my house; you see, not obeying is not an option! This house is not big enough for the both of us. As long as you are physically able, you can work. If not able, the government will help you. If you don't qualify for their assistance, what makes you think you qualify for mine?

Before I met Trotter, I had my children take on temporary

job assignments for the summer and after school. When Job Agencies called, my children knew they had to go. My son is very successful at the shipyard and paid off two trucks and just bought a home on his own with no assistance from anyone in our family. Divine intervention took form; God blessed my son when he got his job at the shipyard. It was a one-day event; they asked for applications; he applied and got it with full benefits. I had told others about it and they waited until that Monday; the job was closed down. I know it was God's voice because that was seven years ago and the shipyard hasn't had a sign up since that time. God allowed my son to be in the right place at the right time to receive his blessing. The enemy tried to stop this great blessing when he was young; I believe the enemy saw his future and tried to block it, but the God I serve intervened on every attack.

I went into detail to show God's Glory. He said my seed would be blessed, so many times society stereotypes our children; all young people can do is sing, dance, and play basketball. Yes, it is good to use your gifts; however, use your potential to the fullest. The world needs to know we have authors who write, managers who supervise, and hard workers in other professions. For some reason, reporters put the drug addict and the killer on the front page, but the attorney and doctor is toward the back. My co-workers at the bank joke that in a crowd of people, reporters will go to the one who can't speak and ask them what happened. My message to children is please, stay in school; listen to your parents; and respect those in authority.

When my daughter received her first Meritorious Service Award, Trotter and I proudly attended the ceremonies in Washington, where the enemy tried to block and hinder her success and the general had to reinstate her orders. Since God had interceded on her behalf, I repeat: it wasn't my daughter's but God's Glory! You see, only God can make a crooked road straight. That's why I must tell this story, to encourage other young children. When the devil says no, God says to all races and colors, yes we can!

It was a long ride to Washington, but it didn't bother me; my baby girl was being honored that day. When Trotter and I arrived and entered the building, we saw the black security guards and other black men and women; the other officers looked at us funny, as if we were not supposed to be there and we had lost our way. Please understand this was ten years ago. She was special, and they selected her out of hundreds of soldiers from all the other branches of services; the best of the best were chosen for their accomplishments. I believe in my heart God interceded so doors could be open for other young soldiers who wanted to excel. At first I didn't pay any attention to the stares; I was use to that kind of attention from when I held my manager job overseas. We were the first to sit down and then everyone else came into the room. Since Tonya was the highest-ranking officer in that ceremony, she was the first to stand in line. When Tonya's name was called, everyone in the room had to stand at attention when she walked across the stage in her blue Air Force uniform; we all had to greet her with a salute to show honor.

She looked like a child of the king of royal priesthood, going to accept her inheritance.

As Trotter and I walked out the door, many people came up to us and congratulated us, but to our amazement, the black attendants and security officers came up with tears in their eyes. I asked them what was wrong; they said they had tears of joy because at that time in history, only a few black soldiers were honored. The security guard said the ones who ran the program asked them to leave because pictures were being taken of the chosen ones; the ones who set up the tables and cleaned their floors had to go also. Tears ran down the security officer's face; she said, "I thought I could stay but they told me to leave also." When they heard the one who got the highest award was black, they all jumped up and screamed. She said they just wanted to shake our hands because the family of the daughter who received the highest award couldn't be put out!

When Tonya became a civilian, she said even though she had the same job as the military and ran the entire floor, when she put in for the civilian award, some people told her she didn't stand a chance because that was a hard award to get. My daughter got it with flying colors; a congresswoman was there for the third one. Tonya went on to get her master's degree in law.

She is one of the highest-ranking civilians on base. My daughter took her boss's job when it was posted; she is now in charge of the employees she was working with. She is equal to a general; when on base, she has to be respected like an officer. God blessed her with a parking space with her name on it.

Tonya's boss in Washington wrote me a letter to tell me my daughter drove five hours to attend the funeral of her father, and the former Secretary of State Condoleezza Rice was there with her Secret Service detail. I later found out her boss spoke of the former Secretary of State visit, as a joke because the people in West Virginia thought Tonya was Ms. Rice when she showed up as a high ranking official. In the letter addressed to me her boss said, "I wanted to tell you what a great job you did raising an incredible daughter." She further said she was a joy to work with, a role model in humility. She thanked me for being a great role model and raising a daughter they all admired.

The letter brought tears to my eyes; she had no idea she was writing to a woman the devil tried to take out. In my darkest hours, I would read the Scripture that said, "My seed and my seed would be blessed." The reason I wrote so much about Tonya's accomplishments was because the high school counselor told her to take other classes due to her color. God still got the Glory!

She had a praying mother. I know some readers will get upset with me, but I'm saying it anyway. Back in my day, in the fifties before they took prayer out of schools, we never heard about shootings and violence. Those who don't want to pray don't have to, but those who want an angel to intercede on their behalf should not be denied their rights to speak to the comforter. I'm fully aware that not all readers call themselves Christians; never forget, your enemy watches you and studies you to bring you down; that's why I write: to show God's power is greater than my adversaries.

The difference was Tonya never accepted the fate of her doubters. She said God had been so good to her; she wanted to give back to her community. She volunteered hours to help children; she stayed at the Air Force Academy an extra year to recruit children from schools all over the United States. She was recognized for helping the underprivileged with their homework. Tonya met her husband when she worked with the homeless at church. That story sounds like the Book of Ruth, how she gleaned in the field and met King Boaz, who became her husband. Even to this day, my daughter remains quiet and humble; she just told me the other day that I didn't have to put her accomplishments in this book and relive her job, since she has top-secret clearance. I honored one of her wishes about the job assignment, but I had to tell about the victory.

My son PJ took three years of ROTC but decided to work for the government instead; he is very good with his hands; from a young age, he liked breaking things and putting them back together; remolding he could also out-think me, and that's hard to do. He is now married and has 2 sons Daivon and Eric and two stepchildren, and is doing quite well. When all odds were against my children, nobody but the hand of God could have stopped my adversaries from getting their way. I feel the events are truly the signs of miracles, of modern-day divine intervention and supernatural powers.

I have spoiled all my grandchildren. PJ's son Daivon reminds me of Tonya; that's why we have him in a special school for the gifted; he will march in his cap and gown this year, he is eleven years old.

"And let us not be weary in well doing: for in due season we shall reap, if we faint not." (Galatians 6:9)

When my grandchildren from out of town visited us every summer, Daivon asked, "Why do you treat them better than me?"

I responded, "I see you every other weekend, I only call and send them packages on special occasions; they live nine hours away. They are mine also. They need more love and attention." He just smiled and said okay.

The dream of a mother, whether her child is by birth or by

law, is a desire for them to have self-determination, to be self-sufficient. Starting now, show tough love. Teaching them is giving them responsibility; instead of giving them a fish to eat and later on they are still hungry, teach them how to fish!

As God promised in His word, "The LORD shall cause thine enemies that rise up against thee to be smitten before thy face: they shall come out against thee one way, and flee before thee seven ways." (Deuteronomy 28:7)

This chapter showed His word didn't come back void. "To give unto them and to their seed, a land that floweth with milk and honey." (Deuteronomy 11:9)

That's God!

Chapter 8

Woman Scorned;
Crime of Passion

October 20, 1991
"Lovechild: Child Out of Wedlock"

I declared my deliverance from domestic violence, which carried a scar. Time has healed the wounds; this month marks the eighteenth anniversary of the chapter that created this book. I called my sister that day and told her I wasn't going to talk long, I just wanted her to know I had left him for good. It was something about the way I said it; she knew I meant it.

The first thing she asked me was did he kill someone. I asked why she would ask such a question. She replied, "For twenty-four years, after he hit Daddy in the nose just months after you married him, I've been asking you to leave him." I didn't respond, I just said politely, "I'll talk to you later," and hung up.

I had papers saying I was still married, but I knew they were just papers. When it was over, he refused to sign the final decree. He said himself he never wanted to sign them. His actions kept us separated for three years. My husband's mistress thought I was holding up the divorce but it was my ex, giving the last and final performance of his life with me as his wife. He avoided showing up for court and left his job when the sheriff came to serve papers to appear. I just couldn't understand why he acted like he wanted to be free so badly and when he got his chance, he tried to keep me from going on with my life. Sorry, I just couldn't wake up the next morning and ask, "What do you want for breakfast?" He had to go!

I had to pay hundred of dollars to get the Commissar of the Court of the state of Virginia to sign it. We had to *force* him to sign so I could be free! He would not sign until after his attorney quit his case. What would cause a woman to become scorned? After she feels betrayed and hurt?

Yes, my husband and his affairs had scorned me. They made me feel inferior and unworthy of attention; my children's father treated his lovers as if they were the wives and I was the girlfriend. Once I found a copy of his cell phone bill and called the lover who ended our marriage; he even came on my job and fussed at me for calling the number (we were still living together and I was paying the bill). He acted up so badly my boss asked me if I wanted her to call security. I guess he forgot there were laws against a woman being mistreated or threatened. I told my boss I'd take care of it and told my husband to leave my job.

This chapter refers to the beginning of what happens to a family after the woman is scorned; it also tells how the victim feels about-facing reality and opening up their eyes when they make direct, deliberate, and open attacks. My faith caused me to hold it together because I almost lost my mind; that's why I had to wait years to revisit the attacks. At the time surrounding this chapter, I was just a sinner saved by Grace (it's funny, that was my mom's name). My test was after our second tour from Germany; my son was given a half brother, which became my living testimony. It was years later when I found God. I never missed a church service but I had to go through a lot before I found God's delivering and healing power. Events and experiences shaped my destiny by renewing my mind and gave me strength to survive and help the Master to heal the brokenhearted through my ministry.

Yes, I was scorned but Paul decided to show them mercy. He said my daughter was in college and my son was sixteen years old; I needed the money to support them. My attorney then said if my ex lost his job or went to jail, no one would get paid and support would get cut off. The judge ordered support, which I received for ten years until I remarried.

They were also offered a plea agreement without my knowledge; after I found that out, I hired another attorney to fight some of my cases so that would never happen again! It will always be my ace in the hole because I can go back to court and ask another judge, "Where is my signature?" The judge left the restraining orders in place; I had three, and one of them was permanent due to the severity of the case.

What caused me to become scorned was going through years of abuse. Just to touch on my life of hell, these events went on after his first tour in Germany, up until the breakup of the marriage. I recall being slapped and spit in the face; I was punched to the ground; he put a pillow over my face while I slept, and placed a gun to my head; a glass plate and a glass cup were thrown from the other side of the room and hit my head until it began to swell (I had to take a towel and rub the pieces of glass out of my face; since the pieces got into the skin, every time I would rub, the blood came out). I had to call in sick; I was too ashamed for anyone to see me. I ended the violence myself after the attack on October 20, 1991, when he allowed his lover to beat me; it became a crime of passion. I give no excuse for my actions; as I said, enough was just enough.

Scorned, torn, and just worn down from the years of abuse and betrayal.

I remember a story of a generational curse that gave my life story some kind of clarity. My father-in-law's brother James told me he and his brothers witnessed a lot of abuse as small boys; at times, he would sit quietly at the table and put his hands over his ears, trying to stop the screams and yells of his mother when their drunken father would tie her to a tree and beat her for hours on the weekends, the houses were far apart in South Carolina. I was also told my father-in-law had words with his father about how his mom was being treated; his father began shooting his gun into the air; he just started running in the cornfields and then joined the service. He never returned. I feel that story is very relevant because the abuse began to make sense; his father had witnessed abuse at an early age, which I'm not at liberty to even speak about, but I know it affected my children's father as he relived it in his mind every time he hit me. Somehow in his mind I became his great-grandmother tied to that tree.

Yes, that happened before he was born, and the unexpected death of his mom, which I refuse to talk about also, out of respect for our family, caused him to be very angry. I could be wrong but it all made sense after James told me the story. I thought I could make a difference and bring him happiness with our children; if I showed love, I would get love in return.

The abuse that damaged my marriage and caused me to be a scorned woman now had a name: "A Generational Curse." My therapist said my ex didn't know the difference between love and hate; since both our mothers had passed at a young age, I realized he could not show something he didn't understand.

The Tale of an Unknown Soldier

Many nameless victims lay in shallow graves with a similar, untold story. Their story would go like this: A war-torn soldier has bruises from the ongoing attacks. She has cutup clothes and shattered dreams; her misdirected and misguided journey takes her to a place with a revolving door as she forgives and returns. Too many uncertainties: not knowing when her attacker would go off or express unprovoked rage. Her body is in a constant alert zone, preparing for an unannounced attack at any time. She knows her abuser is somewhere, skillfully planning the next attack. She has no bodyguard or rich friends to comfort her or give her a safe haven to spend the night for a short time, until she gets herself together. Many battered women are workingwomen, too proud and ashamed to go to a shelter; they can't afford to take time off work to make a speech or appear on a talk show.

She knows the shelters will only house her for a short time; with low self-esteem, after being brainwashed, she stays with her abuser for a stable living arrangement. All of that combined didn't prepare her for the slow death it took to write the horror in her own words; domestic violence was forced to loosen its hold as it let her go. Who was that daughter so strong? Henrietta Trotter.

I saw the writing on the wall; I just wasn't reading it. I tried to be a good wife but after the events I'm about to reveal, all hope was gone. This caused me to be bitter and scorned. All I could remember was staring at a piece of paper that came through the mail that said "Final Decree." These events occurred throughout the marriage; I'm not giving any dates or time, just telling you what happened. I still have my right mind, as God intervened and canceled every plot for my destruction. I referenced the movie *The Burning Bed* (starring Farrah Fawcett) because when I saw it, it reminded me so much of what I had gone though: A jealous, controlling husband who didn't want his wife to have a life, but instead dictated to her and belittled her every chance he had. The part that really got my attention was when he tore her schoolbooks up. My husband tore the pages from my college books and tore up checks from my job before I had a chance to pay for some classes. He said, "You have enough education; you have one degree and that's enough," and he ripped up a $500 check from my job right in front of my face; all I could do was cry. A month before, the military police came to my government apartment. Yes, to some education is a right; the struggle for equality come so easy for others, but for victims like me it was a fight! God intervened and had the end justify the means, when my daughter saw my tears and felt my pain and heard my cries; many nights, her dad left us alone. Her victory felt like my victory, as she grew up and made me proud; she carried the torch to the finish line for the fallen soldier of those that lost hope, like me. Now do you understand why I made a reference to the movie?

My biggest mistake was telling him I was going to leave and not leaving. When I returned home in 1989, a year before I left him for good, I told him I had enough and this time it would be for good. Many days afterwards, my face would be disappointed as I saw unforgettable hatred and mental attacks. He cut up a pile of clothes while I was at work and left it in front of my bedroom door.

My son discovered he had put my broken rings, watches, and jewelry in the cracks of the loosened wood in the attic; he was too young to understand hate in its worst form. My son showed me what he had found with a look of despair on his face. I didn't get upset about the material things his dad destroyed, because that was his "MO," but the thoughts of it affecting my sixteen-year-old son after he saw the torn passports of himself and his sister in the attic cracks seemed unbearable; I wanted to spare him of the pain by removing the items: however, they are still there looking up at us if you look through the crack because they were placed too far down to reach.

That was one of my breaking points; I soon learned of the birth of Ms. C's newborn; she was having my husband's child, my son's half brother. All my thoughts were in disarray; I thought I had nothing of value to say to him. The scandal and pain were just too great. All my sacrifices couldn't spare my little ones of the pain I never wanted them to experience. The lies finally led to our breakup.

When I discovered my ex had gotten another woman pregnant, he knew I would leave him, so he began destroying more of my clothes and my jewelry. One day, I came home and found a pile of cut-up clothes in the hallway; one day, I went up in the attic and my son showed me another loose board he had noticed. I pulled it back and saw all my best nightgowns, most of my jewelry, and my passport all cut up in between the cracks of the attic. I went into the garage and saw some of my ID that looked like it had gotten rained on. When he left, he took my best coats, leather, furs that I bought in Germany, and my best dresses; this was before I got the restraining orders. Now that it is all over, I think it wasn't that he didn't fear me; he knew I cared about my jobs. He knew I wouldn't do something that would cause me to lose it all; that's why it hurt me so bad when he instructed his lover to go after me and lie to get me in trouble. He knew in order to fight me; he would have to fight dirty!

When my son showed me what his dad had done, I just looked in shock and thought to myself, *He's gone mad!* My son just turned around, not saying anything, and I'm glad we both had unspoken words. My son was still in high school. It seemed the demons were all let out at one time to destroy my home. *It was time out for words; action must take form* is what went through my mind.

Yes, that moment started my willingness to want to leave after seeing the cruelty of mental abuse starting to unfold. I did not want it to affect my son; there were warning signs.

A thought for today:

- Wisdom is knowing what to do.
- Skill is knowing how to do it.
- Virtue is doing it.

Reaching Out for Help!

I quickly received confirmation when I saw the following headline on AOL's Web site: "Oprah's Domestic Violence Double Standard" (posted November 4, 2009, by Adam Horne). God shows up and shows out. According to the news story, at the center of the controversy is Debra Winans, ex-wife of BeBe Winans, the forty-seven-year-old Grammy Award-winning gospel and R&B singer. In February, BeBe made headlines when he shoved Debra to the ground in front of their two kids (age ten and thirteen) after a verbal dispute regarding custody issues. A domestic charge violence against BeBe is pending until a court hearing in 2010. It also said Winfrey invited BeBe Winans to appear on her show. It will all be unraveling soon. I feel this relates to my story since my children were about the same ages as their children; Oprah's people rejected me when I wanted to tell my story but I feel the same way BeBe's wife feels: why should he be allowed to shine when he has a pending case? If he was poor, he might be in jail awaiting trial. Is the system just for the rich and famous? Are the poor to be overlooked when they get hit? (Something to think about.) I have to take my work seriously because there is only room on a tombstone for names and dates; there's no room for recognition. All victims should be treated equally.

I was going to take the line about Oprah refusing to see me out of this book, but I got a confirmation from God Himself that it should stay. I did feel bad that she rejected all my e-mails and letters, so I stopped sending them. When I first got an answering machine back in 2001, I recorded a message with my sister's voice saying that Oprah was too busy for me because so many people write to her; that message stayed on my answering machine for eight years. I have always admired and respected Oprah; I feel in my heart that if she were screening her own calls and e-mails she would have answered me. I only wanted my story to help others; I was already established.

I can remember when Oprah first started out, she talked about domestic violence and I would say, "I sure would like to tell my story." I was much younger then, and I was still living with the one who was abusing me. There was no way I could have gone on her show and come back to a man who had just thrown a plate at my head; the plate itself broke all the plastic rollers on the back of my head, only because I had gotten upset with him and went to stay with my sister for a few weeks. One of my tenants had given me a phone bill that showed my ex-husband was calling his ex-lover Barbara in Texas. That's one of the things I will never understand; how can you be dead wrong and beat me? I got beat up for no reason; God help me if he really had a reason. That's why I had to leave him in 1991, years after this attack.

A few weeks after he threw the plate, he threw a coffee cup against the wall, and the pieces from the cup went into my face, all because my daughter ran the phone bill up. I was trying to defend her while she was at school by saying the bill wasn't that much. I will never forget because my face hurt so badly, I just sat on the floor. He ran over to me and acted like he cared that I was sitting on broken glass. I went into the rest room like all the times before to wipe my bloody face, but this time it was just a little different, because the small pieces of glass were imbedded in my face; it would be clear for a second, and every time I would wipe my face, one second later the blood would rush back out. I called in sick; if I had gone to work like that, he would still be in jail right now. That's why my husband told the judge I had done no wrong. His own attorney said in front of the judge he had nothing to work with as evidence against me during the twenty-four years and quit his case before it was over. Looking back, I did the right thing by not continuing to write Oprah, because if I had gone on the show at that time, I would not have lived to tell about it.

When I read about the prophetess Juanita Bynum getting beat up, I tried to let her know the same thing happened to me; when she came to my town, she didn't seem to care, but a few months later, after I had given her all my information, she was abused also and wanted the world to care about her. I had warned her and asked to speak to her; to this day she hasn't contacted me. I forgive her but I'm that scorned woman.

How I First Discovered His Newfound Lover

After the physical abuse started up again, the affairs followed. Now that I look back on it, he started the attacks so it would look like he was so unhappy he had to go to someone else for a listening ear. It was always in that order. It was the same game, just a different partner.

I went back to college when I got back in the United States. I wasn't going to let him stop me! I took management classes; my job at the bank paid for them. However, he felt threatened by me going back to college to get a higher position. Since they were night classes, I could go to school and still watch him; also so that began his cheating with a lady who destroyed our marriage.

I could tell something was wrong. My son began acting differently; he wasn't smiling as much; when I asked him was anything wrong, he would say, "Nothing."

I went to the basement one day and saw an old Army duffle bag that my son had hung on a line with his dad's clothes in it; he began punching it. PJ was a teenager in high school. My ex-husband was beginning to stay out late and change his working hours just to hurt me. He started to do a lot to catch me off guard; I never knew his schedule. Years later the judge asked his lover how long she had been seeing him; according to the court transcript she proudly said, "Three years." My ex-husband began acting strangely, and the signs were the same as they were when he was cheating before. I couldn't prove anything at that time; I only was suspicious, but I could tell whomever he was cheating with wanted me to know who she was.

I asked myself was this girl trying to drive me crazy? One day, I was washing some clothes; I had just put a load of my husband's clothes in the dryer; when I began to fold his clothes, I found a picture of his lover's son; he looked to be five years old at the time, so I knew it couldn't have been his because we had just come back from Germany. I know now the picture was just to taunt me, because I also found a pair of child socks with a high school ring with her name engraved inside of it, to further torment me. I questioned him about it. He just looked at me, shrugged his shoulders, and walked away. Later, the woman whose name was inside the ring would become my worst nightmare.

My daughter called and said she was coming home from college for Christmas. I was always excited when she came home; it always seemed like a real family when we all got together again; however, the happiness was short lived because I wanted her dad to come with me to show Tonya off at my job. She had made a surprise visit and had her uniform on; I was so proud I just wanted my co-workers to see her with it on.

Tonya's dad said he had other plans; he was evasive and acting nervous, which made me suspect something. I caught him driving down the street with his lover; we never got to my job. Both my son and my daughter were disappointed. Halfway to my job, the kids said, "Mom, Dad's red truck just passed us."

I told them they must be mistaken. My son then said there was a lady in the front seat; at that point, I made a U turn in the middle of the road. I knew something was wrong because he took off so fast I couldn't catch him! I was about to give up when the kids said, "There he is!" He was behind the restaurant, so I pulled my Nissan beside his truck; lo and behold, he was with his lover. That's why he tried to hide the truck behind the building;

my children pointed to where he was hiding. He jumped out of the truck but she stayed in and locked the doors and smiled. I asked her in a nice way to please get out of my truck; the ride is over. For some reason, she didn't know what time of day it was. Yes, this was years before I started preaching or having a real relationship with God. I went to church but I told God, I got this. I was his wife and I just pulled out my key and opened the truck door. I said again, "Would you please get out of my truck?"

I was confused about who this girl was (he had many nameless women who harassed me during my marriage with him). I found out later she was some Christmas part-time help at his job; he was giving her a ride home. Since she wouldn't get out, I told her I would pull her out by the scarf she had around her neck. She was very short and when she got out, she was huffing and puffing. I then began speaking to him; she seemed upset to see me talking to him, so she started walking toward my car. I wasn't upset with her, she could only do what he allowed her to do, and so I took his cap off and put it in the mud and stepped on it. When I saw her coming toward my car (my children were still inside), I acted like a mother bear protecting her cubs. I started to drive away as she kept coming toward the car; there was some water in the parking lot and the wheels slipped so she jumped back out of the way. Instead of him leaving her and following his family, he went toward the restaurant where she was. Yes, I was a scorned woman; I broke a Coke bottle against the side of the building and watched it as it broke. They were not near it but it let them both know how I felt about their little affair. About ten minutes later, here comes my husband crying in the living room, saying he was sorry; this was all an act, just like before in Fort Story and in Germany.

I was outdone, he was cheating again and this time my children had caught him in the act of deception. How could he? I didn't know what to do; I began planning how and when to leave him for good.

A few months later, I drove to my brother's house. My husband was angry with PJ for telling me about the phone conversations he overheard between him and his lover. At that point I knew it was time to leave; I was thinking my child might get hurt. My twin brother said he would stay with me just to see how crazy he was; since I had problems with my husband before when I was alone, it wasn't hard to find me. I left a trail of clothes falling out of my trunk toward my brother's house, which was just around a few corners. My brother parked his car behind his own house just to see if my husband would come by to hurt me, since it would look like I was alone. Just as I thought, my husband was angry that I had left. When my husband stopped his truck outside the house, it sounded like he had hit the house; it made a loud noise, and my brother's neighbors ran out to see what was going on. I guess he was trying to scare me and slammed on the brakes.

I screamed after seeing that my husband was about to attack me. My brother loaded his registered gun and pointed it toward the hall where I was standing. My husband didn't knock, he just ran toward me, saying something with an angry look on his face, raising his hands toward me. It was a matter of seconds. I looked to my right and saw my brother coming out from his bedroom with his fingers squeezing the trigger of his gun. I said, "Henry, no!" and I knocked the gun upwards. My husband turned, not knowing the gun was at his face. All this occurred because my husband ran toward me to hit me, but this time he was in for a surprise. He didn't know my twin brother was at home, and he almost got shot for trying to hurt me. My husband ran so fast and jumped in the truck; I was glad nothing happened but that was close. I told my twin brother I didn't want him to go to jail for me.

Henry then said he didn't care if he had to go to jail because he was in his own house when my husband ran through the front door to hurt me; he also said he had heard about him hurting me in the past when I moved away. This time he wasn't going to stand by and allow my husband to hurt me in his own house. He said he would just have to take his chances with the judge.

My husband went back home and called Henry's house about twenty times; at first I hung up; that's why there were so many calls that day. I finally got tired and asked him what he wanted; he said just to talk.

I said, "About what? I'm getting an attorney" (I had gone to see him that day). I told him the attorney told me just how much I would get with two children; my attorney said that he was going to take him to the cleaners. My husband really got upset then and said, "Come home now, I promise I will change. We don't need a lawyer to get in our business."

I guess my own insecurities wore me down. The reason I went back home was I knew my husband would just harass me just like he had done every time I tried to leave him. To him I was his property; at that time, I wasn't as strong as I am now. My son was a teenager and I felt he needed his father. I was weak minded, thinking it would be hard for me to live on my own. I had a good job but he was good at brainwashing me.

Our reunion only lasted for a little while. The same girl kept calling my home, asking for him by name. He bought a cell phone and would not give me the number, and he brought a private phone line into our den just to call her. I've never seen someone try so hard not to be with someone before. You would think she was candy and her house was made out of sugar. When his mistress couldn't get him on the private line at our house, she would call on our regular line just to upset me. She got very bold; she would call my home and my job and say, "Hello, this is Ms. C, can I speak to your husband?" and then she'd laugh. She called my house any time of the day. I told her I would change the number; she said, "Go ahead, he'll give me the new one."

She would call my job and hang up; after she called and left a message, my boss finally told me to tell her that she was violating a law to call a bank and harass me; they would record the conversation and press charges against her. She was getting so bold that if I didn't pick up, she would ask for me by name; her phone number would show up on the phone's caller ID, and they recognized it was the same number and same voice. My co-workers saw my reaction when I would hang up; I did not want to tell others my business but they saw me slowly hang up and saw how it always took my smile away. I still have a copy of a notarized letter written by one of my co-workers my boss secretary to give to the judge stating she witnessed the calls and the harassment. You see I always hid behind my smile. After my boss got involved, the calls stopped at work. I asked her to stop calling my house; she said she was still seeing him. Later on, I was shocked to learn the affair had lasted three years; this was when he was still living in my house.

For some reason, he decided he wanted to make my birthday nice; he invited all my family and hired a limo to take us to a seafood restaurant at the beach. I was all excited; all our family came. As we left the house and got in the limo, just before I closed the front door, the phone rang; guess who? Our friend who needed to get a life! She caught me off guard because I hadn't heard from her in a while; that usually meant he had gotten tired of that one and was trading her in for another model; I was still the queen of the house. This one was like a bug that just wouldn't go away!

She said she knew about the birthday party. She even knew where we would be eating. I then hung the phone up; it was my birthday and she wasn't going to upset me, with my family already on the way to the beach. When he upset me, I acted like he wasn't there, a ghost. To this day, I never told anyone she called to spoil my birthday. That's the way you have to treat the enemy. While they are trying to bring you out of your character, confuse them by acting like they have no power (and will never have any power). The Bible says to forgive, and I'm doing it very gracefully, still holding on to my joy and my peace, which she wasn't woman enough to take!

God was still working on me.

His lover came to my job to harass me. She called again and said she was pregnant, and in three months, my father-in-law would then also be hers; she said the baby would come out looking just like him! I told her to stop interrupting us while we were trying to spend some time together; I said my husband didn't date bears (you must remember at that time I was only going to church; I had not yet given my life to Christ). I called her a bear because to me her face looked like a bear. She hung up; I guess that really got to her because when she came to my job, she got into the elevator and pulled her white sweater up to show me her stomach.

The day she came to my job was just like any other day; I call her crazy because she knew you cannot just walk into my office, you have to have clearance and a special card key with picture ID to enter my workplace. PJ and his friends had seen her many times, following me to work as I dropped him off to school; many times co-workers had seen her follow me during lunch and after work, but I stayed in control.

This day was different; she hated me so much that she got a part-time job delivering magazines to our building. To her disappointment, she still couldn't enter my office without clearance; the security guard told me she was asking questions about me. He told her I had a beautiful picture of my family on my desk. I guess that really upset her; even after she called about the baby, I was still acting like a happy family. When my husband asked me about the picture, I asked him who told him I had a picture on my desk and how he knew which one was on the desk; he then stopped talking about it. Yes, it was shocking; she was so bold as to get into the elevator to approach me. That day what little faith I had at the time was tested. To get you to understand just how it all unfolded, you must realize she did not have it all together. The reason she came to my job was because even after her call to my house, my husband was still living with my son and me; she thought after the call about the baby, I would put him out. She was upset he was still living with me. It wasn't until after the baby was born that I said it's over. She knew my lunch schedule because she would park her car in front of my building and wait for me in the parking lot when I got off. So the elevator was her next shot to get close to me. Because of her, I was really feeling scorned.

Somehow she had pinpointed the time I went to work and left for lunch; that's how she knew I would get on that elevator. It's funny, now that it's over; I wonder how many times she practiced it until she got it right. Anyway, she made sure someone else was with us on the elevator: a white man with a suit was standing to the front and she was standing behind him. The reason I'm saying the man's color is that's one reason I held back from losing my job that day; if I had gotten into a fight, that man might have said, "Look at those ghetto women," creating a scene and losing everything I had worked for. There was another man standing in front of her, looking straight ahead and waiting to get off. At first I didn't pay her any attention and she began to clear her throat; at that moment, she pulled her white sweater up, revealing her pregnant stomach; she looked at me with a smug expression and smiled. That really made her day; she was so happy. I think she did that because when she called and told me she was pregnant, I didn't believe her. When I got off the elevator, my hands were shaking, not because I was afraid of her (not in the least) but I was afraid I might lose everything I had worked for since she came to my job to provoke me. It was divine intervention that helped me get off that elevator without touching her. Nobody but God! I wasn't saved then; I believe that day was my biggest test, not to give into her hatred for me.

Things with her didn't get better; they got worse. I found a checkbook to his new checking account; the return checks were in her handwriting; one of the checks was for Toys R Us. She was buying items for her newborn child. I found many other checks, which were submitted as evidence in my divorce hearing. My attorney used this evidence to help burn him later on.

Crime of Passion

The morning of October 20, 1991, was a little windy; I looked at the clock and noticed my husband had not come home from work from the post office. His mistress had called me three months earlier and told me she was pregnant and the baby was due in three months. I had already seen her stomach in the elevator at my job, I saw the papers my husband had left around the house; he had signed for a house for her.

It was time for me to make my move. I told my son we were going to the store to get him a coat. The store was in the same area as the house my husband had just financed. I made a small detour; it was easier than I thought because his truck was in her garage. There were no curtains on the windows; even someone with nothing to hide would put something up against the windows. It seemed she had been expecting me for a while. As large as our truck was, he didn't need to try and hide it. I had a bad feeling about knocking on that door, even though I knew my ex had signed for the house note. For the safety of my son, I parked the car down the street and walked to the house. I knocked on the door; I really was hoping to see my husband, but she came to the door wearing a see-through nightgown. My husband was quietly sleeping on her sofa; he still had work clothes on. His lover smiled at me and proudly said, "You see, I don't ask him to come; he comes on his own." Those word have rung in my ears for eighteen years; everything else I had to try and remember, but those words I'll never have to write down to remember!

I didn't have anything to say to her because I knew I was about to lose it. I remember thinking to myself, you're not worth it, and I will see you in court!

When she said those evil words on that October day, she thought the last laugh would be on me. But it didn't go down that way; they decided to jump me before I got to the phone. After I begged my husband to let me get off the floor, I ran and called the police from the house next door. I knew the law was on my side; my husband had bought the house; there were no signs of forced entry because she let me in and beat me. That day everything seemed bleary, and my thoughts were jammed like jelly. I never thought anyone could go temporarily insane; until it happened to me, I always thought they made that up just to get out of something. All I can remember is the lamp hit the TV, which made a loud noise; a large puff of white smoke went into the air. My husband woke up and forgot he was holding the baby;

he stood straight up, which caused the baby to fall from his lap (later, the doctor said it only needed an aspirin).

My husband was holding the baby, which is well documented, and grabbed me by the arms and legs. She was so happy that she finally had a chance to hurt me. She grabbed a broom and began hitting me as hard as she could from the top to the bottom of my body, leaving large, black bruises all over my body. I remember seeing her reach back to gain strength to hit me with more force as I lay helplessly; my back was flat on the floor. I can remember begging my husband for my life while he was holding me down with all his strength. Sorry, real life is different from the movies; no matter what I said, they would not let me go. She began hitting my nose, eyes, and ears; divine intervention stepped in because instead of my ex-husband letting me go, he pulled his body over mine to protect my face. She was jealous and got really mad then, because he was protecting me. I believe the enemy had my husband's mind at that time but I don't think he was thinking about me. When he saw her hit me in the nose, eyes, and face, he put his body over my face, pinning my legs and arms to the floor. She began hitting him on the back. Then and only then, he let me go. Years later, as I look back, I think maybe he was trying to protect my face. I was only thinking it was to stop the police from seeing my bruised face after she had already begun to hit me multiple times.

She then said she would get the gun from under the front seat, which really scared both of us. He was only trying to save himself from being involved deeper; he let me go. He knew I had blood pressure problems, combined with another illness that could have taken me away in the excitement of that day. She thought he was saving my face, after it seemed like she had beaten me for hours. After the attack, I decided not to go home but waited for the law to arrive. I began to get flashbacks as they came to my memory; I realized that was what happened in Fort Story years earlier when I caught him with a woman and just went home. He then took the same women, his cook, to Germany and lost his military career over her. This time he was caught at the home of another lady who helped ruin my marriage. This time I had witnesses; he would pay for being caught, I wanted it recorded by the police to help me break free from a tyrant.

My son had driven the car up to the house; he said he was worried about me. He had no driver's license; I didn't even know he could drive. I asked him to get back into the car; I knew I was about to change the events; this time, I would have it on record that he was found at his lover's house with their month-old baby. I had to think and think fast. I went into my trunk and threw any and everything I could find at the windows of the home purchased by my husband. I ran out of things to throw so I started breaking the windows with my hands. I was in a state of confusion just seeing my husband in the house with another woman. I was so upset I began to say out loud, "That love child will grow up poor!" On every word, as I broke the windows with my hands, the blood began to drip down my arms and hands from the cut glass. I felt no pain because my body had already been beaten with bruises from the top of my head to the bottom of my feet; big, black bruises that are on record in court as evidence.

I had been vindicated. I didn't want to hurt anyone; I just wanted them to know I didn't just turn and *run* after they beat me up.

It was great to see them scream with fear since thirty minutes before; I was lying helpless on the floor.

When his lover heard the police cars, she came out of the house; when she came toward me, just before the police arrived, I sprayed mace at her, but the wind was blowing and the mace flew right back in my face. By the time the police came, I couldn't see out of both my eyes; I told my son to drive my car home; I didn't want him involved at all, I then said I would be all right and told him to call my brother. I was so upset; I sat in the back of the police car. I was so tired. I didn't say anything. I was in a state of shock and mass confusion.

The police asked me questions; I wouldn't speak. I was still in a state of denial that my husband of twenty-four years had betrayed me, with no regard for our family. Not only was their baby born on my father-in-law's birthday, my ex had given the lovechild our last name, which she proudly told my lawyer. We had all the information we needed to close my case in court; that's why it took him so long to sign the divorce papers. I went temporarily insane and openly broke the windows; afterwards I went to the neighbor's house and called the police. It looked like everyone in the neighborhood called; it was like *Starsky and Hutch*; police cars and ambulances were coming from all directions!

It was my hell day. Also just moments before the police came, my husband ran out the house where I had just gotten beaten up and left his mistress and their new baby. He didn't answer when I asked him where was he going? I then took a tree branch off the tree and told him he better go back into his lover's house, the residence he bought in secret with marital funds. The police were on their way; how dare he try and disappear after holding me down while she beat me!

The officers arrived; no one even tried to put handcuffs on me. They took me to the station; I voluntarily sat in the back seat of one of the cars. The officer was about to ask me who I was.

After a few minutes of silence, a white man came over to the police car; at that point, there was nothing on the police report because they didn't see anything. The neighbor came to the car door and said, "I don't know why his girlfriend came over there" (meaning me); they were the model couple, he said. "He comes home to his wife every day; they stay to themselves. He's always cutting the grass and doing something around the house, and they just had a new baby."

At that time, I had heard enough! I broke my silence and said out loud in a very professional voice, "I am the wife; she is the girlfriend!"

The man took off and ran as fast as he could!

The police then asked me which way he went. He said he would make a good witness for my divorce hearing. He then said he couldn't believe how my husband was in that house with her and not standing beside his son and wife. It was worth breaking the windows and paying the fine; I had it in writing that the cheater came out of his lover's house, which I could never prove before!

It seemed like every police car and fire engine was out there. I recall there were at least ten police cars coming from every direction very fast. There were so many because when Ms. C's neighbors saw me breaking the windows, they didn't know who I was and they all called the police. After I got beat up, I ran next door and called the police myself and told them they needed to get there right away. I then began to break the windows, which I could have gotten away with; even the police officer that took me to the station said he didn't know who broke the windows. He said it might help me out in court. I knew she had no proof since her neighbors refused to get involved after they found out I was the wife. But I did the right thing and admitted to the judge about the windows; I lost it that day and was temporary out of it after they beat me up (he held me down and she beat me with a broom).

Since she opened the door and let me in, and the house was bought while I was still married and living with him, the judge said just to pay a fine, which I did. In the past with his other lovers, I couldn't prove he was in the house; the officers always said no crime was committed. That's why I knew I had to do something, since this time a baby was involved in his affair. His cheating had just gone too far. For the first time in years, I could prove his cheating while he was still legally married to me. (I couldn't see it in the natural eye at the time, but it all worked out for my good.)

The officer said, "Don't worry, I'm going to put in a good word for you when I get to the jail," and he did. I cried for about four hours; time seemed to stand still, until I spoke to the magistrate. When I was put in a holding cell (because I broke those windows), I refused to speak to anyone; all I could think was, I gave my children's father many chances to keep our family together; now I'm locked up and I haven't ever been in trouble before in my life. The ladies in the holding cell all stopped worrying about what they were there for and began sympathizing with me, since all I did was cry since I arrived. They were tears of courage because all I could think was, Lord, just give me a chance to get out of here and I will sign those divorce papers as soon as someone gives me a pen! Even the lady guard said she had never seen anyone cry nonstop; I cried from the moment I came to the moment I left. She said, "Somebody better talk to you because I am running out of tissue"; she let me go in front of some other ladies. I was so upset; I had long pants and a long-sleeve shirt on; I had forgotten they had beat me, so I didn't tell the arresting officer, but when I showed the magistrate all my bruises under my clothes, pictures were taken. They let me go a few hours later; then they picked him and his lover up and arrested them.

I never wanted media attention; I was glad it never hit the newspapers or magazines. I was a very proud person, and it was just too embarrassing. Now that I'm older and God called me into the ministry, I want to help others.

I don't know when the love left but my hand was forced after he allowed me to get into harm's way, which almost cost my life.

I felt my children had been through enough, so I decided not to run, not to move out of the home. I was paying the mortgage on time every month (it was automatically deducted from my bank account), and my husband was given the rental properties since we are a commonwealth state; he let them go on purpose. He knew we had two liens, one on the rental itself and the other on my house to cover the rental as well. No, it's not normal; my husband had it set up with double liens on the same rental, my house and the rental, so that if I ever left him, I would lose everything if he stopped paying on his loan. He even told me that one-day, but I didn't know what he was talking about; I never looked at what I was signing. You just have to think evil to understand why someone would trick another like that. Yes, a double lien on the same rental property is unheard of. The manager of the rental even called me and said my husband had called and asked why haven't they taken my house that the judge gave me. You see, he never really wanted the rental; he just wanted it to stop paying and since the liens were on both properties I would lose everything if one weren't paid.

We could have gone back to court but I just refinanced, and now my home is paid in full. I'm a strong believer in divine intervention; that's why I have written this book despite the pain it took for me to relive the past, which still haunts me to this day; I could not leave this world before telling others, "There is hope!" Sometimes you have to encourage yourself.

Yes, I'm still talking about being scorned and my reaction to it. A few months after the attacks took place, on my way to church one Sunday, I stopped for breakfast around the corner from my house. To my surprise, that home wrecker was at the fast food place, showing off her newborn baby boy, all dressed in white. I was amazed and could not believe what I was actually seeing; when I saw her with the small child, who was only two months old, I screamed out, "She just had my husband's baby!"

At that point, the clerk at the fast food restaurant quickly handed the baby back to her; she was so furious about what I said that she jumped into her car and drove around to the drive-through; she parked her car beside mine (leaving the baby unattended) and ran over to my car, yelling, "Your husband said he no longer wants you anymore!"

I just looked at her and shook my head. I called him at his job and told him what she said. Instead of him getting upset with her, after she had just beat me with a broom, he asked me what I did or said to her to make her get angry with me. Yes, I had the locks changed the morning after it all went down, but I still called my husband to test the waters at the beginning of a three-year separation. As you see, his heart was cold since I put him out, and the rest is history. My lonely, sad, and misunderstood mind thought just for a moment that an ounce of him still cared; was it because I had two children with him or was I having a hard time dealing with the breakup of a twenty-four-year relationship? Was I just in a dream world? Who knows? My daddy said when you go overboard for someone who doesn't deserve your love, you should look in the mirror and ask yourself, "What kind of fool am I?"

At that point, I knew my marriage was over!

Enough was enough. I filed for divorce. I went to my attorney's office; after I told him the story, he said his retainer fee was $1,500; I told him I only had $100 that the lady next door had given me. He said, "Okay, pay me what you can; my secretary will work something out with you." The next day, my husband tried to come into the house; he followed me from our rental property, which was located behind us. When I walked in the door, I locked it; he pulled his key out and tried to open the door; however, the locksmith had already come two hours earlier and his key didn't fit!

After my husband received the divorce papers, he tried to call me but I wouldn't respond. One night, I was sitting in the kitchen, drinking some coffee, and there was a knock at the back door. I asked who it was; he said, "Your husband."

I said, "Oh, now you want to talk to me. It's too late; it's over!"

Discovering my husband's secret lovechild almost destroyed me; it was the last straw that ended my twenty-four-year marriage. After he received the divorce papers, he moved into the house they bought together. After he had taken everything out of the house he wanted (when I wasn't home), he told the judge all he wanted was a cabinet that had belonged to his aunt; the judge denied his request. That was the price he had to pay for living a double life, which is documented to substantiate my claim of abuse.

His Lover Was Our Best Witness

Listed below are actual statements taken from my attackers concerning the date of the crime of passion in the circuit court. (The Commissioner's Hearing Report was dated May 19, 1993, same year my divorce was recorded in the Circuit Court of the City of Norfolk.)

Referring to the altercation on October 20, 1991, as an incident by the courts, my attorney asked, "At the home in Chesapeake where you saw your husband with the baby, did you take pictures of any bruises that you sustained? And are these four pictures showing those bruises?" My answer was, "Yes sir."

Mr. Wilcox (my husband's attorney) had no objection because it was true how they tried to hurt me.

Ms. C was asked if my ex was listed on the house at all; in her own words, she said, "He's cosigner. He cosigned for the loan."

Ms. C was asked, "Do you have a small child?"

Ms. C gave them the child's name; when she was asked, "Whose last name is that? Where did you take the last name?" Ms. C answered and gave my ex-husband's name; she said, "He is his father."

Ms. C stated that my ex-husband and her son were present at the house, saying, "He was asleep." (Meaning my husband.) She said her son was lying on top of my ex on the sofa because her son "wasn't feeling well." She said, "I pushed her [meaning me] down; I went and got a stick." (That was the broom I was beaten with.)

The judge realized they couldn't prove any harm I did to anyone, so my ex-husband's complaint against me was dismissed on the same page of the decree.

Even today, he can't control his baby mother; he and his new wife don't answer their own phone; they let the machine pick it up. Yes, my husband tried his best to make me a scorned woman; he created the events that led up to the crime of passion. The hell on earth they wanted to create for me backfired; afterwards, they turned on each other. When their child was born, their glory became my hell; the fire was when he got off work and went to her house first, giving her a checkbook to his private account, which created the scorned woman!

The son born out of wedlock and from broken vows just left for the service; now what do they have to talk about together? Nothing! He's now with his new wife. Before I remarried, my ex had to pay me support for ten years; a few months after the support stopped, his job was cut off. Do you still question if God would make your enemy be at peace with you? God let the world

Henrietta Trotter

know he was blessed to be a blessing to me; the Bible speaks of stewardship, further substantiating that I made my mind up; I refused to run from the devil.

The children always spend Christmas mornings with me at my house and the evenings with their dad. That's why I say abusers don't belong in jails or mental hospitals; they need a building all to themselves with trained medical help. Yes, I was still scorned; yes, lives were destroyed because of senseless actions. My claim after seeing His Glory shows everything divinely takes its orders from God.

I would like to ask a personal question: eighteen years later, what was it all for? I love in the movie *Forrest Gump* when he says, "Life is like a box of chocolate; you never know what you're going to get!"

Chapter 9

Being Stalked

1992

"An Uneasy Feeling of Being Watched"

After the beating, the stalking began. When I looked down the street, I saw my husband was sitting, reading the newspaper, parked in his truck on the corner. That was the first time I had seen him since the incident at his lover's house. A few days after the beating, I was in the parking lot at work, and as I got out my car, my husband drove past and stuck up his middle finger at me.

I drove back home, where my son was alone. I'm glad I did because when I opened my front door, I noticed he had gotten a ladder and came into my house through the attic (the locks had been changed). I immediately called the police since the judge in family court had given me a restraining order for my protection; my lawyer got one after I was attacked.

The police officer and I were waiting in the living room as he was walking down the stairs of my house. He looked at the police officer and told him this was his house, I was his wife, and we didn't have a problem, as if he didn't break in, as if what happened to me never happened. I told the police officer that he had been served his divorce papers; he then told the police that all he wanted was the keys to the rental property.

I then told the police officer that the week before, he and his lover had beaten me up, but I could tell the police officer didn't believe me and believed him, because he always had a way of talking that was very convincing. I was beginning to think I was going crazy until a voice came to me and said, "Pull up your dress and show him the bruises." When the officers were called a few weeks earlier at his baby mother's house, I was wearing pants and had to wait until I got to the station to show proof of the beating. But this time, I had a dress on. I pulled my dress up and showed the officers the same large, black bruises that the magistrate had seen.

Another officer arrived; after he pulled the information from the courts onto his computer, he asked no more questions and took my husband to the station and booked him. My husband was very angry with me; in twenty-four years, he had gotten away with almost everything, but because he allowed another woman to hurt me, I pressed charges for the first time. I was so disappointed in his infidelity and the level of betrayal. If I lost everything, then I would just have to start from the bottom up, which I did. That's what this book is all about; I want it to be clear the warrants against them were issued the same day I was beaten, only hours after I cried in that holding cell, because when I was taken to the station, I didn't say anything about the beating until after I arrived. I had only told the officer I was the wife. I was just in shock; that's why they didn't know warrants were out for their arrest. After he came back to our family home, the warrants were discovered and he was taken away; they picked his lover up at a different time. From that point on, my husband began giving orders to the very woman who turned my world upside down. He was angry with me for something I should have done years ago: arrested him for beating me. His lover began to take her orders from him, and the stalking began.

I had decided I wasn't taking any more abuse. Afterwards, he and his lover tried to stop the child and spousal support order; the harassment didn't stop until after the judge signed the final decree; we were legally separated for three years, that's why the stalking seemed so long.

A few months after the attack on October 20, 1991, Ms. C began harassing and stalking me. She sent a letter to the CEO of the bank I worked for just to embarrass me and get me fired. The letter said I was harassing her family; however, he and I were still married at the time. I was working very hard one day when my supervisor called me and said personnel wanted to talk to me. My boss was always cool and calm; we got along very well. She was the same lady who gave me the number to the therapist when she saw the bruises on my legs (one day I had forgotten to cover them up). She always smiled and made me feel like I did a great job. But this day was different; she had a sad look on her face (she usually had a jolly outlook on life). It was not what she said; it was the way she said they wanted to speak to me that made me nervous and frightened about losing my job. I had worked so hard to be at the top of my performance; it was just too much to think about.

Personnel use to call you to the office and fire you themselves; now your boss does it. It was a long walk to the next building; all I could think about was, *what did that crazy woman say now?*

Yes, it was a long, slow walk to the office; I'd taken that walk so many times before since I used to work in personnel at the same bank. I had no idea what it was all about; I decided to just listen and comment calmly, not go all over the place. Before I told my side of the story, I asked the personnel manager how much time she had; she was sympathetic to how I was being wrongfully accused without merit or substance.

I couldn't think of anything; I hadn't seen Ms. C lately following or riding by laughing, which she did on a daily basis. I sat down in front of the head of personnel. She asked if I knew a Miss C. After telling my story about the stalking and her three-year affair, the personnel manager said, "You do not have anything to be ashamed of; hold your head up high." She also said that one day I would come out on top!

The bank dismissed the letter as being written by a crazy lady. That was divine intervention.

I really didn't know his mistress was stalking me but it seemed she had been watching me ever since he met her. She acted like she was given a license to openly make my life a living hell. I began noticing someone was following me. I knew it was her stalking me; it was the same car. She wanted me to know it was her by driving beside me at stop lights; when I went to a store, I would look over and she was at the next rack, laughing; she parked her car in my job's parking lot and parked outside my gym. Whenever I saw her, she would just laugh. She wanted me to see her so she could say I violated the no-contact order I put out on her myself. She always lied and came to wherever I was and said I bothered her. She knew the judge would dismiss it because I never responded to her when she tried to provoke me. Yes, I was both angry and scared. She just wanted to make my life hell; that's why I call my story "Between Hell and Glory."

Strange things began to happen to me. My car was damaged many times while I was in a store. When I would get home, the phone would ring and stop. I would call the operator and ask for where the call came from. Every time, the location was the same place: where my car had been scratched or kicked in. I invested in a very expensive car alarm system, since my tires were being slashed and sugar was being placed in my tank. They were so evil; they would cut three tires and leave one. When they realized that I had a talking alarm system, she began to openly follow me and wait in the parking lot at my work. When I started going to the gym, she followed me to the gym also. She was just sitting there in her car, watching me. I began to go shopping to relieve some of the stress; I would look around while picking out a dress, and she would be there smiling or laughing.

I really did try to avoid her; I took great measures to never go anywhere near where she lived or worked. That's why she would come to me. I remember once thinking; *This woman really doesn't have a life because he is living with her; why is she stalking me?* I was afraid to approach her (not physically; she was short and I knew I could have beaten her, if my husband hadn't held me down that dark day). But her mind wasn't right; I decided I would never bend down to her level. I knew she was jealous of the way I carried myself and wanted to be like me, even though she had my man, she still couldn't compete with me because in the back of her mind, I put him out and could take him back like I did so many times before (she harassed me because she knew he still loved me). You see, she had the body but could never get his heart; that's why she lost him months after the divorce. He told me himself afterwards he never loved her.

Once PJ and I were riding down the road, and she wanted me to see that she had put my husband's name on her license plate (this was while we were still married and going through our divorce). She almost caused an accident by driving her car in front of us just so I could see the license plate. What really frightened me was she drove in front of me very fast and the traffic light turned red; I had to immediately hit my brakes or my car would have hit the back of hers, which put my son and me in a life-threatening situation. At that point, I contacted my attorney and filed a restraining order on her. While it took time for the court date, it didn't stop her from continuing to follow and harass me. Every day when I went to work, she would be at the corner of my house; I would see her at lunchtime when I walked with my best friend; I always went to lunch with someone because I did not want her to make me lose my job (I needed a witness); she didn't care, she kept following me.

Once I saw her just sitting in her car in the parking lot of my job; this was after the car alarm. She began to follow me; it seemed she knew my work schedule. She would try something else to get some sympathy; she began stalking me with her kids in her car, what a sick plan. Divine intervention spoke to me, telling me to move fast, and I listened, so no harm was done to anyone, and her sick plan became null and void. No one could tell me she wasn't crazy. I know because of her actions it showed she hated me. She was harassing me; she was falsely accusing me and having me put in jail, trying to get me fired, provoking me on the highway and in stores. My job wasn't enough; she put her own children in harm's way by taking them with her to harass me; she had gone too far.

I usually go down the road around the corner to get home, but when I saw her children (one of them was my children's half brother), divine intervention stepped in and told me to take off as fast as I could on the interstate to lose this mad woman and to keep those innocent children out of harm's way! I put my foot to the floor; as I entered the interstate, I could see her in my rear mirror. She tried to catch up but she had an older car and I had a new high-powered Nissan. She didn't stand a chance of catching me; it worked, because I lost her.

I never drank or smoked or took drugs; that day, I wanted to do all three. I wasn't scared. I was just tired of playing her game. I knew if I could just get him to sign the divorce papers, all the stalking would be over, but he wanted to regain what he had lost; he just wasn't getting it that this time, it was really over. I hadn't yet declared Christ as my Lord and Savior; I believe that experience brought me closer to God and made me the woman I am today. It seemed I cared about her children more than she did; all I could think of was her well-developed plan went wrong. I really didn't want her children to get hurt on that highway; that's why I was trying to avoid a confrontation with her. I didn't want to see or talk to her again; one of the reasons I left my husband was to get rid of her. But it seemed she was just a bad nightmare that just wouldn't go away.

My ex was just out there being my ex; I was still getting calls and letters from his lovers he was seeing while living with her; she was stuck with two kids (she had one boy by another man before my ex met her); she was still single with two children; the hell on earth she tried to make for me had backfired. Her evil all backfired on her; after my divorce, my ex dropped her like a hotcake and married someone else and built his new wife a home. I have nothing against the son; he is my children's half brother, but like in the Bible, he and his mother were put out to roam; he never got his full birthright; he was never really accepted by my ex's family; they acknowledge he was born but that's about it. He never spent any real time with them and now he is grown. I do not blame him; it was his mom and dad's fault to use his birth to destroy our marriage; he was a victim just like me.

I wouldn't dare write a tell all book if I thought it would hurt my ex-husband's out-of-wedlock child. I waited eighteen years to go into details. He's old enough now to hear my side of the story.

My life was turned upside down; just being a wife made me a victim, while someone with a sick mind plotted against me. It seemed they were just out to get me; everywhere I went, she was there. It was an eerie feeling; I could feel someone watching me at all times. I have to admit it was just plain spooky. Even when I went to church, I would see one of them drive by. When I took my son to school, there she was, driving our car. She loved harassing me; I know she was just trying to get me to lose my cool, like I did that day in front of her house. I can even remember once my father-in-law and I saw her coming toward his house through the side window while I was visiting; I told my father-in-law that I had to leave; he told me, "I don't like her anyways, and I never liked her, and if she gives you any trouble, I will get my shotgun from underneath the bed and be the judge and jury this time."

She was angry because the judge was giving me spousal support and child support; it was automatically deducted from his check (I got this for ten years until I remarried). In the end, the judge gave me the deed to the house, I kept my land, and they granted me half his retirement from the post office. Since he had taken things from the house before we went to court, the judge said he could not get anything else out of the house.

This was something I had dreamed about; those words coming out of the judge's mouth ("You get nothing") made my day! Her little deranged world was falling apart. She fought so hard to make me lose everything, including my mind, and I won every case in my divorce hearings.

One day, the mailman left a birthday card that had our last name on it. I was still dealing with his mistress and his double life with Ms. C, his baby mother, when a letter came in the mail. My son thought it was for him, since he has the same name. He opened it and it was for his daddy. But to our surprise, it was the ghost of the past; it seemed the devil had a contract out on me! The card came from Ms. Barbara, his lover from Fort Story who became his mistress in Germany and took my identity. She

Henrietta Trotter

had moved to Texas; somehow, he had told her about me filing for a divorce; the card said that he could move to Texas with her because someone in her family had left her a house.

I sat down at the table and composed one of the most powerful letters that I have ever written. It went something like this:

Dear Ms. B,

I know it's been a long time since we have communicated; it seems that you heard about our separation. I know that you are very surprised because you tried so hard to break us up in our last duty stations.

I fought to keep my marriage together and I thought I had succeeded; however, I hate to disappoint you but you sent your love letter and the birthday card to my children's father to the wrong address. He is now living with his new lover and their new baby. I know how you feel about me, and you should know how I feel about you, but the communication between you and I have finally ended. I did get your things that were placed in the attic after the movers mistakenly sent it to this house from Germany. I saw all of the pictures of the vacations that you two took together. I saw all of the Christmas cards that you conveniently kept with words he wrote in his own handwriting, each card telling you how he felt about your relationship, words he told all of his lovers to keep them in his web of deception.

He always knew what to say to me, that's why I stayed twenty-four years; the problem was his actions didn't match his words. I guess I was also fooled with my head in a cloud as well; he tricked me by buying me nice things. Like you, I couldn't or wouldn't see what was right in front of my face: lies, lies. I saw both your and his name on brown leather wristbands that you conveniently put in the box along with the new pictures. The one that got my attention was taken in your bathtub with my husband, as he had no clothes on, wearing only his Mason hat. I guess that was one of the times he said he had to go to a meeting, leaving the kids and me home alone. That's how most of them operate: buying expensive gifts. I thought the larger the gift, the bigger his heart was. He knew how to put on the charm. I still have the first gift he gave me: a little man holding a flower saying I love you. I fell for it; unfortunately, when I found out what he really was all about after the charm wore off, I was married and pregnant. I also saw some of your belongings that you had purchased in Germany; I gave them away and wrapped them as Christmas presents to some of my friends at the job; the rest I told my father-in-law to break up into small pieces. I watched him take the rest of your belongings that were mailed to my address to the trash.

Signed, Henrietta

The letter was powerful because the war was finally over. I never got a response, but I felt great after writing it. I felt in control for the very first time; a weight had been lifted; yes, I won the war. Ms. B was the only one who kept popping up like popcorn; every time I thought she was gone out of our life, here she comes again. I could imagine her heart cracking when she read each line. She finally for the first time felt my pain, knowing how it felt to be hurt, betrayed, and pieces of my heart broken and scattered. Sunshine became cold as ice whenever her name came up; I even began disliking anyone that had her name, no matter how nice they were, before God delivered me from myself. Trust suddenly became betrayal. I just wanted her to feel the emotions I felt for years, feeling like a fool. She denied my family the right to collect on his military retirement, which she helped cause him to lose.

Henrietta Trotter

He left us alone many nights, while spending time in her bed at the Fort Story Army base and overseas. It felt good to mail the letter to her with my response; instead of tears from the endless nights she always gave me, I could finally smile with thoughts of knowing my heart had company; this time, I wasn't alone, thinking he got you to this time! My family was destroyed, but the battle of hope for a new beginning was won, because it was on my terms this time. Just knowing I would never have to deal with the women (before his baby mother), the ghosts of the past, again!

The judge had all the evidence he needed; just knowing he committed adultery but not being able to prove anything, like my attorney said, "We don't need the other women's names; we have a baby this time."

I told God if he got me out of my test that I would never complain about anything again. When I went to God's word, I read, "For I am with thee and no man shall set on thee to hurt thee: for I have much people in this city." (Acts 18:10)

Years later, my neighbor Ms. Lambert (who retired from the Pat Robinson Ministry) said it was okay to cry as long as I was crying to the Lord! I had a support system before my calling. I was chosen to endure so others would see His Glory on me when I was delivered from the mad woman and my evil attackers. I had peace in my home; no man spent the night at my house until I married Trotter. I met Trotter seven years after my divorce. After meeting Trotter, all the stalking stopped.

Through God interceding on my behalf, I turned my life 100 percent over to God. I began publishing books; given the situations and circumstances surrounding these, only the hand of God could have released such power; He gets the credit and the Glory! I declared war on my enemies; every tongue that rose up against me was cursed! Chains fell off me. I now see His Glory. I began quoting to myself, "Eyes hadn't seen and ears hadn't heard what was in store for my children and me."

It was hard when I was being stalked, as she laughed at me every time she saw me, but I had too much to lose to throw it all away on her; she had my husband, she should have been acting like a winner, but instead she was acting like a loser. She had no power because she was fighting a blessed seed. I know it was the enemy using him. I know he was possessed and his mind was not thinking, as he should.

Remember Paul in the Bible: he wanted to do good but evil was always present. I'm not making excuses for him; that's why I left the marriage. It's a fact: he was being used by the devil himself. I had to learn to forgive my enemies; I had to grow spiritually, and as long as I hated, the same poison would run down my veins. Their wicked imagination destroyed them after they tried to get rid of me. In the end, they turned on each other by splitting up. Trotter shared with me one day how it was a big mistake knowing Ms. C and how it didn't work out for my children's father because how could she expect him to stay with her when she knew he was a cheater and she cheated with him? My ex actually said afterwards to me, "I couldn't trust her to be a lifetime faithful partner." It reminded me of a story. You get what you invest in: you bought a steak but chose the hamburger to get caught with; don't be surprised when you are left with the lesser grade.

My ex-husband was very angry with me for marrying Trotter; he then left Ms. C, the home wrecker, for good and married a well-respected church lady from his job, in a small secret wedding at his new wife's home. My children's stepmother came to both my children's weddings; I insisted on her taking pictures with our family. She seems very nice and treats them good when they visit the home my ex-husband had built for her. I give respect where respect is due, since she had nothing to do with the breakup.

I stopped thinking about the way I wanted things to be and accepted the way they were and started praying, "God let Your Will be done, not mine." God brought it to my attention; that's awesome, eighteen years later, I can really write in detail about it, there was a time I couldn't even talk about it. If I had met Trotter just after the divorce and he had stepped in and paid all my bills and paid off my house, man would have gotten the Glory.

If Oprah had answered just one of my e-mails before God blessed me with books on all major Web sites and bookstores and public libraries, TV commercials for Lifetime for Women, and newspaper ads, Oprah would have gotten the Glory.

That's why I say I write my pain, and it took me eighteen chapters and eighteen years later to send the full story in for publishing. This tell-all book takes my attacks and the word *struggle* to a different level; that's why in the past, writing poems and short stories was easier for me to express myself. I needed more time to heal in order to reveal the devil himself!

Who am I to tell the Potter what to do with the clay?

I told you how I was being stalked, but in the end, God was watching over me.

Everything happened according to God's plan after all.

Chapter 10

Intervening Lawyer in the Courtroom

1993–1995

"Falsely Accused; Here I Go Again!"

When I first went to my attorney Paul's office, he decided to help me after I told him my story; I had never seen him before, another attorney recommended him. I came to his office just after I was beaten on October 20, 1991. I knew I had to make my case good since I only had $100, which the older lady next door had given me, and his starting fee was $1,500. I had to be very convincing. I decided not to just talk but to show him; I threw my body to the floor, demonstrating how my ex held my legs and arms down to the floor as his lover repeatedly hit me. I then got up and gave step-by-step details of the events which I later told the same story to the judge how I broke the windows of the house that my husband had signed his name to. That day caused me to go to court for three years, trying to end a relationship of twenty-four years.

My husband kept refusing to sign the divorce papers; he would not show up for court in an attempt to delay it. He told me outside the courtroom that he never wanted a divorce. I just walked away; it would be four years before we spoke again.

I knew I would win. I continued to live a respectful life. I didn't want a real boyfriend. That's why I was harassed so much, because there were no witnesses. I was always alone. Yes, I was being tried that day. According to *Webster's,* "trial" is a test or a source of annoyance; this is when it gets a little crazy. You can say the three years of courtroom experiences started when I met my husband's lover and ended after my divorce. She was a thorn that I wanted to be removed quickly, but just like God told Saul, "My Grace is sufficient." He was later renamed Paul after he made a commitment to serving God.

I had to go through a lot in order to be delivered from bad choices. Life sometimes puts you in uncompromising positions and situations beyond your control, if you don't have the right mate. My trials also allowed me to tell others about the knowledge I gained from real life drama and experiences. As a child, I heard about God being a lawyer in a courtroom but not until His divine power intervened, interceded, and opened prison doors and set me free did I become a believer. It made it easier for me to understand victims of physical abuse and also those who get attacked mentally sometimes leave God's protection. Just like the child who left home and whose father took him back after he came to himself, I left my hedge of protection and my heavenly father took me back. I now look back at the road I traveled as stumbling blocks and struggles that molded me into who I am today! It also gave me a humble spirit and strength to help others. The enemies' assignment was to take me out and destroy my life, as I knew it. The black robe on the cover of this book is not the robe of many colors, but it represents the child who had a desire to do her first works over again. It represents a life of many choices that led me to writing this for you. To overcome is to endure; to endure is to overcome. Sorry, that's just the preacher in me.

There is another side of my story, which helped me to become wise. God put special people in my life. My attorney's name was Paul; God touched him after my attack to show favor, to help me get delivered from my captors.

Just before my call to ministry, two-prophets prophesized a word in my spirit. The prophet's job is to teach the supernatural; their prophetic words stress revelation in one's life. They are endowed with a mission, with the power of a word, not their own opinion, which accounts for greatness but also with temperament, concern, and character. There was no resisting the impact of divine inspiration.

The word of God reverberated in the voice of man. The strange disparity of the two staggering facts in the life of a prophet are God turning to him, and man turning away from God; this is often his lot; God puts him through trials. These prophets are chosen by God and are often rejected by the people; the word of God, which is so clear to him, is unintelligible to others.

God used Paul Lipkin to intervene on my behalf in the courtroom; however, two others had a direct connection to God's spirit on my behalf; both prophets were named David. David Paul, who has a worldwide radio ministry, prophesied victory over my life; he called me out by name in the midst of hundreds; he said he saw me leading a woman's ministry. David Terrell, who has a tent ministry that travels around the country, anointed my head with so much oil it began to drip all over my clothes; I was never the same until my bishop ordained me the very next week. At the ceremony, he said with tears in his eyes that God told him to.

It seemed everything was going my way in the courtroom; as if God Himself was giving the orders, the judge allowed my son and me to stay in the house, and since he abused the finances, the judge put me in charge of the rental property for three years. Then the devil got mad and tried to curse me. One day the lady across the street showed me a newspaper with my house for sale. One of the rental property managers called me and said my ex-husband told them the courts had given him the rental property. He collected rent for five months and didn't pay them, and since there was a lien on my house, he asked what they were waiting for; why didn't they take my house? Paul requested an emergency hearing in court, and my ex was ordered to pay the rental notes in his name; since he didn't pay, I could have put him in contempt of court, but God says vengeance is His. Even though the weapon was formed, it did not prosper. Years later, the bank where I worked took over the note.

It was nothing for me to get a warrant on my door; it was a

direct attempt to cause me to either lose my mind or lose my job. Once while I was in court, a man ran up to me (I was carrying a briefcase, like I always did, with my evidence). The man said he needed an attorney and said I looked and talked like one; sometimes when my attorney had another case, I didn't want it postponed so I would defend myself and win. I told him that I wasn't an attorney, and he seemed disappointed.

She was using up my vacation time and trying to bring shame to me every time a warrant was placed on the door for my son to see. She was very evil and very cruel. But instead of making me look bad, God's Glory was elevated and began to shine. Once after I waived my rights and pleaded my own case, a district attorney came up to me and said he thought I was an attorney. While my co-workers were at lunch, I was at the legal library getting prepared to help Paul with my next case.

A few months later, when I went to work, his lover called and told me this time she would set me up for good! She said I wouldn't be able to get out of it. I immediately called Paul and told him that she had threatened me at work. He told me to get a copy of my timesheet and keep it with me. About fifteen minutes later, two police officers came to my job to arrest me.

I worked at a bank and was bonded by the FBI; if one charge had been proven, I would have lost my job and she knew it. Since the letter to my boss didn't work, she took it to a different level. Remember, her boss was the devil himself. Two officers walked past my desk; I wasn't surprised because Ms. C had just called to say that she was about to embarrass me in front of my co-workers.

Now that I look back on it, I knew how Jesus must have felt when the soldiers came to arrest him; he was also falsely accused. Just like Jesus, I didn't say a word, because the favor of God was all over me. The police officers talked to my boss; she told me she told them I had worked for the bank for a long time and she would vouch for me, that I would not give them any trouble. She knew it had something to do with my husband's lover since her name was on the warrant; it was the same name that had been calling and leaving messages. I know it was God's divine intervention; the officers told my boss to tell me to walk with them to their car, which was parked in front of the bank; they said they would not use any handcuffs as long as I walked in front of them and sat in their car, which I did. Ms. C was very upset that I wasn't embarrassed; I went back to work that day after only signing the warrant with a time to appear in court.

I went back to work in the office, and later that evening, I went to cash a check and the bank teller said, "Did you hear one of our employees was arrested today and was taken out?" I just smiled and acted like I didn't know what they were talking about, since I was released so quickly. When I appeared in court on the date requested, the judge looked at Ms. C and said in an angry tone, "Little lady you know her home address, as long as you live, don't you ever send a warrant to a bank or I will have you arrested." And he dismissed her charges after I showed him the copy of the time card, because it was impossible for me to be in two places at the same time. After the judge dismissed that case, it only began a list of false charges with no merit.

She sent another warrant to my house, saying I was calling her on the phone and harassing her, which was another lie. God always told me what to say to the judge. Think about it; this was the same lady who called my home repeatedly, day and night, when my husband was living with me. She even called my job; I had witnesses, and I never bothered her once, so why would I call her after I put him out?

I told the judge, "Isn't it funny that every warrant that she took out, the location was ten minutes from my house to my job, which shows that I never went anywhere near the city where she lived."

She knew she had to put the location close to my home or my job. Whenever I would go to court, I would always be well dressed and spoke very professionally.

Before meeting my husband's mistress, I had never been in trouble with the law and never have since; that's why I'm willing to reveal my entire court record publicly to show you how an innocent person can easily become a victim in a mad woman's world. I'm listing them with dates to show the outrageousness of her attacks on me without a cause, just to humiliate and bring me down to her level of hate.

These dates don't include the three years of back-and-forth divorce hearings that had numerous postponements, due to my husband not showing up for court dates, saying he never got the notice. Many times the judge and his attorney and my attorney would look at each other and ask, "Where is he?" If you notice, they all began the day she attacked me and ended the year of the final decree of my divorce.

Chesapeake, Virginia

Date of Trial	Charge	Disposition
10/20/91	Damaged property misdemeanor	Dismissed 2/11/92
12/4/91	Assault & battery misdemeanor	Dismissed 2/13/92
12/4/91	Vulgar language telephone misdemeanor	Dismissed 2/11/92

Norfolk, Virginia

2/26/92	Damage to private property	Dismissed
2/26/92	Assault & battery	Dismissed
2/13/93	Abusive language	Con't to 4/1/93, Dismissed

I fought to change the law about getting warrants so easily due to the time I lost out of work; because of what happened, they changed the law. I got dressed up the next day with my best suit on and asked the magistrate how she could get warrants so freely without cause. A new law came to play: you would have to pay for a warrant before they would issue it, and that's when the warrants stopped. He also apologized and said that I was denied my rights to see the magistrate. Ms. C's actions were a blatant attempt to waste taxpayers' money on false charges; my only crime was she hated me and didn't want me to win anything in my divorce hearings.

There were many bad language charges. If you asked anyone from my birth until now, you would not find one person to tell you I used bad language; that wasn't my style. She even tried to bring my character and integrity down. But God had the last word; He was a lawyer in the courtroom!

She boldly came to family events and went around my children to provoke me every chance she got; the intent of her heart was to get me in court, she knew I had restraining orders against her, but that was a joke to her; she turned what was meant to be for my protection against me, to falsely accuse me and make my life a living hell. Yes, it was a journey of living hell; other victims of abuse must know how I got to the point of almost total destruction. I survived to tell the story without typing it from a jail cell; now that's God's Glory!

It hurts so bad to remember some of the attacks, like sugar in my gas tank; the car began to act up as I drove down the street; it began to shake uncontrollably as my daughter and I were driving home (she was on a holiday break). I know Tonya was his heart and the love of his life; she was in danger. I looked and saw almost a bowl of sugar was placed in the tank; a handful was still around the tank, the car starched up while I was at work. I had fingerprints taken at the police station that time.

I remember one time going to court and she was with him. It was one of our first court appearances; all I could think of was how dare he help her destroy my home.

On one of my first court cases, when my lawyer went to use the telephone, I calmly took a chair and sat right in front of both of them. I thought, Yes, God, I did bear pain and abuse, but putting my child in harm's way was just too much to endure; they

Henrietta Trotter

crossed the line! I looked at them and smiled just before we all went into the courtroom, letting them know that I wasn't afraid of anything they could do to me. My attorney Paul came back and saw me sitting in front of my husband and his lover in the hall of the courtroom, which was one of our first court cases; he told me to stay away from them, that it was his job to protect me.

At that time, I started going back to church after talking to the lady who raised me. For some reason, after telling her my story, I thought she would have some answers. She told me I needed a supernatural intervention to stop the hand of the enemy from trying to destroy me and take everything I had. I am so glad that I had that talk. I don't think I would have been able to endure the experience that I'm about to tell you if my mind was not in the position to listen and hear God's voice. All my life I knew of the man with supernatural power and miracles, but I just knew of Him. I regained the relationship that I had. After every attack, I gathered strength. I believe that time after time, whenever I faced the judge, he could see the Glory on my face and the strength in my heart. His lover would always look at me and laugh whenever she saw me before and after the court hearings, even when she lost, because in her heart she won because she made me lose a day of work and humiliated me.

One day I received a warrant; with the other ones, I just had to sign my name and they would give me a court date; it would get dismissed, and I would go home.

This one was different. Satan had gathered all of his imps and evil forces to totally strip me of what pride I had left, but it backfired because the experience brought me closer to God.

Yes, this case was different from all the others; this was the first and only time I had ever stayed overnight. The courthouse was across the street from where I worked; other times when I would get a warrant from the court, I would just go by on my lunch and sign a release paper. She must have gotten tired of me getting off so easy, the police officer told me; I thought it was just another one of Ms. C's routine attempts to stop me from being happy. That time, she took three warrants out at the same time;

judging from the past, I thought I would sign all three and come back with my attorney to court.

I had a wakeup call; I will remember the night I spent in a cell for the rest of my life. They took my bag lunch, started taking pictures, and put me in a cell, all alone, for hours. This time, it was not just a holding cell; it was my first and only night I have ever spent in that God-forsaken place. This time, I was arrested. I was shocked; this was the first time that I couldn't just talk to the magistrate and set a date. They said that she checked a box on the warrant and wanted me arrested.

I was set up. The magistrate is the one who makes that decision. I wasn't allowed to talk to her and tell my side of the story, because the magistrate knew my husband and she was working with his lover to have me locked up with no bail. It really was against the law for me to have no bail and not be able to tell my side of the story to anyone! The trial was the next day. They later said I could sue the city, but I just wanted to go on with my life, which was almost destroyed.

My co-workers didn't know where I was; PJ didn't know where I was; my car got towed; they made me wait for hours to call my attorney. After a few hours, they allowed me to talk to Paul. I had to call him at his home because it was so late; his office was closed. When I called Paul, I found out that there was no bail; he said he would see me in court the next day. The jail smelled like someone had peed in it for days. I was denied my rights to see a magistrate. When I finally got upstairs after being booked, my brother told me my husband had called him and asked him to go and see about our sixteen-year-old son. I wouldn't get a chance to talk to anyone that night, and they would see me in court in prison clothes the next day.

When I found out there was no bail, I asked, "What did she say I did?" The warrant she took out said I hit her and broke her car window. Those words ("my car") were what set me free because the car belonged to my husband; we were still legally married and not divorced yet!

She was accusing me of damaging my own marital property.

It wasn't until the next day that divine intervention revealed to me that she had lied to get the warrant; the property was not hers at all. My head began to spin; just for a moment, reality hadn't set in. I truly believed I was dreaming and I could go home and come back.

Then they took me upstairs; the lady police officer looked at me and said, "I don't know who you are, but I know you have an attorney." I looked at her and didn't say a word; I just smiled because of her kind words of encouragement. I had a silk dress on and she said that few ladies come in there with silk dresses on, so she would give me a jail outfit that didn't have any numbers on the back; she felt that I would not be in there long. We then walked upstairs to the holding cell. I hid under the cover because I didn't want anyone to see me. There were no more beds so I slept on the floor; the bugs were crawling around the mats. Later that night, someone turned the television on and I sat up. I looked over and saw a shower; it didn't have any curtains. I had never in my life been in a place like that. When we first had problems, I was only locked up for a few hours and let go, but this time, pictures were taken and I was brought upstairs to be in a cell with about thirty women, with a shower with no curtains; all I could do was shake my head and wonder if I was dreaming.

That night I walked over to where the television was; a girl asked me when had I gotten there. I had been hiding underneath a cover on the floor all day, hoping it was a bad dream and I would just wake up! No one saw me come in. She asked me my name and said usually when someone comes in, they get an initiation: the girls would punch them on the arm. At that point, I really didn't want to talk to them anymore. This one girl told me to come and sit beside her, because if they thought I had a friend, no one would bother me. I said okay and we began to watch television. I will never forget that night; the movie *Scarface* was on, and a lot of the girls had been picked up for prostitution; for some reason, they were so excited when Scarface put the drugs on the table and began laughing and jumping up and down. The noise of them yelling had woken me up earlier. I just sat and watched in amazement. I then got my thoughts together.

I wasn't in control of anything; when the phone was put in that nasty cell downstairs, I could only make one call. I picked my attorney to call. The officers set the time for the next call. I had to get in line with the girls upstairs later that day. I was able to call my brother, who said that he had spoken to my husband. My husband seemed very excited and happy that she finally was able to get me arrested and said, "This time, she's not playing with you." My brother told me how my husband knew I was being set up.

At that point, I really didn't want to hear anything else. I just told my brother to go to my house to take care of my son because his own father didn't seem to care. I wanted to say more but there was a long line of girls yelling and a large lady standing right behind me telling me to get off the phone. It's not like what you see on TV; I didn't see a guard in that room watching us until we were brought back to the holding cell. I looked at that lady; I didn't want any trouble to add any time to my one-day stay; I was hoping to get out the next day, so I gave her the phone. I went back and sat with the girls, not really saying much. One of the girls asked me what was I in there for; I pulled out one of the warrants that said damaging property; the next one said assault; and the next one had something to do with something I can't even remember. But I will never forget the expressions on their face, because when I pulled the first one out, they just said okay. Then I slowly pulled the second one out, without saying a word.

They said, "You must think you're bad."

Then I slowly pulled the third one out. The girl said, "You all better leave her alone; she got three warrants, most of us have been in here for six months waiting on a trial and we only got one."

Since they looked like they were afraid of me, I spoke for the first time and said, "Six months? You must be kidding!" I said I would be getting out of here tomorrow once the judge heard my story.

Henrietta Trotter

I told them how I worked at a bank and that she only bothered me because she knew if I got in trouble, I would lose my job because the FBI bonded me. One of the girls said you work at a bank and you're in here with us? I said yes, I work right across the street. I then told them this woman had been harassing me for about three years and she finally got me where she wants me; she was making my life a living hell. One girl said, "Just give me her name; we have people on the street to beat her up."

I looked at her and said, "That's not my job, that's God's job; she will get hers in the end."

I will never, as long as I live, forget the noise of those prison doors every time a new prisoner came in. It just brought chills down my spine. It was something right out of a horror movie. When the lights went off, it seemed like the guards disappeared. The only comfort I had was that I had made friends with the girls before I went to sleep.

The next morning, I woke up gagging and choking from the smell of those boiled eggs. Can you imagine smelling thousands of boiled eggs all at one time? I will never forget that smell. They woke us up, and we walked down the hall. I refused to eat; one of the girls asked if she could have my food; I told her yes. The night before I didn't eat; that morning and evening of the trial I didn't eat. Another girl told me if I stayed there any longer I would starve to death because I hadn't eaten anything yesterday and I hadn't eaten anything that day either. I said I would just starve to death because I'm not eating any of that food.

When I went back upstairs, they called my name. A group of us girls went downstairs; now I know how Daniel must have felt when he was in the lion's den; that morning would forever remind me of that Scripture. As we walked downstairs, God was all I had on my mind, how he was going to deliver me from that lion's den. As I walked past the men prisoners, they were all screaming and hollering with their arms hanging out the cells because the lady prisoners were passing. They put you downstairs in the den of the jail, underneath the courtroom, before they called your name to go to court. It really felt like I was in the lion's den for real.

My lawyer came for the first time and I was thinking that he had good news to tell me, but instead he broke my heart; what he said made me depressed. He looked at me and said, "They have Sacks and Sacks, one of the most powerful and expensive lawyers in our town, and this time we have a problem because they have the commonwealth attorney; she said that you hit her." And he walked away.

As he walked away, I held my head down in sadness but as I looked down to the floor of that prison, I looked back up to where my help came from, and through divine intervention, God gave me a word. He said to tell the girls down there with me to join a circle and we would pray, and everybody in that circle would be set free that day. We all joined hands and began to pray. And as I began to pray the first thing that came to my mind was that "whenever two or more are gathered in his name, there he will be also."

I looked to my right and there was a girl with a cross around her neck; it blew my mind because they had taken all the jewelry away from us. I looked to the left and saw a girl with some sandals on with the letter "D." A voice came to me and said that "D" stood for Daniel. And I looked straight ahead of me, and there was a girl wearing a T-shirt with a picture of a lion on it. I began to shake, and God's voice came with power, letting me know He had never left me or forsaken me. Every person in that circle got freed that day and went home, which God allowed me to see that because my name was the last one called. When I walked upstairs in my prison clothes, the courtroom was full of people. I later found out that she had requested an open court, unlike the last court cases.

It seemed my life and careers were flashing before my eyes all at once. My attorney and her attorney went back and forth. I was hurt because I had never worn a prison outfit in my life, but what hurt me the most was that my children's father, the husband I had not yet divorced, was standing beside his lover in a three-piece suit, and we were still legally married. I knew I had to get myself together so divine intervention could step in, and it did so gracefully and told me what to say. I raised my finger up in the air; the judge looked at me and said, "You can't talk, you have an attorney."

I looked at my attorney and wrote on a piece of paper, "Can I speak?" He said in a loud and angry voice, "Go ahead because they already have their mind made up; there is nothing I can say." I stood straight up, looked straight in the judge's face, and began to tell my story. As I began to speak, you could not hear a pin drop in the courtroom; everything got silent.

I said, "I went to his lover's house; she stood at the door in her see-through nightgown in the middle of the day telling me to come in, with a smile on her face. She said, 'you see, I don't ask him to come; he comes on his own.'"

Then I told how I saw him holding a baby that he previously said he knew nothing about. I described how he held me while she took a broom and brutally beat me from my head to my toes, and when she said she was going to get the gun, he let me go. And I told how she had me coming in and out of courtrooms while the final decree has not yet been signed. I then said she falsely accused me on many occasions, like today. I said, "If you notice the warrant, it said my car was damaged. The reason why I'm here today is because she lied to get the warrant."

The car was never hers; the car was marital property and was registered in our name since I was still his wife. Her name was nowhere on the registration. I was locked up for nothing; I was at work and she couldn't prove otherwise. And at that point, I could see that the judge was beginning to be sympathetic to my situation after realizing that I was still this man's wife of twenty-four years and the mother of his two children. Her attorney realized at that point that he was losing the case, so he angrily said, "What about the windows? And what about you hitting her?"

I looked straight in his face and said, "I don't know what you're talking about."

Her attorney really got upset then and said, "What do you mean you don't know what I'm talking about? Are you saying you were not there?"

I said, "That's what I'm saying."

At that point, the commonwealth attorney turned around and walked out of the courtroom. Everyone in the courtroom that day stood up and gave me a standing ovation; after the standing ovation, the judge dismissed both warrants. I held my head down, reached in my pocket, and pulled out the third one and said, "Excuse me, Your Honor. I have another one."

He then looked at me and smiled and signed off on the third one. I had tears of joy, thinking to myself. *The devil was defeated once again with his lies.* The people in the courtroom applauded just to see that justice was done that day. My husband was so angry that I had once again won that he hollered as loud as he could, "What about my car windows?"

The judge then said, "I see you are admitting that the car is yours and not hers. You get your own windows fixed."

My nightmare was all about Ms. C, saying our car was hers and I had broken the windows; that's why they took my bag lunch and locked me up. She just added two more charges to make that one look good. But without the charge of damaging of the car windows and putting me at the scene, the other two didn't make any sense. That's why all three were dismissed at the same time. I was never at the scene in the first place. I was really happy that God had stepped in and showed his power. He even made my husband mad enough to tell the truth at the end. However, since I was the last person that day, my paperwork was held up; it was night time when I got out and I didn't want to call anyone because it was so late. I was so angry that she made me miss a day of work. I walked home from the courthouse that night. PJ was very happy to see me when I got home.

The next day I got my car out of towing. I went back to work as if nothing happened, never telling anyone. I thought that was the end of her trying to scandalize my name, but another warrant came to my house the same week. This was one of the last ones before I got the law changed. She was in a state of anxiety. I found that very strange because I had put that no-contact order out on her so she would not bother me (and she turned it around against me, with no proof again). And she took the same case to general court and I just won; everyone was so proud of my courage, even the police officers hugged me. This crazy woman was taking me to civil court to be tried all over again. My attorney met me in court; you can imagine, it was all twisted just like her behavior; I was outdone with her conduct and demeanor. I stood there wondering why I was even there after the charges were just dropped a few days ago, but now she took the same case to civil court, claiming I contacted her after the judge had just dismissed it in the higher court. I stood there in awe, knowing she would lose but having to go through it all over again, as my husband stood beside her again just because she couldn't take the fact that she lost.

The judge asked me if I had any contact with her. I told him the contact I had with her was seeing her in court. At that point, I began to get one of my seizures; my hands began to hit the wood in front of me, my teeth began to chatter, and I collapsed on the floor. The police ran over to me and picked me up, and my attorney helped them. The judge said he would postpone the case; I then stood up and said, "I'm okay, please continue." I explained what had just happened in the higher court, and the judge said I could go home.

She ran out of the courtroom with her hands up in the air, hollering, "Not again, not again!" She was clearly a distraught and deranged woman. My ex-husband was so shocked that she left him standing by himself beside my attorney and me. The judge asked who he was because he didn't get a chance to speak; my attorney told the judge it was my husband.

The judge was so upset and said, "How dare you come to court against your wife? Don't you ever do that again or I'll have you locked up for trying to lie on her."

He was so confused because his lover had dropped him off, and he didn't know what door to go out of, so the judge called the bailiff and told him to escort him out of the courtroom. She falsified court documents to get me arrested by saying "my car" when the car was registered to us. If I were to file for pain and suffering, I could be a millionaire (after my divorce, my attorney sued my husband's lover for me as a counter suit and won).

The judge asked me how much I wanted! She didn't even show up for that final and last trial. I decided to let the Lord vindicate me. I felt as long as she owed me, she would stop all her lies and attacking me without cause. It worked because that was my last case with her.

I just wanted to live in peace. It was my test before I went into the ministry. I'm dedicating part of this chapter to Pastor Jones. I minister at two churches on Sundays and I love them both; I was just finishing up on some of my writings when he called; I gave him a preview of what God instructed me to type and asked his opinion. He said it sounded like, "Here I go again," because God had delivered me from the enemy so many times. I had to call on a higher power for help again!

The courtroom drama almost took its toll on me; some events I know were divine intervention because I narrowly escaped from statements that were proven to be false. After that, my ex-husband's divorce lawyer was so upset with him about what he had done to me that he quit the case. I got the commissioner to force him to sign the divorce papers, and the rest is history.

In more of the courtroom drama, the final decree of my divorce papers says he is guilty of adultery beyond a shadow of a doubt, referencing to him giving his newborn son our family name while we were still married. While married, he had six lovers total that I knew about because he admitted to them; I guess they all thought they were special. He was still dating while he was seeing his baby mother.

I just needed more proof; that's why I never mentioned anything about the other six women he was involved with in our twenty-four-year relationship in this book. During the marriage I was sent many pictures; some women I recognized, some I didn't; phone records of calls; and cards in his handwriting to some of his other lovers. I could have asked PJ, my niece, co-workers, and family members who saw him with other women to go to court, to tell what they saw, but I needed something more solid. Adultery is hard to prove; like my lawyer said, he didn't need other names; he had a baby! For the first time the ball was in my court and God showed favor because his mistress was my best witness at the hearing; her hatred for me overtook her loyalty to my husband. In court, she gave us more than we asked for. Paul and my husband's attorney, and the judge just sat back and listened as she revealed details we were not even aware of. For example, we were still married when the baby was born; I didn't know the baby had the same last name as my son. Her statements allowed me to get more than I asked for.

My lawyer called him a womanizer on our separation papers and proved it. Paul was very rude at times but that was good because no one wants a nice lawyer. He was a Jew and would sometimes use bad words. One time my son asked him why he cursed; he smiled and said, "Because I like to," which broke the ice because my son was having an uneasy feeling about testifying at my divorce hearing. He had been through a lot and saw and heard a lot; he was only sixteen years old and had to suddenly grow up overnight and get two part-time jobs after school. I had to get a weekend job as a secretary out of town to make it, because I had to pay three mortgages: my home and two rental properties, plus utilities. After the divorce, my son and I could quit the extra jobs and live off what the judge gave us from his dad. Our daughter was in college, and he even had to pay an extra $100 for her. Paul was the best thing that ever happened to me. He was God-sent, and I'll tell anyone that. He became our family lawyer.

Ms. C was our star witness; she came with her mini skirt on and those thick glasses and told us all we wanted to know; she was so proud of the fact that she had been his lover for three years while he still lived in my home. She even told the judge the name of the baby. "Nelson" is our family name; she tried to give him the same name as my son's middle name; it was just one letter off but sounded the same. She was our best witness; my attorney really didn't have to ask her anything; she just started talking and wouldn't stop. It made my lawyer's job so easy; as she talked, the clerk of the court typed. For the first time, I felt that I had the last laugh because she was too stupid to know when to shut up. On their way out of the courtroom, they were arguing (they had arrived together).

My father-in-law was there also at his son's request; however, I told Paul to tell the judge he knew nothing and saw nothing and he didn't need to be there; the judge told my father-in-law he could be dismissed at my request since my children adored their grandfather. My son was there and the drama of seeing his granddad there was just too much, I could see the relief all over my father-in-law's face as he gladly walked out. We were already close, and from that day, we became closer. He was another reason I never married while he was alive. I waited ten years; I would not do anything to hurt my father-in-law; he had treated Tonya like a daughter instead of a granddaughter when I lived with him when her dad went off to war a year after she was born. I would not betray the trust he had in me, not even for money.

The final hearing was wrapping up, and our daughter was graduating from the Air Force Academy the next week; I had a plane ticket for the next day to leave town. They needed more time to end the final decree and asked me to come back the next day.

I quietly said, "No, I can't."

Even my attorney looked at me strangely; the judged asked why; I said I had to be at my daughter's graduation. My ex knew nothing about it; for the first time, I saw guilt in his eyes because as much as he hated me, he loved his children more than life!

When I returned, my husband tried to trick my attorney; he had included some money he was to give his baby mother. My attorney threw the new statement of income across the room in anger; at that point, the judge got mad also and said, "Okay, you have so much extra money to give your baby mother, then you have more to give your wife and your two children born in your marriage."

The judge awarded three more hundred than what I had asked for; it was to be paid as a payroll deduction. I received it for ten years, until I remarried. My lawyer was very good at what he did; I had the best (he later became an assistant judge in Virginia). However, it was hard to deal with all the lies and deceptions. I would go to the legal library on the days it was opened; God's voice had told me I needed the law on my side when I danced with the devil in court. I remember after my ex had lied so much in one court case, my lawyer asked me if I had any more evidence. One by one, I handed him copies of evidence and copies of the Virginia Code of Conduct to back it up. It was so bad that my attorney turned around in the courtroom and asked out loud, "What else do you have in that black leather briefcase?"

One example I told the judge was how he had given his girlfriend his checkbook to a checking account he had in his name only while still living with me. After Paul showed the judge copies of the checks in her handwriting, my ex said it wasn't true. His attorney said the copies could have been tampered with; at that point, my attorney gave the judge the original copies of all the checks paid out to her mortgage, her utility bills, and toy stores (one was Toys R Us).

His lawyer looked at him and saw how much he lied; that was the last case for him; after that day, he dropped him and he started going in the courtroom alone. I guess his attorney couldn't hurt me even for the money. I know that was a divine intervention; nobody but God, sometimes. My husband's attorney also said in front of the judge he had nothing to work with after twenty-four years of marriage; my children's father held his head down in court and said she did nothing wrong; it was all him. This was the confession of a man who lived a double life. The judge said after years of working the bench, he had never heard of a case so brutal as mine and the woman survived to tell the story.

The judge not only granted my request, he gave me two more restraining orders and said one would be permanent, for as long as I lived. That was eighteen years ago. Few people could have endured the horror of having warrants on your door when you come home from work. Many women gave me their phone numbers, asking for help; my attorney Paul and I gladly assisted them.

After fifteen years, I called and spoke to my attorney the other day. Paul is retired now but he always came through. When I asked him if he missed me, he just said my case was interesting.

I can still see God's Glory; there were many cases in the courtroom but not one time did any police officers ever put handcuffs on me going to the station, getting out of their car, or walking into courtroom while in custody not once. Also, the lady police officer refused to put a number on my back (this is unheard of; I must have had a glow on my face, something made them not want to touch His anointed). To this day, the devil didn't get any victory. No, my daughter's father didn't make it to her college graduation because of the court drama; however, a few years after the divorce, he and my father-in-law attended another ceremony to honor our daughter. They allowed her grandfather to pin the captain's bars on. I have the pictures of all of us together; everyone thought we were still married at that time. That day, we put all our differences on the side and acted like Mom and Dad; no one can ever take that title from us.

This chapter showed God's favor. He put a hedge of protection around my children and me. Man drew up the paperwork; God sent the orders to set me free! He was my attorney in the courtroom.

Chapter 11

Searching for Mr. Right

1996–2000
"There Can Only Be One
King and One Queen"

As I heard her speak, I could hear the desperation in her voice. Torn, she spoke, in a very cloudy voice, of present and past pain; past loves, in particular, from years ago.

"He loved me, he really loved me, even though I've had one failed marriage, he really loved me." She really just wanted to be seen, heard, appreciated, and recognized. But no one saw it, so she thought. Her life was one twist, two turns, and three sheets from anything normal. She wanted the best in life and expected it. Drama, however, kept going itself, with no problem.

Jesus restores your ability to love again. There are different levels of brokenness. I shared with you my life story, revealing how a relationship that was healthy at first became broken, mainly because it didn't have a good foundation. Ruth is my favorite chapter in the Bible, because she just kept gleaning in the field until she meets King Boaz. Never forget harvest time is right around the corner.

The Scripture released me from an adulterous and abusive relationship. I always like to encourage victims not to give up on finding their soulmate; seven years after the enemy destroyed my home, I met my Mr. Right, Trotter, and fifteen years later, I feel the same way I did when I said, "I do." No man is cute enough, smart enough, or rich enough to make me jeopardize what God gave me.

People go through emotional stages during a breakup. The victims who chose the wrong mate experience denial, then anger. Some seek revenge, and then accept their fate. That's why most men will not confront a woman in person when they sever a relationship. Ending my marriage was met with emotional trauma and the presence of violence. I had to adjust to the absence of a mate as the bitter reality of splitting up. There are hurting people out there looking for answers. Some survived and some are still going through it. The reason why some battered women feel they have nowhere to turn is because some Christians act like they have never backslid or ever had a past of wrongdoings (holier than thou attitudes). Having a proud spirit is sin. Yes, God cleaned them up, but not to look down on others that haven't been delivered from the devil's tricks of abuse and self-destruction.

We all have had weak moments before God touched our lives. Yes, it's okay to look for your soulmate, but you must first find yourself, and we all need encouraging words to get there. No one wants to be around anyone who's depressed and without joy. You must prepare yourself by having a positive attitude to draw others. Learn how to like yourself first. It's all about the way you carry yourself; your lifestyle can encourage someone to bring others close to you.

The following stories will reveal the outcome of living and sleeping with the devil. You need to understand how to know the difference between Mr. Wrong and Mr. Right; they have different traits. The Bible refers to the first as wolves in sheep's clothing. In my experience, there were two kinds of wolves. One admits he harmed you. The other blanks out in a form of rage and says it was an accident. My ex admitted his affairs to me. He also admitted the abuse to the judge. The judge had a shocked look on his face before he issued a lifetime restraining order in family court.

Unfortunately, too many women find Mr. Wrong first, before finding Mr. Right. My assignment is to help you avoid the wolf, which is the silent abuser. He puts on his best behavior at first as if he was a sheep, but after you are married and get pregnant, the wolf personality comes out. In the church, he only has a form of Godliness; everyone thinks highly of him, especially co-workers; he has to win points somewhere. But behind closed doors, the wife and children are terrorized, living in fear. From out of nowhere, they are beaten, slapped, choked, and hit in the face repeatedly in unprovoked attacks, never knowing when he will just go off. I say it was the deadly kind because they are the ones whose wives end up in the graveyard or are never found; even his wife's family didn't believe he did it because he made his family keep the secret. The attacker even consoles the family, knowing very well he did it. Dead women can't tell stories.

I must tell you how to resist Mr. Wrong before you can even think about finding Mr. Right. You see most victims didn't see the punch coming. Most abusers have a dark past behind that smile. The misconception is the wolf approaches you with an evil look and an angry tone and hits you the first time he sees you. That is the furthest from the truth; he gains your trust first and then goes in for the kill. I'm referring to killing your spirit and your self-esteem.

They are attackers; you can't control their anger. They hear voices of demons on a regular basis. Most of them don't like themselves; that's why they complain all the time. Within seconds, they can go off for little or no reason. They go into rages; a warning sign is their eyes turn red. Their faces take on a monster-like expression. Their voice begins to crack and is clearly evil; they are possessed and taken over by demonic spirits. When they come out of the devastation of the storm, the victim is left with broken items in the home and injured bodies; when they say they don't remember, some really don't until it happens again. Do we put them away or do we get them help? Try to help them by getting them into a church home and some counseling, but they must be willing to accept the counseling and not turn on you. There is warning before destruction; the devil doesn't want you to see the warning signs that are blinded by hate. To win this war on violence, you must study the nature of the beast.

Mr. Wrong shows you acts of disrespect. To all those whose husbands have always been 100 percent faithful, never had words or fights, and never had to suffer tears of not knowing whether your spouse would come home that night or spend special occasions, holidays, birthdays, or just time with the family. If you've never seen the sadness in your child's eyes when Daddy didn't show up for a school play or hearing their Mom cry all night long not knowing what happened and knowing they were too small to do anything about it, maybe this chapter is not for you; feel free to go to the next chapter.

My only crime was I wanted to keep my family together. No one needs to feel ashamed, and somehow it was all his or her fault. I paid a high price; my home was a battlefield. I had to endure hardship to raise my children; they are the loves of my life. I wouldn't take anything for the journey to keep them safe and out of harm's way. After the breakup, it took me four years to talk to him again. When trust is lost, there are no winners. I had so much bitterness and anger until my daughter got in a car accident years later; I felt as though I had to tell her dad, since it was his child.

You will now read about how I was deceived for the last time. The wolf can turn into a sheep anytime and begin treating you kind, nice, telling you what you want to hear. It's easy for them to deceive you because they know what you don't like, so they just turn their actions to what you do like, knowing all along their cheating heart will tell on them!

I gave Mr. Wrong another chance. We started talking again; one night I saw him at my father-in-law's house. There was a really bad storm so my father-in-law asked me to stay for a little while until it blew over. The thunder and lightning were frightening in that trailer but having my ex in the same room without his lover and our lawyers was more frightening. He was having a problem with his girlfriend, the mother of the child, who had made my life a living hell. He was now staying at his father's place. I hadn't spoken to him in four years. We began to talk; I told him I would give our relationship another try. I felt none of us were married, as long as he wasn't living with her. He promised he would never cheat again. This didn't mean I wasn't still upset about what I went through. I just needed closure. We dated for a year.

That one year he treated me like a queen; I really thought he had changed! I had a better time in that one year than in the whole twenty-four years I was married to him. I really thought that we could make it this time. Nothing was too good for me: expensive clothes, expensive perfume, and vacations at the best hotels. I know what you are thinking: "Hotels?" I still have the pins. Remember, I wasn't saved yet nor was I trying to be at that time. I only knew my family had fallen apart, and I was trying to get it back together the only way I knew: showing love.

Please keep in mind; I was not calling myself a Christian at that time. It was a year after the final decree and we were both single.

Remember the verse "Sinned and fallen short"? All I was thinking about was he was my ex and the father of my children. The judge had given me most of the money, and that was the biggest problem; the women liked his money. Another reason was I knew I made the decision to break up but others thought he left me, which he never did. The truth was he wanted to come back home the next day but I had changed the locks. I was thinking in a strange way I could somehow get my self-respect back; this played a big part in rekindling our relationship. At that time, I hadn't dated in twenty-four years. I wouldn't know where to begin; just like most victims, the unsafe place seemed safe (familiarity). I was trying to reunite my family and find closure. I'm still on the theme of this chapter: abuse victims don't think like others; we don't live in the real world of break up and it's over. Somehow, our minds always wonder, was it my fault? Was he Mr. Right and I did something wrong? I had mixed feelings. I was feeling guilty that my family broke up on something I might have said or didn't say.

Since age fifteen, my Mr. Right was Mr. Wrong. Even though I was divorced and he had hurt me so many times in the past, I still felt that I would be cheating on him if I had a serious relationship with someone else. It took therapy and church to get me out of my self-made guilt. It was a struggle to mentally let go. I just didn't know how to go out in public with someone other than him. I was tired of looking back to see if someone was following me, afraid to date.

Only someone who has survived such an experience would understand.

Even though I was divorced, a shadow of fear still hung over me. Please understand, this book is different from any other book. It looks in the mind of someone who once loved someone, as my therapist said, loved him more than I loved myself. I went to church all my life, all over the world; however, there was a time I was merely going to church—I didn't understand how to trust in God or depend on His word. I was still struggling with putting my total trust in God. When the storm came, I didn't understand I had to go through the storm to gather strength; everything seemed to be going fine. At first, it seemed like the joke was on her; I thought he was just confused and misled; he really loved me, and that October day was part of my imagination; he had lost his mind that day when he should have protected me, his wife, but instead engaged in a horrible act of misconception. He lost who he was that day, since he had played the double life for so long. Now the tide had turned; I was the other woman, yes! But I soon found out I was betrayed again. The difference is this time he would pay for deceiving me; he would lose me for the last time and this time, forever. Yes we dated a year but he never spent the night over my house we would only go on weekend trips not totally putting my guard down.

One day, my father-in-law called and said to come over; he needed to talk to me just before one of our weekend trips out of town together; he said he didn't know which one of us was being played. I asked him why he said such a thing. I thought he was happy for me since he had always loved me like a daughter, treated me like his own daughter, and respected me. My father-in-law told me how his son was still cheating.

I can hardly explain how I felt without choking. He said, "I know you're off work every other weekend, and the weekend that you're not off, I'm babysitting their little boy while he takes her out of town." I told my father-in-law what he said couldn't be true, because he had moved out of her house a year ago! And he knew the promise to be faithful he gave me in front of him on that stormy night. I looked at him again and saw the disappointment he had on his face, because I know he never liked Ms. C and wanted us back together. After weighing the pain of his son's betrayal on his face, which I will never forget, I had to believe him. This was the same man who watched my firstborn while I went to school and to work, just months after our child was born while his son went off to war. I stayed with my father-in-law and not once did he lie to me; not once did we disagree. I had no choice but to believe him; he was a reliable source.

I said to myself, "Oh no, not again. His past sins are catching up with him." I asked myself why couldn't he be the man I wanted him to be? Why was my Mr. Right so wrong for me? I know my father-in-law thought that I would end the relationship right away when he told me that, but instead I went on the weekend trip. I acted like I didn't know that I was being played. I could have gotten an Academy Award for my performance. I went along with him, acting like I was the most important thing that ever happened to him. We went out of town; I stayed in a hotel while he took care of his business. I drove the rental car around that day; the only thing different was I was acting like I didn't care because I knew that was the last day I would see him alone (but he didn't know it).

Just to get back at my children's father, I began playing the role of a scorned woman; however, I'm not recommending this behavior to others, by no means. I'm just telling you my story before I found Christ. This book is different; I'm revealing how the devil used me when I tried to fix my situation on my own.

I'm still reflecting on the hell put on me; I haven't gotten to His Glory yet.

I went on the trip to show strength; I just wasn't afraid anymore of his web of deception and deceit. And for the first time, I wasn't going to bow down to what had a hold on me: the curse of returning to familiar territory would finally be broken when I had the last dance and the last laugh.

No, it wasn't God's voice. I knew it was the devils when I went to the store and charged the most expensive items I could find to his credit card. I went back to the hotel and ordered the·most expensive items on the menu like lobster, steak, and the best desserts. At the time, I didn't care about his money; the judge had given me most of that. I only wanted revenge for a broken heart.

Save the Last Dance for Me?

I then drove to the event in my new black high heels and gown. I even went out and bought some fancy stockings to go with my new shoes; my ex was the vice president, and I met with the president of the union for the first time; we even dropped him home. He always treated me very nice and wished my ex and I could get back together. That night the DJ played the song *Second Time Around*. I was on the ballroom floor with my best gown on (I was always a good dancer; however, he never allowed me to go to a club, but I still knew how to dance from TV).

That night I took the floor. I gave the performance of a lifetime, because I knew that would be the last dance that he would ever have with me. It was almost as if I was dancing with the devil. Everyone clapped as we got off the dance floor. That night seemed so special to him, but I knew I would never spend another one with him.

We left the next morning, and we were on the way back to Virginia when I saw the sign that we were close to his father's place. I felt brave talking about it because my father-in-law always protected me if he was around.

I told my ex that I knew that he was still having an affair. He denied it right away. I told him it was from a very reliable source; he asked who and I told him. My ex said that he wasn't telling the truth.

I said I believed him, and he would never lie to you. I tried to give our marriage another chance because of the children, but this time it was really over; how could he cheat on me and we're not even married?

As Tina Turner said, what's love got to do with it? I'm saying I found a new direction! I really went on the trip to show my father-in-law that after twenty-four years, it wasn't his fault the trip that was to be so right went so wrong. I just wanted him to know I tried my best and was brave enough to take back my heart that day, as I just smiled and walked away!

No matter what my critics may say, that one- year of happiness was worth the revisit. The memories of the good are mine, and no one can take that away. It seemed so real before I found out the truth about him. I will always have unanswered questions. Was my mind completely gone or did I just revisit a comfort zone? I make no excuses. My ex's spirit of lust for other women destroyed my home. I'm still wearing the battle scars. On the journey it took to be set free, I declared my self-worth. My only crime was failing to hold my family together.

I'm not saying my one year of dating my children's father before I decided to move on was the right decision, I'm just saying I found closure.

After my ex-husband began cheating again, I ended the relationship for the last time. A movie with Meryl Streep just recently came out, called It's Complicated; it's about a lady who was divorced and dating someone else and the ex-husband still wanted to see her. I know self-righteous people will judge domestic violence, and counselors would say, Why did you go back just to get disappointed? But I made a lot of wrong decisions; I had to go backwards to step forward. My mind was in disarray with no sense of direction after the divorce decree was signed. You see, I had divorce papers but no one sent a notice to my heart and mind. What my children's father put me through was definitely wrong. It took me years to find someone that I could call "Mr. Right." After we broke up, I decided to tell myself no heavy dating or commitments for a while.

After the word released me in Scripture and the judge put "guilty of adultery beyond a shadow of a doubt" on my final decree, after giving it one last shot on weekend trips to unite for the children, I finally gave up and moved on.

Yes, after the Seventh Commandment was broken, it seemed my husband did me a favor because if he had not messed up, I would have never started looking for Mr. Right.

I tried to heal the pain myself; I stopped watching TV for three years. All I would do was to go to work and come home to feed my son, read my Bible, and go to sleep until love found me.

I started dating again. My first boyfriend was very nice looking with blond hair. When I went to my brother's house, my sister-in-law almost dropped her groceries when she saw me getting out of his car. My neighbor called me and asked me whom that white guy was playing basketball in my backyard. I told her he was a friend of mine. Even my tenants never saw me with a man; I never became serious because I was so hurt by my husband's betrayal. My friend would come over to cook dinner for me or take me out to dinner. Even though he was nice and wrote me nice poems, I broke off the relationship with him. He kept calling but I wouldn't return the calls. I just wasn't ready at that time. It took me a while to get myself together and even think about looking for a husband. I just needed someone to talk to.

One of my tenants thought that I made it up when I said I had a boyfriend so no one would ask me out. Later, a very dear friend who worked with my ex, called Mr. M, was very supportive; he won me over when he said, "Why do you want a fifteen-dollar-an-hour man when you can have a twenty-five-dollar-an-hour man?" He was my bridge over troubled waters. Our relationship lasted for five years. I only saw him two times a month because I was not ready for a real boyfriend.

To summarize, it takes time to catch the right fish. You have to throw some back into the sea. I had three years of separation; after one year of divorce, I dated my ex-husband for a year, which I wrote about so my readers can see just how confused I was, calling wrong right and right wrong. But if you talk to any battered person, five minutes into the conversation it would become clear to you when they give their answers. In your mind you want to understand but on a real note, you are thinking she's just crazy. Even on some talk shows that I have watched, some ladies were in denial that their man would do such a thing, until the media uncovered all the ugly details. Yes, in looking for Mr. Right, only the strong will survive.

I then dated casually off and on (more off than on) for a year, still looking for Mr. Right. I dated Mr. M for five years but he never visited my home, although we spoke on the phone daily. I was still looking for Mr. Right seven years after I broke up with my children's dad. I went to work one day and told a friend of mine I was giving up on trying to find "Mr. Right."

She said, "Don't worry, he is probably out there as lonely as you and looking for you also." Those words gave me hope and comfort and strength to wait on the Lord. I stopped looking and started going back to church and becoming the Christian that I use to be before my marriage fell apart. I asked God to forgive me for all my mistakes that I committed trying to find Mr. Right.

What I Wanted in a Man (the Application for Mr. Right)

Mr. Right came along as a blind date.

Yes, there is a miracle with your name on it, but faith is action. You must venture out on your dreams; they will not come to you. A friend of the family, Mark, said he would introduce me to someone but he might not want me. I took the challenge, because I was so picky. I didn't want a man who drank, I didn't want a man who cursed, I didn't want a man who smoked or took drugs; I wanted a man to stay at home with me and be faithful, a man who when he got paid we would control the money together;

when others saw the husband and wife's names on the check book, they would back off.

Most abusers and stalkers don't want witnesses; I'm happy to say all the harassment stopped after I meet Trotter. I know you are saying: just how did Trotter get into my life? I feel it was divine intervention; our meeting was no accident. I was introduced to Mr. Right because at the time I just needed a movie date; he became a lifetime partner. I really didn't want to go on the blind date because my daughter's father had been a blind date; I wanted to pick the next person for myself. But I wasn't having any luck in finding someone since I was so picky. I said okay. What got my attention was Mark said something I would never forget; he said, "Every time I try and introduce you to someone, you say you don't like him." He didn't understand; the ones I refused to talk to have it going on, one of them even had his own shipyard business, one was president of a bank; money was not the issue with me. I just wanted someone I could trust and spend the rest of my life with in peace. I had a hard time trusting any man.

Rita told me to keep busy, and that's what I did. It really worked. I got two part-time jobs; one was out of town. I got involved in the product called Amway and went out of town to conventions. I also went to church and just had fun. I was getting child and spousal support, worked at the bank, and was doing well. Yes, Mark said he would introduce me to someone. I said to myself, *Why not?* My life was filled with unpredictable events and outcomes. One more wouldn't hurt.

I always liked a challenged, so why not? Years later, I told Trotter about it; he laughed and said, "If I was a bet, did you get your money?" I then said I wasn't trying to get anything materialistic from the bet, but if I got someone who fit my qualifications and high expectations, I automatically won because I got my man.

I asked him what he liked about me; he said that I told him I had to go home and comb my hair before we go to the movie. He said that was a sign that I liked him because my hair was looking okay when he saw me.

Meeting Mr. Right for the First Time

When we went to Trotter's apartment, it was nice; he was a handsome, good-looking Spanish man. I later found out his last name—Trotter—was his stepfather's. He seemed friendly, but I had to wait to tell because I learned in the past most men put their best foot forward at first; they can only put up the front for so long. My daughter and I sat on the sofa, as her friend and Trotter talked about some business at the shipyard where her friend worked. Trotter walked over to us and asked us if we wanted something to drink; remember I never drink or smoke or did anything negative. I had asked God to just give me someone like me, who would stay home and love me as much as I loved him. I also wanted someone to love my children and wanted them to love him as a stepfather. It seemed like he had it going on, until he asked us if we wanted a drink; I had already told myself he wasn't the one; not only did he ask me but he asked my daughter; I couldn't wait to get out of there, but to my surprise he came back from the kitchen with a glass of Kool-Aid. Okay, he was back in the game. We talked about going to see a movie that weekend; he told us he had to go to Florida that night and he wanted to buy the movie tickets before he left; okay, he impressed me again. He had only seen me for ten minutes and he was paying for all our tickets. I had been told I would be introduced to someone who might not want me. I took the challenge.

He then said, "Let's go to the theater and get them"; it was a new movie that was just coming out for the first time: *Waiting to Exhale*.

He was to meet us at the parking lot, and he was on time; another plus. He got out of the car wearing a long black leather coat, suede shoes, and a suit just like the one my father would have worn. The theater was full; we either had to sit in the back or all the way in the front. Tonya sat in the back and Trotter and I sat in the front. I noticed Trotter was quiet; he didn't say much. When I saw Angela Bassett burn the man's car in the movie, I said, "Go girl!" He gave me a strange look, maybe because I was loud.

After the movie, we went back to my house; we sat in the

dining room and talked for a while. I asked him if he was married; he said no. I asked if he had children; he changed the subject (I would later know why). Trotter asked me if I had a boyfriend. I said yes. He said, "Call him up and tell him you don't want to see him anymore" (because I had met him). I just didn't want to lead Trotter on; I was seeing Mr. M twice a month but every time Trotter called, I was always home. It was as if I wasn't dating, because I was always alone. I believe Trotter thought I was lying; because the relationship was so casual, it seemed like I was talking about a ghost because no one ever saw Mr. M; my children and brother only saw him once or twice in five years.

My friends and neighbors never saw Mr. M; I know it seemed strange; how could I be so head over heels with my children's father but refuse to give anyone else the time of day? Years later, I still can't explain. I guess you can say between the rental properties, my children, and the church, it took up most of my time. Because of my lifestyle, Trotter could easily take over my heart. But I didn't tell Mr. M good-bye; I just stopped answering his calls and stopped calling him. I didn't know how to say good-bye to a friend I could always talk to when I was down, so I chose not to. Years later, I called Mr. M from a phone booth in front of my church to tell him why I just stopped calling. I told him I had met someone else, and I never spoke to him after that conversation.

Yes, Trotter won my heart. I asked him what he liked about me. He said when I had to go home and comb my hair before we went to the movies, it was a sign to him I liked him because my hair was looking okay.

Our relationship started off as friends; in the beginning months, I didn't know Trotter was a preacher back in his hometown. I believe that's why our relationship has lasted. On Sundays, he could never reach me (I didn't have a cell phone at the time). One Sunday, I asked him to go with me to my church (I was going to three services a day). When I stood up and began to clap my hands and move like I was really happy, he said my church looked like something he belonged to. Months later, he told me why he had to travel; he was sending money home to his children for years. His work hours sometimes got in the way of him going to church on a regular basis; after meeting me, he found God again. I then took an interest in helping him with his children, because we were of one accord and not unequally yoked, like my children's dad.

My Sunday mornings were busy. I would take the lady next door to our church and take her to buy food, and then I would go to Trotter's apartment to cook breakfast and go to church with his children. Then I would cook dinner and go to an evening church service and go back to my house across town to spend time with my family. During the three years Trotter and I dated, we went to church all the time. I told Trotter I had ran from my calling years ago. Now that I was single again, I was going to run as fast and hard as I could for the Lord, because when I needed Him, He was there for me.

Finding Mr. Right: Asking Myself Was He Really the One?

Trotter came into contact with my children's father twice; the first time, they were standing next to each other at the airport but didn't know each other until years later, because I hadn't introduced him yet. The second time was at my father-in-law's funeral; that time they both knew each other. This story begins with an unusual meeting while I was still dating Trotter. A chain of events that were not planned left me with an eerie feeling of choosing my own destiny. My daughter became a captain; while I was still dating Trotter she had a ceremony. I bought tickets for my father-in-law and her father, but I had no idea they would be on the same plane with me at the same time. I hadn't spoken to her father in quite some time after I met Trotter, but I found myself in a situation that they were standing side by side at the airport. Trotter had no idea who he was. I tried to hide when I saw them. When they called the flight number I had to come forward. My future stepchildren were with Trotter when he waved good-bye to me. I was walking fast trying to get on the plane so I wouldn't have to speak to my children's dad; that wasn't the time for a meet-and-greet; no way, not that day.

Going forward everything seemed okay; I was on the walkway heading to the opening of the plane door; when a little lady told me that she liked the perfume I was wearing, I smiled and said thank you and turned around to wave to Trotter one last time before I stepped on the plane. I was thinking my ex and his dad were walking behind me, but to my surprise, Trotter and my ex-husband were standing beside each other. Trotter didn't know who he was, and he looked at me with that sneaky grin and smiled. It's funny because my ex knew what was going on, but since I had just met Trotter, he and his two teenage children had no clue my ex was standing beside them.

My ex even tried to show off his power of control after the game was all over. Instead of just walking behind me to board the plane, he stood beside Trotter at the end of the walkway, his shoes almost touching Trotter. Trotter stood there looking like Denzel Washington in his gray and black suit. My ex could have missed boarding of the plan just to see my reaction to him standing beside a man who was a vision he never wanted to see. Instead of a full wave, I did a half wave and quickly took off.

Since I was fifteen years old, I had to deal with his affairs, but the sight of seeing me with someone else was just too much for him. He just stood there with a mean look on his face, making me feel he was still in control. That's why I quickly turned around and walked onto the plane. It was all like a bad dream, a nightmare. I just wanted to wake up. All I could think of was, how could this happen? All I was trying to do was get some good plane tickets for my daughter's grandfather and her dad, but being on the same plane was not part of the deal. They were on the same plane and sat on the same row just opposite sides of the plane. I know my ex could tell I was trying to avoid him when I saw them. I had a great deal of respect for my father-in-law and respected his feelings. I really didn't want my father-in-law to see Trotter; even though I was divorced, I waited until after my father-in-law passed before thinking about marrying Trotter. I didn't say a word on the whole flight until we had a layover. I walked over to my father-in-law and spoke to him as if it was the first time I saw him. He said hello; I asked where his son was. He said, "Over to the bar getting drunk after he saw you."

I walked over to him and apologized for being rude but I wasn't ready to introduce him to Trotter just yet. He said that's okay; we got back on the plane.

Later on that day, we both were happy to see our daughter; the ceremony was great; my father-in-law really loved it. The general even did something different and let my father-in-law pin my daughter's captain's bars on. That made all of us very happy. I have to admit my ex and I did have a great time those days we were visiting our daughter. We took pictures and went out to dinner with her grandfather; since it was in Texas, the steaks were bigger than the plates. At first we went places with Tonya and then we just started touring the town alone. You would think we were still married. It seemed being far away from the baby momma drama and courtroom scene eased the grief of the destruction of direct attacks by the enemy. After the ceremony took place, my ex helped me with my bags. He thought I was going back to Virginia but to his surprise, my ticket was for Florida.

My ex looked disappointed, mainly since I was single at that time. However, reality came when my ex saw my ticket to Florida; he just looked at me in disappointment. It seemed I had hurt him for the first time since we were fifteen years old. I couldn't fix the pain on his face, because I had no idea getting away from our hometown after the divorce made that much of a difference. It seemed we both felt free. When he looked down and saw the return ticket on my luggage, he didn't say a word, and neither did I. All of those thoughts were short lived when he saw the tag's destination: Florida. It seemed my heart and the tickets were in two different places.

The loudspeaker called for his plane to go back to Virginia. As he left, I ran to the window and watched his plane take off with him and his dad. As I looked in the sky feeling very confused, I had tears in my eyes; I thought, what have I done? Was there a chance that his cheating heart finally wanted me as his own? Did it take him seeing me with another man a few days earlier before we took off for Texas? Judging from the expression on his face, did he think he had won me over in Texas or did he think he still had a chance to talk to me on our way back to Virginia? Something haunted me about that trip for my daughter's awards ceremony. As an angel of forgiveness and hearts touched and wounds mended, it went from the joy of my child's dreams coming true versus the rise and fall of my relationship with her dad. It didn't get us back together, but love was released and a hate spirit was suppressed.

I had just met Trotter; he hadn't had enough time to prove himself. It began to look like the ticket I purchased before leaving Virginia was the deciding factor. The next day I would be at Trotter's daughter's high school graduation; I was on my way (she would later become my stepdaughter after we got married). When the plane touched down in Florida and Trotter met me with his two beautiful teenage daughters, I was still in a state of confusion. My body was there but my mind was back in Texas on the events of the days before. After meeting some of Trotter's family, I took the car and just rode around Florida for about five hours—not getting out, just riding; not even knowing where I was going (at that time, I didn't know anyone there). I just wanted to be alone.

When I returned, Trotter was very upset and asked me to never leave without telling him where I was going again. It sounded good but only months later our relationship was tested again. Trotter and I went back home; months later, we got into a disagreement. He was allowing his ex-girlfriend to call his apartment; when I asked him about it, he told me it was his phone and she was still his friend and could call anytime she wanted to. That didn't set well with me, and we broke up for a week. Don't get me wrong; I understood about the children's mother calling. I was there on most of the calls, but an ex-girlfriend? That was just too much. Again, I wasn't saved then, and even if I were, it would have taken a lot of prayer, especially when the girl began to curse me out in Spanish.

During that one and only week of our break up, my sister-in-law called and told me my father-in-law had passed away. I hadn't seen or talked to my children's dad in a while and I had a foolish idea that we could communicate and try and get along. I felt at that time we had a common bond: the love we had for his father, and Trotter and I were having a few problems, but again that was short lived. The night before the funeral, Mark (the same friend who got Trotter and me together) tried to keep us together by calling Trotter to come over to my house. Trotter was dressed up in his suit with some nice-smelling cologne, looking really good. But after they finished playing some games, I told him I was going down to North Carolina to help my former sisters-in-law, Addie and Rita, with the funeral. He got really upset and asked me why I was doing that. I asked him why did he care since we had just broken up a week before.

He left and went home; the next day I went to North Carolina; that morning I cooked breakfast for everyone. I even spent my own money on the food. I talked to the funeral director, who gave me great discounts. I even rode in the limousine to pick out the flowers. It looked as though my ex and I were back communicating with words only again. That night I got the shock of my life: someone said Ms. C was coming down the road. This time I didn't feel afraid of a confrontation because my sisters-in-law always had my back.

As she drove up, I walked out of the trailer, thinking my ex would stay by my side just as he had the entire day. I was shocked that he walked over to her and grabbed her by the waist and introduced her to my children's family from South Carolina as his woman. I just stood there, looking stupid and feeling disrespected, rejected, and betrayed. All I could think of was, how could he? Not after the great day the family had together. I quietly got into my car and drove back to Virginia, alone and disappointed. After I arrived home, I got a phone call from the funeral director; his sisters had wanted me to ride in the limo, because they knew the children's grandfather loved me like his real daughter. I only wanted the program to read "grandchildren's mother"; I was told that my ex didn't want my name on the program at all and didn't want me in the family car. He had secretly made other arrangements after the family talked.

Yes, I fell short, lost it, didn't understand how to depend on His word at the very time I needed it. I was almost too ashamed to come back to God and Trotter; nothing happened between us physically that day but I still felt guilty, like I had disrespected Trotter; even if we had broken up, I shouldn't have seized the opportunity. My ex-husband had said the night before that I would not be allowed in the family limo with my children, since we were divorced. At that time, we were single but I realized I was still the underdog. That feeling I was on top and somehow had an edge faded very quickly after he embarrassed and rejected me on the program.

I had to get Trotter back, because I saw that my ex-husband was just mean spirited. I called Trotter the next morning and told him I wanted to speak to him. He said okay. I drove over to his apartment. When I saw him, I asked him if he would go with me to my father-in-law's funeral. He looked at me as if to say, you've got to be kidding me, but he didn't say it (even though I saw it in his eyes and I would have deserved it). He grabbed his gold shirt and began ironing it very fast, with the hope that we'd be getting back together.

My only request to the funeral director was that I'd be allowed in the next car behind the family limo, where my children were. Before the cars drove off, my ex looked at me straight in the eyes; I stared back at him without emotion.

I just recently told Trotter why I stared back so hard; for years Trotter thought I was still in love because of the way my ex and I looked at each other. It was in front of everyone at the funeral at the time, including Ms. C. The reason he looked at me like that was because I was with Trotter, and he knew that if I was bold enough to bring him to his father's funeral, this time it really was over. I wasn't just using words I was using actions.

I told Trotter it was an emotionless stare because I knew that look on his face; I had seen it so many times before, just before he would go off in rage, but the difference was we were not alone behind close doors. This time all the cars were lined up, my children and his family were looking out of the limo windows at me; it was if the world had stopped for a few seconds, because not a car moved. No one moved; all eyes were on my ex and me. I looked at him as if to say, It is finally over; when he made the decision that I could not sit in the family limo beside my children the night before, I gathered strength I didn't know I had and proudly got back into Trotter's car and made the decision it was over for good!

They asked if I was going to stay and eat. I told them no, I was only staying for the burial; I only came to show my respect and be with my children since they were so hurt. They really loved their grandfather very much, mainly because their grandmothers and the granddad on my mother's and father's side had all passed before they were born; this was the only person they had ever called a grandparent; that's why I knew I had to be there to comfort them, even if it had to be from afar. Just like so many times before, I couldn't let my pain and hurt feelings stand in the way of doing the right thing for them. An unselfish act to show them love was greater than hate; I'd known my father-in-law for twenty-four years; he would have wanted me there. My children sat in the family seats in front of the casket as it was lowered to the ground.

My ex made me feel like I wasn't part of the funeral way before I decided to bring Trotter and act like a guest. I stood in the guest line as my twin brother Henry and Trotter stood on the opposite side and talked. I shook hands with the family, as if I were a guest, as I walked past the casket, but just as a last-minute attempt for him to get the last stand of control, he grabbed my hand and held it for about five minutes, holding up the line. He began to smile as my face showed panic. He then let my hand go, and the line began to move again. I could not believe that he would cause a scene as if he were still in control of my life, after he made the decision to introduce his lover the night before to the family from out of town. Ms. C was not allowed to sit with the family; his sisters requested that because of the way she treated me. As I walked to get in my car, she was stomping her feet on the porch, because she was upset that he still showed signs of caring about me. To me she didn't have a thing to worry about because his actions made me sick; he only acted that way because that was the first time he had heard about me being with anyone, but as you see, his past actions drove me to Trotter. That was the last time I saw that evil woman. I guess after she saw me with another man for the first time, she knew the game was over; that was the beginning of my relationship with Trotter, and for the first time I felt safe!

Trotter and I had gotten to really like each other, but I still was distant toward him, not wanting to get hurt again. What impressed me was my children liked him; Trotter and I began to see each other more often. I had to fix the gift God had given me. He just didn't trust other women. He had dated women who had cheated on him before. He also didn't understand there were times I just didn't feel like talking or seeing anyone. I would look at the caller ID and not answer. My job as an account manager at the bank was very demanding, and I needed my rest. I know that was strange but that's the way I was before I found the Lord. I was in my own world. To other people, it seemed I was lonely, but to me I was okay, because most of my marriage I was alone. Sometimes if I needed to just get away, go shopping, or go to my brother's or to where my dad's people lived for the weekend, I would tell Trotter I was going out of town. He didn't understand at first but later said okay.

For years, Trotter worked on government contracting jobs and military duty, which took him out of town. Before meeting me, he never lived with a woman more than two years. Years ago, before he found God, if a woman began to cheat, my new sister-in-law Rose said, "He would just say, 'I'm out of here!'" He would not give them any warning, no forwarding address, and never looked back. I was the opposite; I tried to hold it together.

One night there was an eclipse, and I wanted to go in the house. Remember, he never spent the night or went into my house at night, so he wanted me to stay outside in his car longer to look at the sky. I said no, I was tired after dinner and like always I would say good night, but this time was different. Trotter wanted to hold me a little longer, so I sat in the car for about a half hour in front of my house. I was thinking, what is he up to? He was acting like he wanted to get closer.

One day after we had gotten back from the store, he offered to help me bring in the large flower he had just bought. I said yes. It seemed I was beginning to lose my control of being in control; we were just getting too close. Remember, I never wanted a serous relationship. I said, "You know, I don't need a man." He reminded me of that a few years later and laughed.

What impressed me was my children liked him, He asked me to go with him to his family reunion. It was getting close to the date and he had told some of his family that he was bringing me down to meet them (some of them, for the first time). I said yes; he had been nice to my son and me, and a real plus was my son liked him, He even got my son a job at the shipyard, another plus: an eighteen-year-old boy making good money with full benefits. I was so happy I had finally found Mr. Right!

I remember thinking we had a few rough roads but because of divine intervention, we were okay now. Another twist: his mom was keeping his children at first while they were in school. On school break, they came back with us. We all had to get used to each other, but it wasn't so bad because the three years we dated, we both had our own places. One day, we went over to his mom's house. I saw a picture of a handsome man in a Marine's uniform by the fireplace. I saw it as I walked in the door, but I tried acting like I wasn't looking at it. I couldn't stand it any more; I asked his mom whom that guy was.

She smiled and said, "You already have him."

His children came back to Virginia with us. It took some time for me; I had been dating him for a while before I found out he was a preacher and had children. He stayed on his side of town at night and I stayed on my side, until we decided to get married, but because of the children, I came over and cooked, cleaned, and taught them how to clean. I met their teachers at school and took an active role in their lives.

His girls and I get along fine; when we first met, it was a little hard for them to accept me, which is understandable. For fifteen years, there had been no mother living with their father, and the last time they saw her, they were too young to remember. I have devoted years to bringing my blended family together. After I found out that his children would be living with us, I realized he needed me more. If you look at the wedding pictures, both his and my daughter favors each other. I'm blessed to have a beautiful family.

For fifteen years, he was looking for a wife; going by what he told me, the other ladies who wanted to marry him had a problem with the children being of mixed heritage. This was fine with me; they blended easily with my family, because my niece (my twin's daughter) who looks just like me is mixed. I have cousins with blond hair and blue eyes, and in the pictures they look like me in the face but a lighter version. Some of my boy cousins even passed for white years ago; they say most people couldn't tell my father had some black in him. My stepson looks just like my cousin's son. My grandmother was full-blooded Indian; that's why my daughter looks the way she does with her long hair (her childhood sweetheart used to call her "squaw"). My twin is even lighter than me. I never thought my niece looked like me until one day she got a tan. I took the color of my mother. I'm just saying all that to say my family blended in just fine. Even after we got married I would come home and find a gift he had left me. Like my therapist said, my breakthrough came when I learned to love myself more.

I had written a letter to the base and requested some soldiers attend my wedding, since we had soldiers at my daughter's wedding and it was impressive. It would be my gift to Trotter; I asked for two and they gave me six soldiers. Yes, the Marines were at my wedding.

My children's father then married a lady who had nothing to do with our divorce. She came to both of the weddings, and I will publicly say thank you to their new stepmother. I gave her a hug after each wedding for being kind to my children when they visited their home.

Yes, there are many unanswered questions; I still have some myself. When he saw Trotter for the first time, it was not a trivial encounter; his reaction was that of rage, and he had fire in his eyes. Remember, he had never seen me with another man since I was fifteen years old. Before my first child was born, I had never been with another man, and no one can say otherwise. A man who had so much to say about me to justify his affairs went in shock when I decided to close the door to my last chapter with him. Game over; the player played his last hand.

I have shared what I learned from my past failure with you. I just gave you the secret on how I repaired my heart and built a solid foundation to receive His Glory.

In my books, love is action. I know I found my soulmate, Mr. Right. For fifteen years, God has blessed Trotter's and my relationship. My children love Trotter. They never forget his birthday or any occasions; they treat him like a king. My brother-in-law Junior said, "My family must really love you," because he said he had a hard time getting them to come to anything. He said I gave them two months' notice of my son's wedding and the entire family came down. I thank God for my new family; when I was about to give up years ago, happiness was right around the corner! My children were kept out of harm's way by a divine hand and His power. My children were never harmed physically; they were my seed. They entered the land of milk and honey just stepping into God's promises.

Everyone wanted to know my secret. Last weekend, Trotter's Uncle Robert and other members of the family were in town for their granddaughter's graduation from Hampton University. They told us they were so happy that after all these years, we were still together. The phone rang and it was my stepdaughter Dionna (I always call her my daughter). Mariea called the next day, wishing me happy Mother's Day. His Aunt Lucille looked at me and said she had known Trotter since high school, when he played baseball and football, and she had never seen him so happy. She then said, "You have been good for him." I smiled and she said, "I really mean it."

Trotter and I are in the ministry together; we are like glue. We have learned through trial and error. We will never do anything to jeopardize the relationship God gave us; however, his past tried to haunt him when we first started dating. (It wasn't him; it was them.) Trust me, I've had some try and break us up while we were dating, even churchwomen (some of them were the worst). They couldn't even get close. Trotter said after we got married; if a woman couldn't call him at my house phone, don't bother calling him. If someone asked for money, he would say, "Ask my wife first; the funds are marital funds, we both make decisions on every dime that has come into our home." God always had the last word; like the Bible says: "What therefore God hath joined together, let not man put asunder." (Matthew 19:6)

God is confirming His word. My favorite song is *What God Has for Me Is for Me*. I asked God to get Shirley Caesar to sing it at my wedding, but she was not available at the time. God still honored my request; my friend Shirley Hoskins sang it. Mrs. Caesar's husband is an elder as well; I spoke to both of them a few years later. She asked me about my book sales; I told her they were okay. Years ago, I wanted a movie on Lifetime for Women but instead I've had TV commercial on both Lifetime channels; I have been doing business with them since 2007. It's funny; I was born with the direct communication with God but sometimes I have to be specific. I asked for Shirley; I got my friend Shirley; I asked for a movie on Lifetime; I got a TV commercial on Lifetime. I'm still trying to understand the gift God gave me.

When I met Trotter, he was my Mr. Right; however, he was a broken and wounded soldier, he didn't trust women, since they had hurt him so badly with their affairs. Divine intervention mended his heart. Sometimes God gives us the desire of our heart; it comes with a few bumps and bruises; it's up to us to heal and enhance them, mend the broken in heart. "Get your house in order" means what it says? Some know the word; they just don't understand it. That's when you call for the elders of the church! If I had given up, look what I would have lost; my blessings were around the corner.

When I was young, I would hear others say, "One man's poison is another man's gold; one man's trash is another man's treasure."

I have to reveal something to you; Trotter treats me like his treasure.

He is everything I wanted in a man. My Mr. Right is Mr. Perfect. Sorry, ladies; he's taken.

Chapter 12

Call to Ministry: Behind the Glory

2001–2002

"Born with a Veil over My Face:
A Gift to See Visions"

"The Spirit of the Lord is upon me, because he hath anointed me to preach the gospel to the poor; he hath sent me to heal the brokenhearted, to preach deliverance to the captives, and recovering of sight to the blind, to set at Liberty them that are bruised." (Luke 4:18)

All my writings were composed on small pieces of paper from notepads and anything I could find at the time to write on. I put together writings from a voice that divinely spoke to me whenever and wherever I was at the time. When I was young, I was doing fine when I was obeying God's voice. I could see things in the future. God deals with me through visions and dreams. The voice would even wake me up at all hours of the night; I was compelled to write. Once I was tired and asked Trotter to write down what I was saying from the voice that was instructing me to write (he said I was going too fast). All my poems were written in less than five minutes.

The Dream (Warning before Destruction)

In 1981, I had a dream showing a small boy running around in a trailer. The same month ten years earlier in 1971, October, my first child was born. Because the voice had told me it was my children's brother, I immediately told my children's father I had a dream that we were going to have another child. After I described what the boy looked like and what the inside of the trailer looked like, we both dismissed it as a bad dream.

Ten years later, October 20, 1991, I saw that same child in my ex-husband's arms but he didn't belong to me; however, he was my children's brother and it was his son. God has always tried to warn and protect me from danger (I now question if I had understood the dream, could I have somehow stopped what took place that dark day? Could somehow the events that led up to that day have been changed?) If you add twenty years to 1971, when our first child was born, you get 1991. October 20, 1991, was the day of my attack. My first born's month of birth coincided with when her half brother's mother attacked me exactly twenty years later. Also his lover's child had been born the same month and day as my father-in-law's birthday: September 11. I just thought of something; wasn't it September 11, 2001, a ten-year difference from 1981 and 1991, the same ten-year difference between my dream and my daughter's year of birth, when the enemy decided to attack this country? My daughter was assigned to the Pentagon but didn't get hurt. God said, "Not so!" Was this a coincidence or divine intervention? Exactly twenty years after Tonya's birth, her half brother would be born.

Remember what I said about the eerie feeling of how my twin and I were born on the 28th; both my mom and dad were born and died on that date. I'll give you one last mystery to think about: I opened up with the date 1981, the day of my dream; take the year I was born, 1953, from 1981 and you get twenty-eight.

The Vision Became Reality

Years later, a child out of wedlock was playing in a trailer that my children's great-grandmother bought; he visited on a regular basis. I had an eerie feeling when I discovered the dream was true; I went to the trailer I had visited so many times myself to see my father-in-law. One day I screamed and asked, "What happened?" The trailer had been remodeled to fit the same layout as the dream, the same month the baby was born. My mother-in-law simply said she just redecorated the place. At that point, my gift became reality.

When I was a small girl, some of my friends called me a witch, only because my dreams came true and it scared them. I just warned them; I didn't want the dreams to come true. If the dreams were bad, I could walk past someone, discern evil, and know if they were sick or if something good or bad would happen. A feeling would come over me to call a loved one when I felt danger in sight.

My daughter inspired me to write after she was impressed with my gift. She said, "Mom, don't just keep the gift to yourself." She then said, "Mom, I have a master's degree and you can help me solve everyday problems that I had no clue what to do." She then said, "When I tell you my problem, you make it seem like it's nothing, which makes me feel like it was nothing, and I soon forget what was said or done."

In every job I had, I have excelled to the top and had so many letters from customers. My job was to give advice to customers on their finances.

I attribute my success to the voice of divine intervention; I would only speak and preach and give advice of encouragement when I heard His voice; that way, I knew it was His voice. I began to tell others that when I was a child, they turned on me.

When I was a young girl, I asked God to take the gift away from me because it would scare me and I didn't want people to dislike me. If they listened to me, they would have been fine, but some disobeyed and things didn't go their way. Then I said enough was enough; I begged for the gift to be taken back and the next time, it didn't come so easily.

Years later, my sister-in-law in Florida took me out to dinner. Her granddaughter asked me why I smiled so much; I said everyone asks me that and I say that's how I stay in control of my emotions at all times, so no one can catch me off guard when I'm in the spirit and flesh can't take over. I went through so much after my ex-husband began to abuse me, many times, not just physically but mentally also.

Yes, years later, I became an ordained elder and received my license to marry couples; I was authorized to celebrate the union of marriages in the Circuit Court of the City of Norfolk. I'm proud to carry these licenses.

Our church loves helping the less fortunate. I've always celebrated Thanksgiving with my family; this year I told my family I would be feeding the homeless all day. Both my husband and I are in the ministry together; the name of the church is New Trinity Pentecostal Holiness Church.

My husband has been a prophet for years. I know God called me because the date typed on my elder's license is December 28. That date has always been a sign to me; in the past, it has always represented greatness or loss in all areas of my life. The twenty-eighth of November, my mother was born; December 28 my mother died. March 28 my father was born; February 28 he died. December 28, my twin brother and I were born after escaping the hand of death, since my mother died the same day. Just like Jabez, my written words were written in pain, but I never made excuses; not even my closest friends or co-workers knew of the tragedies in my life. You see, that's how the enemy works; he makes you give up just before you get your blessings or a breakthrough. My daughter asked me, "Mom, did you know you were born on Denzel Washington's Birthday?"

I replied, "No, Mr. Washington was born on my birthday."

When I look at Trotter's Marine picture, it looks just like Denzel when he was younger.

When I was between ten and seventeen, my duties included being a Sunday school teacher, church secretary, and youth minister, along with writing and directing plays; all that at an early age. After marrying my children's father at eighteen, I stopped serving God. My ex wouldn't allow me to get involved anymore; he said it took away from my duties at home, and I believed him. I went to church, but I knew if I had stayed involved in the activities,

I would have gotten into the ministry sooner, because everyone was always asking me to speak. Every time I would feel pressure, I would stop going or change churches. It was easy to avoid the offers because my ex-husband was in the military; we were always moving. I felt, how could I help others when I was having issues and looking for answers myself?

I always knew there was a calling in my life; I missed that voice that gave me a way to tread on serpents. Eve's mistake? She began to listen to the serpent. I know God, not man, chose me.

Years later, my pastor called me. I was already sitting in the pulpit and serving God when he gave me my license. The events were all in the same year. Before I retired, when things on my job would begin to stress me, I would remind God of my service to him like Hezekiah. I began to walk in my calling; it wasn't long before my plate was so full.

Trotter and I spoke on the radio on Saturdays. We visited the nursing home; we visited the hospitals every time someone called us. It didn't matter whether the patient belonged to our church or not, anyone who needed prayer, we would be there whether they requested us or not; that's our job: vice president of the youth committee, wrote and directed plays, put on programs since 2002, taught Bible study, preached at revivals, opened the church for noonday prayer (Monday through Friday), fed the homeless, worked on nonviolence. I was not just speaking at my church, but other churches requested me to be a guest speaker on a regular basis.

The engagements wouldn't just be in our town but also in other states; I am a motivational speaker for battered women's shelters and schools, licensed in the circuit court to perform weddings. It seemed after retirement I had more engagements.

My schedule was full. The devil began to try to hinder my assignment God gave me to help others. But I knew I had to follow God's instructions. I had three surgeries in between books, and I didn't want anything to go wrong; if the enemy won, this would just be a book that was never published if God called me home before the assignment was over. I e-mailed my daughter and my niece to carry on with my work just in case something happened to me. Because of nerve damage, I had surgeries on both my hands, which slowed my typing down. I still believe in divine healing, and I trusted in God when the x-rays showed the entire side of my back had nerve damage as well. I'm refusing to have surgery on my back because He is the same God that healed me so many times before.

One cold day, I went to the library with my friend Cynthia; I noticed there were some homeless people reading books. Many servants of God who have best-selling books say they are called, but when I checked to see if their best seller was released in the libraries or given to battered women and homeless to read for free, I was disappointed. Since 2001, as soon as my books are published, they are put in the library, before they hit the malls, stores, and Web sites.

When I first started preaching, I would give the speaker's offering back to the church or someone in the congregation after God led me to who needed the money the most. On many occasions, I would not even count the money first. My co-workers never understood why I was still working and giving money away. I would get up in the middle of the night and give someone some food. Trotter and I helped many people who just needed to get themselves together. I allowed many people to stay for free in my rental property until they got themselves together. I've gotten people out of jail and put thousands of dollars for a lawyer on a credit card more than one time. I've paid for cars for people, gave away cars, and gave away my dad's house just because someone needed it. I live what I preach; I preach for the love of God, not the love of money. I have never accepted any kind of offering from my own church. God never told me to take from his people for my own agenda. I'm not driven by money or greed. My Bible tells me money is the root of all evil; through the years I've seen a lot of evil.

Yes, I have fully accepted my calling; some of my readers have e-mailed me, one man found my phone number; I've run into fans in the stores who would remind me of something that I said that changed their life, something God had me write.

Now that you understand what kind of preacher I am, allow me to minister to you. The way you know someone loves you. Love doesn't hate, love builds up, and it does not tear down. If you are the attacker, you have the power to stop your mind from thinking evil. If you are a victim, you have the power to change the way you handle a hopeless situation. Take control of your life in a positive way; stay away from negative things and negative people. At the end of the day, know who you are, know your strength; build on your weakness to help you grow and gain power after every attack. The reason you started the journey was not to sabotage your mission. Stop letting the enemy undermine your purpose by listening to loose, fast-talking women or men who don't have your best interest at heart. Learn to believe in yourself.

There is a life to live off the church pulpit; both my husband and I feel the same way about being of one accord. If you can't talk to my husband, you can't talk to me. Even the Bible says, "The flesh is weak to strive to stay in the spirit and not to lust in the flesh." Your sole purpose in going to work is to support your family, not break up your family. The work place is just that: a work place! The reason why I decided to minister to you about the work place: that's where my ex-husband found most of his lovers. If you were like me, I needed the money from his job; we had children to support; however, drama that went with the affair was not needed. You can protect your marriage; it takes two to tango. Most relationships can survive if you keep the home-wrecker out of your home business.

Ironically, divine intervention tells me it's my season; my Bible tells me, "in due season I shall reap the harvest." Now that I'm retired, I know it's my time to reach out more to those who are abused and misused. Years ago, my husband told me my ministry would be like Joyce Myers's. At the time, I didn't understand what he was talking about; ten years later, I now understand I just have to have the heart to want to help others; it's God's job to open the doors. I have the full revelation of what the Prophet David Paul said. I still remember how he said I would have a great woman's ministry. He called me out by name when he came to town, among thousands of people. I met Prophet David Terrell in Florida; he poured a handful of oil over my head; after Trotter and I left his ministry tent, riding down that long dark road, the voice of God wouldn't let me sleep. God's voice just kept flowing, and I haven't been the same since. That was in 2001. I'm thankful that God decided to put His trust back in me to help lead His people by guiding my footsteps. (It's funny; my attorney's name was Paul also.) They gave me words of encouragement just days before I was given my license to preach. That's why I know I was called.

As I was typing my last lines to this chapter, Chris Brown appeared in another interview. As I looked up, he was asked how he felt about what happened in his domestic violence case. All he said was, "I'm messed up." He asked forgiveness. A good Shepherd loves all his sheep, even the ones that went astray, but if you keep it up, He will cut you off!

Even Peter had issues; he lied when he said he didn't know Jesus; he cursed and cut off a man's ear—yes, he needed counseling. God put His trust back in Peter when He allowed him to preach on the day of Pentecost. He preached repentance and said the people are not drunk; they are filled with the Holy Ghost.

Please don't come against others that confess and ask for forgiveness. Stop acting holier than thou by not forgiving; you might be shocked to know what's in the closets of the ones who throw the stones. That's what this book is all about: being real with you. "He slew two lion-like men of Moab: he went down also and slew a lion in the midst of a pit in time of snow." (2 Samuel 23:20)

God is telling us that to overcome your fears, sometimes you must be like a warrior and defeat a lion.

Sermon
War on Domestic Violence

My enemy's hatred wasn't worth me losing His promises. When they began lying on me, falsely accusing me, backstabbing me, plotting my demise, I was still marching. I'll stop just for a moment and say did you read Deuteronomy 28? The verse says that they came against me one way and I had to flee seven ways. I'm still marching. When you hit me and hurt me in the dark, Jesus was watching. I'm still marching. Please put your ear down to listen closely; you thought I was praying that you would stop hitting me so hard; I was praying that I don't lose my anointing and take you out the same way you came into my life: like a thief in the night. God ordered you; orders of my enemies are to be revoked; their assignment was canceled. I won because my assignment was to save you from yourself.

King Balak offered Ba-laam a house full of silver and gold to curse the blessed children of Israel: "If Balak would give me his house full of silver and gold, I cannot go beyond the commandment of the LORD, to do either good or bad of mine own mind; but what the Lord saith, that will I speak? And now, behold, I go unto my people: come therefore, and I will advertise thee what this people shall do to thy people in the latter days." (Numbers 24:13–14)

Just like in the Bible, my enemies were sent to curse me but had to bless me. This assignment could not be trusted to just anyone. I was chosen because God said he needed a strong soldier. You might think you are strong, because you are physically stronger; if anyone underestimates His power, tell him or her, "For unto whomsoever much is given, of him shall be much required." (Luke 12:48)

Money and material possessions can't fix what's broken if the reader is with Mr. Wrong.

My story shows that color, financial status, notoriety, and looks have nothing to do with the way you are treated. Living in violence is a way of life when you meet Mr. Wrong a trap that you just walk into blindfolded. His sickness has no outward appearance. The abusers wear fine clothes as well as torn jeans; women of abuse have fine cars; they live in fine homes; and their children go to the best schools. My children were in military schools most of their lives.

Stop playing the blame game.

Maybe if I was with him when he worked out of town … if

it gives you any comfort, I moved with my ex-husband to every duty station, even took my children to live in a foreign country for ten years. I tried to keep him faithful; however, to him it was just another move, another opportunity to make my life a living hell. It didn't make a difference: a cheater is always a cheater (unless they get help). This seems crazy: he is no longer with any of the women he used against me in twenty-four years. Does he or she care? This is a question you should never have to ask; if you are asking or even wondering, that tells me you have already experienced some form of disrespect or abuse.

I wrote a letter one night concerning me wanting to end it all during my divorce, which I quickly destroyed the next morning (this was before I started going back to church). I'm thankful my children never read that letter, which was addressed to them.

With God, All Things Are Possible

My dreams for my children were right around the corner; the victory line was on my blind side; the promises that had our names on them were the gift that was waiting to be opened. You will read about how He has enlarged my territory in the last chapter of this book. I had no idea I would meet a preacher and God would give me a loving new family while keeping the love and respect of my old one. He gave me another mother-in-law, other sisters-in-law, other brothers-in-law, and a promotion on my job before I retired. And my children have great jobs. My daughter has always had a humble spirit; if I didn't tell you her accomplishments, you would have never known them. Even when she was chosen to represent her school to talk to Secretary of State Henry Kissinger, she got an award and her high school received a trophy when she answered a question on abortion to his satisfaction. She only told me she was selected to attend after she received the award.

My son has a house, trucks, land; it seems he received more than he had. And most of all regardless of what I might think of their dad's actions, I'm grateful to him that my children still kept the love of their father. Since we both have remarried, we don't communicate like we used to; however, I kept the love of my ex's family because my children have the bloodline of their father. God even added a bonus: Trotter accepts them as family when they visit our home. My family was blessed in the city and blessed in the field. The enemy tried to stop my new beginning after my ex refused to sign the final decree. Sometimes, he just wouldn't show up to court or ducked the sheriff when he tried to deliver the court papers. I didn't understand. He didn't know how to treat me, but he didn't want me to go on with my life.

The commissioners made him sign the papers after I paid hundreds of dollars. The weapons formed but never prospered because I learned to depend on His word. God didn't give up on me when I went astray, so why should I give up on Him? When Job was tested, his wife wanted him to curse God and die, but I say I shall live and not die but declare the works of the Lord every chance I get.

I decided after being delivered from many near death experiences to become a living testimony and tell my story all over the world through my ministry and making motivational speeches; I'm hoping after I'm gone on to Glory, a legacy though my writings will live on as a guiding light and a torch for others to carry. I'm hoping the future generation will realize, at the end of the day, the plan was to go through the fire and get delivered by a supernatural power. Always remember: it's not the attack; it's how you react to the attack! I saw His Glory and so did my attackers when He released His superiority. My enemies were defeated when He revealed to the world His awesome power!

Henrietta Trotter

Chapter 13

Dealing with Abuse as Individuals

2003

"How Communities Should Approach Domestic Abuse"

October 2009 marks the eighteenth anniversary of the day my life changed forever: October 20,1991. Eighteen years ago, my life flashed before my eyes. Not only was I attacked but also, after the divorce was over, I received everything I wanted but didn't find fulfillment. That night I wrote a letter to my children (which I never sent) stating I wanted to end it all during my divorce. I was strong enough to fight but not brave enough to survive on my own after twenty-four years in an abusive relationship. Even though I was abused on a regular basis, he was all I knew. Yes, I loved my children more than life, but at that time I had no idea what faith was all about. I knew about God, but at that time didn't know Him as a comforter.

I spent three years not watching TV in temporary desperation; I had more than one night of depression before I wrote the letter. I needed more than a feel good service. I needed something I didn't have; that was the Lord in my life. Money and a good job weren't enough. As I cried myself to sleep, all I could think was some other woman had my man; even though I put him out, I just could not get the thought of what happened that dreadful day out of my mind. I later communicated with him for a year and found closure, which I wrote about in detail in an earlier chapter. I know now, in order to carry myself over those lonely nights, I had to be alone with no desire to entertain anyone, not even myself.

No one really knew just how lonely I was; just weeks after I got my divorce decree, I heard the song *You Are Not Alone*, by Michael Jackson, come over the radio. I asked God to forgive me after the bottle of pills didn't work. I woke up the next morning in a daze; I tore up the letter and turned my life 100 percent to Christ. I felt sorry for myself in a crazy deranged moment, a thoughtless act of stupidity. The enemy had me believe if I ended my life, the bank that I worked for would pay my children my 401K pension plan and funds from stocks, CDs, and life insurance policies—more money than I could give them at the time because of the bills he had left me with. I thought I was worth more to them dead than alive. Afterwards I told myself my ex and his live-in lover weren't worth abandoning my children. Everyone who knows me will be shocked to read what I just wrote, especially seeing me always smiling and always having an encouraging word for others. The smile was the mask behind my pain. I promised God I would not have a spirit of fear of all the things my enemies were trying to do to me. I thanked God for sparing my life; after realizing I had a lot to live for, I went back to my church roots. I started going back to church on a regular basis and never left God again! I became stronger and wiser immediately.

With the help of God, I put together this chapter to tell you what to do as an individual in the war on violence.

Family and friends should be told so they can help; if you don't tell them, how can they help? In the past, my courage was built on the satisfaction that I would never lose the hold I had on our family's togetherness: having both a mother and father in the home was my stronghold, or so I thought. I thought we could pretend we were the model family and that we were an example of what a family looked like, but I was living in a glass house full of lies and deception. I was revealed and uncovered when my family and friends found out. By this time, he was out of the military and in our hometown. This was just too embarrassing; for the first time I felt ashamed; I was living alone, feeling like a fool. I had spent over a decade fooling others and myself. Many co-workers and friends called me and asked what happened because I had hidden the lie of deception for so long, hiding behind a great job and a military lifestyle. I can't believe I have written a tell-all book, but if one abused person gets delivered from a sense of false hope, it would be worth the scrutiny I will be facing afterwards.

I know now it takes self-control to stay calm when dealing with abuse. My strength was rehabilitated from the heartbreaking pains of the past. Today I preach this message: "Just Want to Bless You!" I'm hoping the future generation will take heed and see the warning signs (focusing on His will for me, not mine).

"And I have filled him with the spirit of God, in wisdom, and in understanding, and in knowledge, and in all manner of workmanship." (Exodus 31:3)

I began going back to church with my children; when I was trying to cope with rejection on my own, I never kept them out of church. I believe that saved my life because when I had lost hope, I began to feed on theirs. They always lifted me up. I called my daughter, who was in college at the time; she had no idea what I had attempted because I never told them. I began to share for the first time words of self-pity; she talked in a very strong voice. I later learned she was attending the church at the Academy on a regular basis. Her level of faith took her to higher highs and deeper depths; she became the new director of the gospel choir and even led it on graduation day.

I began to complain about the struggle to maintain the bills whenever the mailman came; I told her I paid the bills as soon as they arrived but didn't have much left over. She brought to my attention I had a figure of a man called a husband; she then said he was good to them but continued to reveal the characteristics of a deadbeat husband. She said she remembered when I told her the utilities were about to be cut off because he was hiding the mail; he even changed his checking account, allowing all the checks I wrote to bounce.

My daughter asked, "Why are you worrying about not having

enough money after they are paid? When he was living with you, they weren't being paid by him anyway."

I knew it was hard for her to talk against her dad but I guess she had kept quiet long enough. And PJ said, "Mom, I will get a job after school," which he did. When he finished high school, he got three jobs, and after the money started coming in from the court order, I told him to quit; we would live off his daddy's money. And the rest is history.

I feel our communities and churches need to get more involved in domestic abuse. The Bible wants you to go in the byways and highways and compel them to come in out of the cold and get help. Most victims don't seek help; for a long time, I refused it too. I was embarrassed and ashamed for others to know my business. With the pain of grief that was almost irreversible, I nearly destroyed myself with grief, until my children gave me a glimmer of hope to want to live.

The Church Needs to Tell Others

When your heavenly father blesses you, take the favor; you know you don't deserve it; make Him proud by not beating yourself (or your partner) up!

God said, "Touch not" His anointed. In the past, the events were too hard to talk about. Years ago, in the month of October, I was struck repeatedly and violently, many times, across my body by my ex's lover and mistress, who was proven to be out of control. Even though he had other lovers at the time of the attack, her brutal attack would be the last chapter of the broken vows and his cheating heart. Later some friends told me after my divorce they use to envy me; they had no idea what I was going through. It seemed I fooled everybody; I only told them what I thought they wanted to hear. The children we had together kept me strong during the marriage, and after the attack, they kept me alive after I almost took my own life. I had said I would take that secret to my grave, but if this book helps one person not to give up hope when all they see is darkness, it's worth revealing and repeating.

I also feel that employers should get involved, like my boss did when she saw the bruises; sometimes, all the victims of abuse need is to know someone, anyone, cares. You see I had it all: a good job, two beautiful children; what more could I ask for? I lived a life of lies. I hid my pain, I wanted others to think we were the ideal couple; I never wanted others to see my failure as a wife. My love for him couldn't stop him from cheating. I thought when I became a GS7 overseas that the money would make a difference. My picture on the Exchange wall as the manager, my impressive office with others working for me, my Mercedes, my BMW and Volvos, my college education, my fine clothes, and expensive perfume weren't enough to hide the face of abuse or keep my man. Again, worldly goods suddenly have no meaning when the loss of pride takes form. There is help out there; you must make the first step by seeking it.

Self-control is more easily said than done. It's something you can't plan or practice. You must live in a do-right mind to achievement and have a willingness to change if the need is there. You must show that you are bigger in intelligence than your opponent by the way you carry yourself.

Have your thoughts fully effective to be more positive when it comes to controlling your own behavior; reckless behavior is always out of control. To demand respect, you must respect yourself. You must out-think your enemy. "Believe in yourself" is what this book is all about.

My advice to those who get to the point of no return after depression sets in, and to avoid suicide, is thinking survival is its greatest form of deliverance. You have to encourage yourself. If you notice, the winning horse always has a better chance to win a race as long as no one ever breaks his spirit. Years later, my unsuccessful suicide attempt is a constant reminder and a driving factor that pushes me to talk to others and encourage everyone I come in contact with.

I wish I had someone to talk to in my darkness hour that lonely night. I wasn't the type of woman to just go straight into another serious relationship or have someone in my bed to hold my hand and replace a body.

That was one of the reasons I was so unhappy for a short time, not because I had done bad things but because I had tried to do all the right things all my life, and it seemed God had turned His back on me. My miracle was oh so close but my mind was oh so far from believing in myself. If I had given up, I would have lost it all. What would my children have done? My son was only sixteen years old and my daughter was in college. The stalking, the harassment, and the pain from seeing my ex standing in the courtroom beside the very woman who had beaten me, while I was being falsely accused. He knew I was innocent; this was just too much. The judge had freed me of the lies but I was in a prison with no bars afterwards. God allowed me to retire after years of faithful service. I left Germany as a manager after working for the Air Force and Army Exchange System and as an account manager for the bank.

Just see what I would have missed, if darkness had overtaken me.

My mission is to help you develop self-control and to answer your unasked questions.

My assignment was to reveal my struggles: the torture and unheard screams; I tried to redirect my attention to the sufferings of others. I'm hoping you will attend real antiviolence and awareness training classes with specialists in this field. Find a credible domestic violence counselor to stop the cycle of victims falling back into a familiar territory of settling for your situation, thinking no one cares.

I challenge all Christians to be the same on and off stage. In this fight for closure on abuse and domestic violence, it's not a one-person show; it will take the joint efforts of all who come your way that are concerned and asking for help. The Bible talks about being thirsty and you didn't give me anything to drink; remember the next stranger who asks for help, men and women of God. It's okay to get media attention but remember the sheep that walks up to you. We are in this world, but not of this world. Christians are a peculiar people; some don't act like they must show love to the world. To some of your fans, you might be the only church they ever see. I'm not doing kingdom work to advance my career. I worked on a 9 to 5 job for thirty-four years, nonstop; the final chapter of my life is almost over. I have nothing to gain but the respect of God when I obey His orders and spread His Gospel. I just don't want the media to trick Christians in believing right is wrong and wrong is right in these last and evil days. (I thought we were in the business of saving souls, not ratings.)

Know that if you handle yourself in His image, accordingly others will rise up with you and help fight with you. "And mine hand shall be upon the prophets that see vanity, and that divine lies: they shall not be in the assembly of my people." (Ezekiel 13:9)

Sometimes I wonder, are we reading the same Bible? Is the word *love* blanked out? Yes, I had to quickly develop self-control and not let the rejection of a few with their own agenda hinder my quest to help others and carry on with God's mission. I have met many others that made up for the few lost sheep. It's just an example: the stranger you are talking to; you never know who you are entertaining. I just looked up and saw Steve Harvey talking on TBN; I was about to delete what I just typed, how people they look up to can't be reached when needed; Harvey felt those in the ministry needed to reach out and care more. It seemed to me God was giving me a confirmation that it was okay to put a statement of a proud spirit, which is the only thing in the Bible that God says he hates. I'm reminding those who don't have time for God's little ones, I'm adding it just in case you were not aware of your behavior.

I promised God on stage and off stage. Before I turned my life over to God, it was my children who gave me a reason to live. Physical and mental abuse, all unfortunate occurrences of domestic violence, and the cowardly and heinous acts couldn't just be talked about; they must be fought against, not turned away from. My heart goes out to the victims living under the weights of structural and systemic injustice; we can find God working on behalf of the "least of these." There are so many women and men who currently find themselves in violent relationships, who need phone numbers to abuse hotlines and women's shelters; they are forced to live in pain and fear on a daily basis. Having said this, I'm hoping the churches and community leaders will take a stand to walk the streets and hand out information—phone numbers to shelters and resources for those who need the information. Tragedy and abuse don't have a set time; they usually strike when you are alone, late at night, when neighbors are asleep and you are too ashamed to go and knock on their doors to wake them up.

Most victims hide the abuse; there are several approaches to stay out of harm's way. Invite your pastor to your home for spiritual guidance; one-on-one is always good. Start talking on the phone when your abuser begins to yell, so you will have a witness. It is hard to make a 911 call when the abuser is looking at you.

Here are some other suggestions:

- Have a family member call often; it throws your abuser off guard if they want to hurt you.
- Keep your keys and money with ID all in the same place; if you have to run, be able to have your credit cards with you for a hotel just in case the shelters are full or closed for the night.
- Keep a spare key on you at all times. Most violent incidents occur after the abuser has established a pattern of intimidation and control in your relationship.
- Your spouse can also inflict emotional abuse by putting you down, making you feel bad about yourself, calling you names, playing mind games, humiliating you, and making you feel guilty; these are all signs of abuse. They can lead to physical abuse.
- Don't fall for the blame game; when they say you

caused it, don't respond, just take control by seeking help.

- Remember, they just want power and control; if you don't give it to them, they can't take it. Let them talk to themselves; until you get to safety, never tell them what your next move will be, just make it until after you get to safety.
- If it's just talk, then everyone should go to another room to sleep or go to another floor until they calm down. I found out I had the power to defuse the situation.
- Don't fight the person; attack the evil spirit. By disregarding negative attacks, you can avoid most physical attacks by not responding to verbal attacks, and if you can, smile and then watch them walk away.
- You can even turn your situation around by calling him "Baby, Honey, Sweetheart." If a fight breaks out, move away from the kitchen, bathroom, or any place where there are dangerous objects.
- Plan the easiest escape. Decide on a door or window to exit quickly and safely. Find a neighbor, friend, or family member you can trust to help you and your children, or call police. Yes, you can be in control.

Individuals must realize how to deal with things, when what seemed so right goes so wrong. Domestic violence has warning signs, if we want to see them.

My ex reminded me in the courtroom after we broke up that one day I had told him I would never leave him; that's why he pushed me to the limit. That was just like him, still blaming me to the end. We talked; I smiled and walked away and had peace ever since. After our one-year reconciliation, I didn't speak to him for years out of respect for his new wife.

Trotter said he prayed for a good woman; he will tell anyone how blessed he is to have a faithful woman of God to share his ministry with. Just last night, I overheard him tell his son on the phone how much he loved me.

I never drank, smoked, took drugs, or stayed out of school or work for no reason; I never wanted to marry someone else's husband; never questioned who was my baby daddy. I was never lazy; I always worked all my life, thirty-five years nonstop.

It seemed I made all the right moves, but all the bad girls hated me and wanted my man, who did nothing but encourage their actions. With all of his lovers, I tried to save the marriage, but the last affair he had was out of control; I'm just grateful to God for interceding and allowing me to keep my right mind and to now live in peace. I'm not going to put all the blame on the other women. Most affairs wind up in tragedy; however, some end up in court or death. Remember, the one who starts the affair is always the one who throws the blame.

Throughout my book, you have read about how I was a victim, being beaten and attacked, gaining deliverance through divine intervention. I was allowed to withstand the fury of those who hated me without cause. Writing and speaking about my trials was a healing process for me. It has helped me regain both focus and perspective on how it's not a one-man show; it's a joint effort for us as individuals to gain strength from our co-workers, church, family, friends, and relatives. Where there is unity, there is strength.

I'm hoping this chapter has provided you a way of escape. As individuals you can deal with abuse, if you exercise the right approach. Trotter and I have proven, it takes two; no one can break up your family unless you allow it.

Henrietta Trotter

Chapter 14

Spousal Role in Christian Marriages

2004

"Only Those Who Risk Going Too Far,
Will Ever Know How Far They Can Go!"

Taking risk involves taking chances and hoping others will change. The ball is in your park; it's your marriage, and you and only you will have the last word as a couple. Yes, it is very important to know how men who cheat think; most women and men want answers after the affair is over. Why not start asking questions before it takes place? Trust me, your partner didn't just decide to have the affair. Someone could have invited them out to lunch at work or they may have given the person a ride home and were asked to come in for a drink, or a dinner was cooked the night before in hopes to lure them into their bed after they got drunk and forgot your name and your children's name. That's the reason they came home the next day; they must have forgotten where they lived. When you discover the affair, the guilt sets in only because they got caught; you forgave their bad behavior and the cycle starts over again, until the next partner or the next duty station, as in my case. There was an old TV show a long time ago called *It Takes a Thief*, meaning only a thief would know how to rob you and take everything from you without you having a clue what happened. My book is on the same level; only a cheater can tell you why a cheater cheats. And a victim of abuse can tell you how it feels to get beat up. If I had never been hit, how could I tell you how to avoid the punch?

Sometimes you have to look in the mirror. Our emotions can get the best of us; we begin to develop an intense behavior that we don't understand ourselves. You can help yourself before the violence takes over and the cheating begins. There are times others can see demons in you before you are aware of it. That's why throughout my books I tell my readers to get upset with the enemy that is controlling their abuser, not the person. You can fight an evil spirit better than a person; with a spirit you can win, but with a person you might wind up dead. It keeps your marriage together longer; your spouse would rather hear, "I hate the spirit in you" than "I hate you." When you put it on a third party, they feel you want to help them, not condemn them.

That's why the abusers begin defending themselves and going into your closet and pulling out your dirty laundry. Why do I say such a thing? In my experience, when a person attacks me, sometimes they are being taken over by an evil force out of their control. They follow every command; a voice speaks to them, whether it's good or bad. If you are happy, the enemy has no power to tempt you; it's harder to provoke you. Your attitude makes all the difference, it can give you power or bring you down. Please stop acting like your life is a light switch, going on and off, whenever he pushes the wrong button. When pressure comes your way, when your partner provokes you, then watch your reactions and moves.

Sorry, your enemy doesn't fight fair; he waits until he thinks you did something wrong, or something he doesn't like, and the voice is on his side; the attack command is easier to follow when you are mad or upset. Why? He wants to hurt you anyway, and it gives him courage to do so. If you look at him funny for any reason, it's his opportunity to get violent. You should begin speaking back to the voice when it's telling you to do wrong or say evil things against your loved one (if you know it's not true).

The choice to stay or leave is yours, not the media's. In the past, I played the role of a humble, passive wife, who took anything, only to get disrespected time after time. I began doing things to let him know I was getting my strength back, and I was taking my peace back. I would be making moves and letting others know that this time, there was no turning back for me. I moved my dad's body from our land to where my mother was buried, and I planted some red roses behind the grave, to show my ex I meant business. The funeral director said those roses would never grow because the dirt had sand in it, but remember I had a gift; when God talks to me, it always comes true. Not only did the roses grow but also to this day, eighteen years later, they are the biggest roses you have ever seen. A year later, I went to the grave and there were so many roses they had to trim the bush; the roses were as big as a small ball; what others saw as God's Glory seemed to speak; other family members grew roses behind their loved one's graves also; that sign from God set me free from those nightmares of my dad with a sand bag over his shoulders.

Yes, it's your decision to try and work it out. In today's world, divorces are decided by what someone else says or feels; for example, the media discovers your spouse had an affair; immediately you call your attorney without talking to your spouse; a third party is involved. Some talk shows and TV programs allow the mistress and lover to have more to say about what went on in your marriage. I say immorality is on the rise. Did the wife just hit herself without knowing she did? Did she cause the man to forget where he lived? Who is the victim, the girlfriend? If the home wrecker is so innocent, why did she return his call? What does she want for the out-of-wedlock child? Think about it: she took their dreams, the other family's happiness; not only is the partner upset, but the children from the other family are also upset. The hurt and embarrassment wasn't good enough; they have to sharpen the blade and take money from the other family.

It was her choice to live recklessly and irresponsibly; they weren't thinking about the welfare of the unborn child. The child was born in an act of uncontrolled lust of the flesh; this was a sin last I checked. *Webster's Dictionary* defines *reckless* as a state of being careless and rash when doing something. They got caught, but now she wants sympathy. For what? Making the other family's life a living hell? That's ridiculous; my grandmother would turn over in her grave. I grew up in the old days of self-respect and moral values, knowing the cheater is getting the attention of a cheater. The concept of right behavior must be taught.

All couples should be happy and not divided. Churches today forget that grandmas stood for unity and love in the home.

Yes, the abandoned children left behind in love triangles should get support; the one who joined in the act must pay. Man's law and God's law both have to be obeyed, that's what the Bible is all about. "Thou shalt not," means just what it says: Thou shalt not. Don't get upset when the judge says, "Thou shall pay ..."

In most cases, the man sleeps around but has to be forced later by a judge to take care of an act done in the heat of the night (was that love or lust)? Just answer one question: where in the Bible did the one who had the affair with someone's spouse come out smelling like a rose? But the media gives them a spot to talk about the wife.

Woman-to-woman, I'm not talking to the one who threw the punch but the one who caught the punch, like me for many years. You have nothing to be ashamed of if his lover tries to scandalize your name after you uncover their affair and little love nest; she is just pretending she is happy. How can she ever trust a cheater? That's why she wants the media attention; she's home alone most of the time, he is out looking for another unsuspecting victim. I've watched many talk shows; not once have I seen the lover or mistress say, "I'm sorry" for hurting the other family. The devil doesn't apologize for destroying your home. Don't worry; I'm here to encourage you. Dreams always come after some nightmares; your role is not to worry; weeping endures for the night, but joy comes in the morning. After they break the Seventh Commandment, God will judge them; they have to answer to God. Just move on; how can God bless you with more when you are still holding on to what destroyed you? There is a difference between a Mack truck hitting you by accident and driving straight into you

Henrietta Trotter

to take you down. Let's not get tricked into a web of deceptions; take control of your mind.

Churches need to take a stand. Preachers don't seem to preach against it anymore; they accept bad conduct and the corrupt character of a person who knows right but chooses to do wrong. Churches need to be teaching the right concept of behavior. Churches also need to contact the victims and reach out to them more whenever they hear about it, instead of turning a deaf ear. It's clear in some cases they are more focused on ratings and offerings, not you. Unless it gets personal, someone began to beat his or her daughter or she was found dead. At that point, they feel they are losing control with the devil, and the enemy attacks them in their home. Don't get mad with the reporter who gives out misinformation and makes the cheater and his partner come out smelling like a rose.

Believe it or not, I feel your church's silence gave them the control. Most people don't care unless it happens to them. Some of the ones who are doing the reporting have infidelity issues of their own. The Bible says it's wrong to break the Seventh Commandment; you must let them know it's wrong, and a change must take place; however, the decision to stay or leave is totally up to the spouses themselves, not the media. If your partner had a one-night stand and no physical abuse was involved, the media is nowhere around when your child cries for their mom or dad. That's why as an elder, I'm reaching out the long arm of love to those who were abused.

The reason some church folks skip the page on adultery is because they are doing it themselves. Someone has to take a stand; I guess that's me. It took me years to heal and speak out. It was not an option to speak to anyone about my ordeal in the past—it just wasn't happening; at the time, I had too much pride. I'm a firm believer that your spouse must have a willingness to change. They must ask God to forgive and then ask you for forgiveness. Everyone has a different level of taking; yours could be less than mine; all I'm saying it is the couple's decision, no one else's. I will say it's okay to leave if your hand is forced, like mine was; if your partner refuses to change and continues to disrespect you, never says they are sorry, or does not ask for help or forgiveness. Even Jesus said, "Go and sin no more."

Don't Play into the Devil's Hand

In life, tragedy happens but the role of a spouse is to try and stay in control of your emotions at all times, because others are watching you. Go buy yourself a new dress, a new pair of shoes, a feel-good item. That's why I said not to play into the devil's hand, by acting and looking defeated. Look like a million dollars; you will begin to feel like a million dollars; the outfit doesn't have to cost a lot; just match everything up, so when you look in the mirror, you can smile at yourself. That's what's wrong with many of us; we wait until others praise us. I found out when I began to act like I was somebody, others would treat me like I was somebody.

Begin to give to others. My dad use to tell me if you close your hands, it doesn't leave room for anyone to put anything in it. You must make up your mind not to give up. Life is all about choices. If you want to change your life, you have to change your way of thinking.

Here are a few basic reminders of what I've been through and the role I played. The kids and I stayed overseas an extra two years, alone, with no child support from their dad. (Years ago, there was no support system.) But God provided for us, and He had the last word! Even though I had to survive on my own, God took care of me. After I had decided on my own to stay an extra two years in Germany, the military told me that my only ticket out of the country had been given to my ex's lover to move her things. The movers made a mistake and sent some of her things to my home in the United States: pictures and personal items that confirmed their affair. I could have fought it; my ex-husband was out of the military (remember he was prohibited from re-enlisting). I still decided to come back to the States only because I had already given my notice to my boss and my employees had given me a good-bye party; I decided to just sell my furniture and most of what I owned for plane tickets back to the United States. Yes, my role as a mother outweighed the betrayal I felt as a spouse. I felt like a war-torn raggedy soldier; all I had left was hope. Divine intervention came through for me again.

My last tour in Germany, I was a GS-7 Exchange Manager. I was too ashamed to let my family and friends know what was going on, how the devil had just stolen my rights to even leave the country. I knew a lot of people, and I soon found out the power of God and the importance of people knowing me and watching my lifestyle! His lover (Ms. Barbara) had caused me so much pain.

One day, I put a sign up to sell all my worldly possessions just to get a plane ticket to bring my children and myself back to the United States. One of the managers at the Exchange where I worked also lived in the same apartment building; he asked me why I was selling everything. I replied I needed a ticket home. He was German, and I didn't even know he spoke English until that day (he owned the dry cleaners there). He said, "Take the sign down."

Then he said, "I'll be over to your place after work."

I just gave him a funny look, not knowing what to expect. He was on time; I had neatly placed everything in order. He said, "I'll take all of it; how much do you want?"

I gave him a price; he then wrote me a check, smiled, and said, "Don't worry, it's good" (meaning the check). Then he just walked away. I never saw him again.

I wrote this book to show you just because someone betrays you, it shouldn't give you an excuse to give up. If your enemy takes you down, he has a party with you being the guest of honor, and the price is your emotions and your ability to think beyond the moment. If your enemy takes you and your children down, he'll have a yard sale: two for the price of one.

After I left Germany and was working at the bank in the States, I told my therapist my story; when I mentioned I had gotten back with my ex before we broke up for the last time, she asked, "Do you like him more than yourself?"

I said, "No, I do not."

She said yes, I did, because I was allowing my ex-husband to control and beat on me and get away with it. She even saw fresh bruises on my visits, which she noted in my files. She repeated that I thought more highly of him than myself. Those words got my attention; it was just weeks before the October 20 attack, which broke my heart into so many pieces; I tried on my own to mend it but God Himself had to recover me from past mistakes of wanting to hold onto my children's dad.

I had to rely on divine intervention when my house hit the newspaper. I listened to His voice of divine favor, allowing me to make the right moves and decisions. It was worth repeating some of my attacks so you would know; I received power from on high when I understood as an abused spouse my role of survival was exercising faith in myself. I finally realized I could do all things through Christ, who strengthens me!

Sometimes you have to take a risk and just move on. It seemed my love couldn't hold him; the thought that runs through your head as guilt sets in: sometimes you just have to let go when you tried your best to keep yourself out of harm's way! Nothing you did was working.

I was single seven years and Trotter was single fifteen years before we found each other. God released us from relationships where both our partners committed adultery and had other children. Trotter and I tried to keep our wedding vows to ones we thought were right for us, but our partners had their own agenda. God says, "Touch not my anointed"; it directly applies to the abuser's angry spirit to hit you. Stop allowing them to misquote the Bible; Satan's trick is to brainwash you. God is a protector, not an abuser. God is love, but He also gives you a way of escaping attacks on your life.

God's Glory began to shine, and God showed me signs. My future daughter-in-law picked the same wedding day as I had with my son's father. She told me she could change it but I said maybe the rings and that date would have more meaning and maybe she could make hers work; that was two years ago. It all worked out because I was able to give her the same rings. I stopped blaming

God for my problems; I know now that I was attacked to make me strong. I would never say that was my plan but His purpose. Yes, a spouse's role in a Christian marriage isn't easy.

Tips to Help Keep the Peace

- Point out a healthy marriage that has no abuse.
- You can use the same thing it took to get them to keep them.
- It doesn't always mean cheating; you can spend too much money, stay away from home too long, not pick up your phone, show disrespect around others, and remember something caused your partner to seek the home wrecker's advice.
- Communication is the key: stop the opportunist from advancing.
- Become your own cheerleader; always know you get out of life what you deposit in it, and no deposit, no returns.
- Never forget one person's poison is someone else's gold.
- You can throw a good man away and some patient, humble, forgiving person is right there to catch them.
- I've heard women say he wouldn't work for me but he works for his new woman. You should ask yourself why; maybe she gives him something to come home to. If God gave them to you, it's your job to ask for help to fix them.
- If he walks in the door after a hard day's work and he's not smiling, you need to go back and do your homework because the other woman makes him smile.
- As a rule in relationships, if someone wants to provoke you, leave the room or change the subject to a kinder and gentler subject, something you both could agree on, and do not go back to that subject that might require unwanted thoughts.

- After you have fed him and made him feel like a king, he is more willing to talk to you.
- Add a little sugar; say words like "Baby, Honey, and Sweetheart." You will be surprised what a difference it makes to treat them with respect; if you give respect, you are more likely to get it in return.
- If you get up in the morning and you are still tired, get a drink of coffee or some tea; relax before you speak to your partner.
- Don't be ashamed. I was in an abusive relationship for twenty-four years. I'm not telling you to stay, but if you are still there, then it's possible you can turn it around with a few helpful tips, but again they must be willing to seek help and go for counseling.
- Start going to church you must stop entertaining the devil.
- There's hope for everyone; we also talked about holier-than-thou Christians. Think about it: some of them married someone who cheated on somebody else, and they still think they are better than you!
- My books are about keeping it real so God can help you. The words *repent* and *forgiveness* should be taken out of the Bible if they don't believe that God is a forgiving God.
- Don't have that poison of hatred in your heart. People want to throw stones and they live in a glass houses themselves. In some cases, everybody but them knows their man is cheating.
- Arguments mainly start when a person is tired, hungry, or sleepy.
- Even if both of you have had a hard day, learn to compromise.
- While you are cooking, make him a sandwich; you might be surprised after he gets that sandwich and you talk to him nicely, he might say, "It's okay, baby,

you don't have to cook; take your time. I can wait," because you have satisfied his hunger.

- If you see your mate is sleepy, don't wake him unless it's very important; he'll be in a better mood when he is rested.
- Every once in a while, buy a card just to say I love you.
- While going to get food, pick up a dollar rose, or something special; don't pay a lot for it, because in the minds of most spouses, the larger the gift, the more they think you are guilty about something.
- Remember you have to out-think your opponent; that's how you gain power and victory.
- Stop saying you don't know what to do after messing up. One of my favorites is if the day starts off bad, that evening (or if you see them during the day), don't mention what was said earlier; always make the subject anything but what got them upset, and if it's important, try a better way or better time to say it.
- Turn your situation around; say, "What if I did that; would you like it?" If the answer is no, then you know he understood how you felt about an uncomfortable subject. You might say that's old school or old fashioned; check out the numbers and dates on breakups.
- Try another strategy; sometimes if they think they got to you, they will try it again, sometimes in the same day; just pretend it's a buzz in your ear; that always works, because they can't talk to themselves but so long.
- They can't get mad with something they said themselves or something you never said back; an argument needs fire! Don't give them anything to work with (tit for tat never works).
- You will never know how far you can go; it's your house. You make the rules.
- Make sure you always have something scheduled so a

spouse will not have time to cheat; remember if they haven't started, you can take control of the thought process, most men cheat because they are bored at home. Make coming home exciting.

- Call him before he comes home; if you don't, a girl or guy who would like to take your place may paint a visual picture of what they can look forward to. Make him think he really needs to be there, and when he shows up, you already have a baby sitter so the two of you are alone.
- Rent or buy a movie you think he will like.
- It's easy to train him to want to come home; if he's with a friend who's not married, tell him to ask his friend if he is hungry; you already have his favorite dish ready. Single people get tired of eating out, and his friend will convince him to go to your house afterwards; than find a way to get rid of the friend in a nice way.
- When you get through filling up the schedule, they won't have time to cheat; cheating is an art, a science, and a game with no rules.
- Plan a quiet day at home with the family doing family things: a day at the beach, at the park, bowling, and so on.
- If you don't have much money, talk to a friend with money who's having problems also; they will be glad to chip in and help you save your marriage while saving theirs, as you plan trips together as friends.
- Losers can be winners in a game of chance, when you make the rules.
- You just don't lose a good mate, your children lose their father; it's a package deal. Try to save it without putting the ones you love in jeopardy.
- If it's not working, learn to let go and move on.

- Sometimes you have to get advice from the opposite sex to understand how they think.
- When I was an account manager, the number one cause of breakups and divorce was financial not cheating.
- You see it wasn't the foreclosure notice that destroyed the home, it was your reaction to it; he is the same man who provided for your family in the past; stop putting him down. Give him words of encouragement.
- That's how some of us lost our man to another woman; he just needed someone to listen and try to understand.
- I'm not saying my first marriage could have worked out if I had tried harder, I'm just saying to try something; don't just say it's okay to take my man and he didn't even want them in the first place; again, his sin is for God to judge.

I left because of the beatings and the money got funny; I did my best to keep it together. God can change anybody if they want to work with you (my ex didn't); it takes a willing partner.

I'm not selling myself short; I still kept him for twenty-four years, but as I said, you know your level of endurance; if you feel like leaving in one week, go! You may say, "If you know so much, why did the enemy come into your first marriage and destroy it?" I admit I was too blind to see the answer was right in front of me: a mirror. I had to understand myself first, and then I could help others. Most tell-all books make the other person they are talking about look like a monster; I've said the enemy was using him. My lawyer said he was a womanizer but I say he was a woman hater; he wasn't faithful to any of them. I know this book is a little different but I'm in Scripture; throughout the entire Bible, it speaks of fornication and adultery in relationships. I know it was a generational curse. I've said if he received help, we might have made it. Know that you are empowered with inner strength to kick the enemy out of your life; put authority over them that fight against you without cause; let him know who's in control and who has the power; never forget there is only one king and one queen in your home. All through history, the wife and the husband are recognized as the head; everything else has to get in line.

To measure your relationship, the good should outweigh the bad. You see the children are watching us, seeing what role we play during adversity (why do you think most spouse abusers saw their parents being abused?). They were too small to defend them and the next woman or man who came along, they only saw the face of the abuser who abused their loved ones.

They are our future marriages; if you train them while they are young to respect authority and values in the home, they will grow up respectful and not part of the jail system and domestic violence. Ask yourself, is the temptation worth me losing all my blessings? The reason I told you that because just those few lines have kept me faithful to Trotter the entire length of our marriage; I haven't seen anyone I would jeopardize my blessings over. It's a lot of things to consider before you break your vows. You have children to consider when you uproot and change; other lives are affected also. You say you love your family; put the words into action.

Know Your Partner; Also Know the Warning Signs

If you call their cell phone and your partner doesn't answer, that's a problem. (I must say my advice for single people living alone is sometimes different from married people). When I was single living alone, I just wanted my privacy. I didn't ever have to answer a phone if I didn't want to. I stopped watching TV for three years; I just read my Bible and highlighted every page. My situation was one of depression and frustration until I turned my life around. I didn't want to talk to anyone. I didn't let Trotter into my world until after he gained my trust and we made a commitment to live together in a marriage relationship; this chapter is about commitment, folks. It's important your partner feels you have nothing to hide: security, trust).

If your partner picks up the phone and no one speaks unless you answer, that's a problem.

If you want to beat or hurt your partner just because they ask where you were, that's a problem.

If money is spent on someone without your partner knowledge that's a problem.

If your wife doesn't know your cell phone number, that's a problem.

If you lie all the time about working overtime and the boss has no idea what you are talking about, that's a problem.

If you never have time for your family, that's a problem.

If you are only thinking about how good you look and your family are wearing old and raggedy clothes, that's a problem.

If you never show up for family reunions and birthdays and the holidays, you are nowhere to be found and sneak away easing out the door for hours (or sometimes return the next day), that's a problem.

If you never show up for school events, and the teacher and the babysitter think the child only has one parent, that's a problem.

If you disrespect your partner in public or around family and only show your partner love and attention in the bedroom, that's a problem.

If you don't have a family picture on your desk at work or don't ever talk about your family, that's a problem.

If you can only say "my wife" or "my husband" around the ones who like your spouse and the ones who like you, that's a problem.

If you talk to others more than your partner, that's a problem.

If you treat your friends better than your partner, that's a problem.

If you don't have time to listen to their concerns, that's a problem.

If you always think money can buy love, that's a problem.

If you think the TV is more important than your partner, that's a problem.

If you stop looking good but dress up for others, that's a problem.

If you stop appreciating family and begin taking them for granted, that's a problem.

If you stop giving and got others to mistreat your partner by taking, that's a problem.

If you stop praising and start bad mouthing them, all the time, that's a problem.

The humble sheep changes into a big bad wolf and the sweet talking gentleman or lady turns into a monster, that's a problem.

No one would willingly get into situations like those! God Himself said, "I would never leave you or forsake you."

But just a mere servant says I'm out of here; he has no power or courage to withstand the storm or the fiery darts! Stop changing uniforms when the going gets tough.

I'm not recommending a spouse stay with a partner who committed infidelity; it's up to them; again, God is their judge; whether you feel you need to leave, or if you want to stay and hope they will change and never do it again, it's the couple's decision.

I promise you in most cases, couples that look like they have it all together (some even in Christian homes), one of the partners has fallen short of God's Glory. I recommend *never* going outside of the relationship or marriage; it will be less complicated and cut down on mass confusion.

When I go to the store or when he goes on vacation, we can trust each other, knowing if we get approached, it's not the ring that stops the other person, it's the vows we made to God and the commitment in our hearts, the deep-rooted love to never hurt each other.

You must stop agreeing with the opposite sex in front of your spouse at anytime; your spouse doesn't deserve belittling and disrespecting.

If you are not at that point or in that place yet, you can start being a vigorous woman or faithful man today. I'm just giving you advice to help you.

Jesus himself said He gave the word and later went about His father's business.

The other person will soon find out you were taking and enduring more than they could ever stand.

Stop displaying wolf characteristics by running your spouse away!

You must start being your mate's best friend right away. Be their listening ear even when you don't feel like it; just try to understand. Remember how you betrayed the character of a sheep to get them; it takes the same thing to keep them.

Chapter 15

Supernatural Interventions

2005–2006

"Setting the Captives Free"

Amazing Grace

I'm so excited about this chapter because time after time, God provided a way of escape for me; I survived adversity and turned my life back around and began trusting in God again. I stopped trying to fix everything myself, I just said this thing is bigger than me and turned my situation over to a higher power. I began listening to His voice as it supernaturally intervened in many situations, which I'm gladly sharing with you. I accepted my calling into the ministry, and I will dedicate the rest of my life to helping others heal open wounds and broken hearts inflicted on them by the enemy. When I look back over my life, I ran from a storm that came with no warning; sadly, the eye of the storm was in my back yard.

I hid from the wind with the strength and force to uproot and overpower my home. How could I get out of the way when my attacker had the key to my house? How could I stay out of harm's way when evil was looking in my eyes when I woke up? Instead of feeling love, I wrestled with hate on a daily basis. The enemy fought me every step of the way, to the point in later years when I almost abandoned my assignment.

I felt I was unworthy to lead His people, because at the time I wasn't fully delivered myself. The struggle was hard; being attacked with such force hindered my mission to escape. After living in denial for years, the very thing that had me bound wasn't easy to break loose from. I put a superficial smile on my face every morning after my spirit had just gotten vexed the night before.

Their senseless acts of hatred were the root cause of my divorce. I felt the power of darkness overwhelming me and bringing me down, feeling broken, betrayed, every time my ex's baby mother laughed and stalked me. I know now she followed orders from the devil himself to attack me. She carried out her plan to ruin me; when she told me on that day she was getting the gun to blow my brains out, those words alone caused my ex to let me go after I began to pray, laying with my back to the floor.

Thinking he was protecting my face, she began attacking him, leaving welts on his back; the pain from her attacking him made him release me from the floor. My story is like no other. I lived to tell about how God touched my husband to show mercy and let me go while I was being attacked. No, he would not have let me go if God had not intervened. It was the enemy that told him to hold me down in the first place, no matter what reasons were in his twisted mind. I was still the victim because the events that led up to that day should have never happened; my car drove to that house but they had driven me there with all their evil plans to destroy me long before I rang the door bell. The jails are full of people with excuses, why they hurt or allowed someone to be hurt; again the question that should be asked to my enemies, what did my abusers do to ignite the fire? My children's lives and my life were turned upside down. When you pray, let thy will be done. My husband might not have released me from the floor, if she had not started hitting him, thinking he was starting to feel sorry for me.

It was a power much greater than me that sealed Ms. C's fate, as he left her just like the bondwoman in the Bible was left to fend for herself. He told me himself, years later, he was just using her. My ex married someone else, just months after the divorce decree.

A supernatural voice came to me one day in a divine

authoritative voice and said, "Go back; get others in captivity." The road to recovery wasn't easy; the journey carried some pain; just like the Hebrew boys, I was thrown in the fire but didn't get burnt. Laying in my bed many sleepless nights, wondering where my ex was, if he was going to come home to me and my children, turning over many nights discovering he had already left the house while I was sleeping and when he walked in the door, instead of hugs or kisses, trauma to the body. God Himself stepped in and turned my situation around. At the time, I could not see it. That's why I must write about His Glory; God's word tells me to.

"'Return to thine own house, and shew how great things God hath done unto thee.' And he went his way, and published throughout the whole city how great things Jesus had done unto him." (Luke 8:39)

God's Miracles: What Manner of Man Is This?

In past chapters, I spoke about God's mercy and God's grace. I will now talk about something that shows God's supernatural power. God's words tell us after we get delivered and are set free, to go and tell others of his Glory. This morning I got a vision, and it really made me think. A strong messenger is only as good as the carrier of the news. Think about it: in my line of work (the ministry), many are called but few chosen. A famous preacher is known by how many know him; that's the only difference. The attraction: An elder is ordained by a bishop and is required to perform the same duties. Many times in my engagements with my partners in the Lord, I'm asked to help them pray for the people, which I do with no problem. That's what we do in God's world; it's not about our titles, it's about whom we represent. You see pastors on the TV and radio (such as TBN, the Christian network) are my partners in the Lord when we come in one accord to save souls, heal and deliver, and set free. Jesus had many followers, but it was His miracles that he told them to go and tell others about, not his title. So much talk about who's who, how well we dress; as long as Jesus knows me, I'm okay. I know if I take the Glory from God, I'm in trouble. I've always been humble; I believe that's why God has blessed me, so others could see His Glory.

Some think to get what you want, you can just write a check, many would say. No one wants to hear of the Glory; the evil is more interesting, but I beg to differ. What manner of man was that who overcame hunger with a few loaves of bread and a few fish and fed a multitude with manna from on high? Showing God's Glory in your life will help deliver others. God needs to be glorified, edified, and honored for His great works. My life story is about storms that came from out of nowhere. Here's something to think about and then I'll go on with my stories:

> And there arose a great storm of wind, and the waves beat into the ship, so that it was now full. And He arose, and rebuked the wind, and said unto the sea, "Peace, be still." And the wind ceased, and there was a great calm. And He said unto them, "Why are ye so fearful? How is it that ye have no faith?" And they feared exceedingly, and said one to another, "What manner of man is this, that even the wind and the sea obey him?" (Mark 4:37–41)

After the enemy took me through, I began to live a life of destiny and divine purpose. I know now the journey was to position me in a place to receive my blessing. After my enemies rose up against me, God touched my life, my children's lives, and my ministry. God gave me supernatural favor. We have a husband-and-wife ministry. I take my work seriously; we also visit other churches as guest speakers and speak at marriage seminars, nursing homes, and hospitals. We stay on call all the time for funerals and speaking engagements. When I was the vice president of the youth committee at my previous church, I loved getting them involved in plays and activities. I'm also a motivational speaker and spiritual advisor at battered women's shelters. God showed me His Glory; he has given me a slot on Lifetime for Women, which has run my TV commercials for the last three years.

To some I should dismiss the events as if they never occurred. If the devil had succeeded with his curses, it would have hit the front page, and the talk of the town would have been how I was brought down into captivity. Yes, this book is not about glorifying the works of the enemy but the narrow escape from a life of destruction. Yes, I was in the valley of the shadow of death but my story tells you how I feared no evil for my God was with me, showing favor and positive outcomes.

I know it sounds like I am being vain but I am just telling of God's Glory. If blessings were handed out like candy everyone would have something good to talk about. When you pick up a newspaper and honor, not dishonor, is shown, that's God's Glory; my readers have learned how to have tunnel vision and shine in the midst of trials and a storm that came from out of nowhere.

God Recognizes a Humble Spirit

After I had been employed at the bank for ten years, my boss asked me what kind of classes I'd taken in the past (the only classes I took with them were in my files). The next day I brought a briefcase full of certificates in management and business classes, letters, and newspaper clippings from my last jobs. I then told him I had more at home. He was outdone. He asked why I didn't show them to anyone before. He said in all the time he had been a manager, he had never seen that many awards and acknowledgments. He then said some people wished they had one paper to add, but I had so many he had to combine them in a category. I was immediately given a raise, and since I had been a manager in Germany, I was promoted to account manager at the bank without even filling out an application (they were downsizing anyway and I had priority). I attribute all my success to having a warrior's mentality with a humble spirit. When my boss asked me why I didn't come forward sooner, I said I simply wanted to be judged on what I did for him.

I have been blessed. The radio (where I enjoy speaking) held a dinner for us, and I met the Rev. Jesse Jackson; when he walked in the door, he gave me a big hug. I was trying to take his picture and dropped my camera; my husband just smiled, as he always does when I see a celebrity. I love posting articles in my local newspaper for special events and holidays. What inspires me most is helping others; working for a higher power keeps my schedule full. I've talked with other Christian soldiers such as Shirley Caesar, Bishop Noel Jones, the Caravans, Kirk Franklin, and many others in my walk and journey in this ministry. Like in the song, I said I wasn't going to tell nobody but I can't keep it to myself what God has done for me. God uses His people in a mighty way, and I'm blessed to have met some great women and men of God.

A good leader is always available. The reason I write about my jobs in this book is to show you how God can deliver you out of the enemy's camp. Many people have set out to retire from their dream job, and the enemy stopped their progress. God shut the liar's mouth and will give you jobs you don't qualify for; God will speak to you after you are blessed and tell you how to excel above them all. No, it takes more than skill to out-think an evil force that tries to discourage you. Talk to the ones who gave up; many of my co-workers did. Sometimes you have to get up from the inside and believe in yourself when others have given up on you! That fight and struggle was part of how God intervened and made a difference. He put a standard against them as I held my ground.

I learned at a women's seminar in Germany to never worry about what you should have done but work on what you will do; if you had the ability to do something better, you would have done it at the time. I also encourage others not to beat up on themselves. Never get discouraged by tragedy. For God promises us passage to this vast and great unknown. In these last days, people are looking for real answers; they are fighting wars overseas, wars in their backyard, and wars in their home. Like Steve Harvey said, stop being too busy for the ones in need to contact you!

I know there is strength in numbers but sometimes you have to go alone if your partners in the ministry only wanted a voice to raise money for their personal gain or make a personal attack that forgets about the cause after their wounds have healed and the fame and notoriety have worn off. My ministry is not about my own agenda. If I have to walk alone, pray, fast, seek God for advice to help my people (all colors, all races, poor, rich), so be it. Man picks and chooses. God gave me a vision; just this morning, He told me to spread my arms out wide. I obeyed and He said I have good children, I have bad children; some obey, some don't, but they are all mine! God was telling me not to turn my back on anyone that needs help; even the guilty can repent from their evil ways if they have a desire to. From those very words, I know my redeemer lives because all hurt is gone, as long as I have breath in my body and love in my heart, the cause will never die. My cry is "Use me, Lord, use me."

I've gone through too much; my deliverance price was just too high. I can't look back, I must look forward; as my husband Trotter preaches, and your past is only one step behind you. Yes, we can endure, but please don't leave out the main ingredient: that's faith in yourself, which empowers you and gives you hope. When my ex-husband tried his best shot to get me to return to the United States, all he said never made a difference because of the pain he put my family through in Germany. But then he said we had to put our differences aside and go back home to the States to give our daughter and son a chance to go to the military academy, because we didn't want to take away their hope.

I reluctantly yielded to his lies and deceptions. I struggled with the decision to put myself back in harm's way after God had blessed me and the children so greatly to live overseas alone for two years without a dime of support from him; I was disinclined to return back to the devil's den. All I could think about was God had delivered me from Egypt; why was I going back into the enemy's camp? Could I trust him a man who had lied so many times before?

Through a supernatural power, he started going back to church with me. I gave in. The first four years were great; he even developed a relationship with my father before he passed away. I thought I had gotten my family back. Only God could have changed my children's father; however, it was short lived. God blessed him to get a better job, making more money than he had ever made; then the devil got back into his mind and the old man and his old nature of lust crept back in. He went back to his old ways; the rest is history and the reason I'm writing this.

May the work I do speak for me. When I walk down the street or go into a store, people often tell me my work made a change in their lives. When I go to the library, where God led me to place my books for free, and I see a homeless person reading one of my books, it touches my heart and brings tears to my eyes. Before I retired, one of my co-workers came to my office and thanked me for writing the poem in my first book called "Satisfied By Just Getting By," telling the children not to accept that fate, and they can do better; every child so far who's read it has turned their grades around. They needed to know they were not just doing it to please their parents, they were preparing for their own success. Whenever I read an e-mail from one of my readers, or get a call from a stranger, when I hear living testimonies, I'm forever mindful to give God the Glory, not me. Because I know I'm nothing on my own, without His divine connection and favor speaking to me on a regular basis since I came back to Him.

I was rejected by the best of the best in the ministry; that's why I know it was God who opened the doors for me. Yes, the devil wants me to leave out this chapter telling "how great thou art," but the ones like me who wanted to end it all need hope to know God is greater than the whole world against them when they are going through it. I couldn't see the future or His Glory at the time I was depressed. I sat in that jail cell for hours crying a river of tears, not saying a word; I thought God had forgotten me, but a divine voice came to me and said, "My child, I didn't leave; you left me."

From that day, I began trying to live the best life I knew how so my good works would help others in distress. You see the soldier who got wounded and received the Purple Heart was not looking for recognition; he did not think he would get an award for courage after he saved his unit from attack. The reason I believe God stepped in and helped me was I had the mind-set that I was not looking for a reward; my heavenly father is in charge of that, when I get to those streets paved with gold and walk through those pearly gates. I survived my biggest test and pain eighteen years ago; at that time, I could have come forward in full detail when this message was straight off the press, but I wanted God to get the Glory. Also, at the time, my mind was in disarray; I needed to heal first, lean on a power I couldn't see first, and hear His voice first. I make no excuses for the delay. As I said, anyone can write a check after they are blessed but for my family, friends, neighbors, and co-workers to see His Glory and power, when nothing is coming in, now that's God!

One day, I visited my neighbor Mrs. Banks; when I walked into her living room, it touched my heart to see she had one of my old books on her coffee table for anyone who came into her home to see. I've sold many books, but I will never forget seeing it displayed. They say one person can't make a difference. I beg to differ; yes, I can make a difference. That's what makes His Glory so amazing; no one can hurt you unless God allows it; He is in control.

We all are tested; some just have bigger tests than others. He has to do something to get our attention. He can intervene and work modern-day miracles on your behalf. I believe God wants the cries to come through this book to help end all domestic violence.

How could someone else tell a story of a hit if they never felt a slap, they were never spit in the face, they never experienced a punch (most cowards hit you behind closed doors when no one is watching). I've always known I had more to offer than a Sunday service and just speaking on the radio. When my books went worldwide on all major Web sites and stores, it gave me a great sense of accomplishment, just to know I'm reaching those beyond the walls of my church, because my life was a sermon. A testimony of the greatest of God and all His Glory!

Setting the Captives Free

Events I remember as a child: I was born in the fifties; I was young but I remember going to visit my cousins in North Carolina in the summer; my father drove in the middle of the night and woke us up and took us back to Virginia.

My cousins told us later men in white sheets were cutting out some people's tongues. I should have been happy we got away safe, but instead all I could think about was what about my cousins? I went to segregated schools and only had old books with writing all through them; we went to separate movies; our movie theater had rats and roaches. I was young but I remember. I also saw the signs on the water fountains: "White only."

When my daughter was three years old back in 1973, her dad was stationed in Fort Knox, Kentucky, and the next city was Louisville. They had a large trashcan on every corner as we drove by. We saw them burning books because there was something about a black man in them. What amazed me more was when I got back to my city; there was nothing on the news about the burnings that night.

My grandchildren are my heart; they all are smart, but I have to tell you about Daivon because he was a seed from the union of when the devil tried to curse my son. He is a very brilliant child and at age ten, he is gifted with a high IQ; the majority of students in his school are white.

Trotter and I went to see a play Daivon was in; I will never forget. It took love to a different level. Dr. King wrote a speech about little black and white children walking together in love. I never thought I would see that in my lifetime. In the play, they went over the speech word for word; the children acted the parts. Yes, his dream and God's prophecy are being fulfilled. The play was about our history; they included Dr. King's speech and even did a skit on Michael Jackson as history in music. I took a picture of my grandson and his best friend, who is white (his friend wore an afro wig and had a shiny glove on); his friend's father smiled as I took the picture with them standing arm in arm. God will show up at His appointed time. Through God's intervention, I met Dr.

King's son, Martin King III, when I was on a program and did a speech on the 911 attacks. God has a way of showing up and showing out!

Yes, King's dream and God's prophecy are being fulfilled. My life is an open book; I admit before I met Trotter nearly fifteen years ago and went into full ministry, I tried to take my situation in my own hands and made a mess out of it. Through divine intervention, God had his angels positioned in the right place at the right time to save me from total destruction and disaster.

The following story shows how His Glory saved my life, and afterwards, not even a soldier who was trained for duty to fight for our country could help me.

One day I decided to take a break at work; I only had fifteen minutes. I was in a hurry, so I ran across the street to beat the light. I saw that it was green but I ran anyway, because the approaching cars were far down the street. I thought I had plenty of time to make it; I slipped and fell to the street face down; my purse and money and credit cards went everywhere as my legs and arms hit the street. I turned and saw the cars in all three lanes still approaching; I tried to get up but both my legs were swollen at once, and I could not move. I had given up and felt hopeless; as I looked up all three lanes of traffic stopped suddenly, my face was on the street with my body and the front wheel of a car was inches from my face. I did not have time to get up. Yes, it was the enemy that tried to take me down so quickly and so fast, even the soldier who was watching it unfold from across the street couldn't handle the near death disaster on a moment's notice. After the cars stopped suddenly, the soldier who was watching from across the street ran over; she said she saw me fall but it happened so fast; if she had tried to grab me, the car would have hit her also. Nobody but God!

Doctor in the Hospital

Back in the eighties, when I was an Exchange manager, I was alone in my office; my employees had left for the day, and I needed God's supernatural strength when I was almost killed by an injury. I had been painting the baseboards getting ready for an inspection; I saw a large wooden pallet on a platform full of large glass sections that were to be installed in another building. I knew by the size of the pallet it would have been impossible for me to move it alone, so I got on my knees and attempted to paint behind them, which almost cost me my legs when the entire pallet fell down on my legs. I tried with my natural strength but they would not budge; since I was all-alone, I called on Jesus and got some supernatural strength from somewhere; His voice told me to take deep breaths, and his strength helped me lift the glass off my legs. I crawled up the steps, called my manager and the military police, and before I passed out; they told me it took five men to move the same pallet; when God intervened and rescued me, it only took me seconds to move it.

The doctor at the military hospital said my legs were too swollen, black, and bruised to operate; gangrene was starting to set in and they might have to cut the legs off. I began to believe in God's power; I begged them not to amputate; the doctor and the military officer couldn't understand where my strength came from to survive. After I came home, my legs made a full recovery as divine healing took place.

God intervened when my children's grandfather, Mr. Nelson, was in the hospital and the doctors had given up all hope; he was very ill. As he was laying there about to give up on himself, I said I had to get Tonya here right away from the Academy. Tonya had just gotten off an Air Force jet belonging to a general, and I drove as fast as I could to get her to what I thought was their last meeting. He must have heard us praying and held on for Tonya. While her dad was fighting in the war, we lived with him. He had another granddaughter and always treated her the same; however, Tonya was the only granddaughter of his bloodline; that day he had a glow on his face. God stepped in and saved him; he lived over ten years longer. My bishop was in the room next door visiting her sister, and she said God had the last word, and guess what? He did!

God once again moved in the hospital. The son of a friend

of ours was in a coma for five days. When I found out, they had almost given up on him; they had tubes everywhere, and no one could enter into the room, not even his stepfather (who raised him since birth). His mother called for me, crying. I prayed with her and told her to go back to the hospital room; she did, and all the tubes were out and her son was sitting up on the bed when she got back. He said he was hungry and hadn't realized he hadn't talked in five days.

That story reminded me of another supernatural miracle in the Bible: When Jesus cried after his friend had died: "Jesus wept." (John 11:35) "And when he thus had spoken, he cried with a loud voice, 'Lazarus, come forth.'" (John 11:43)

I myself had many brushes with death; once in the emergency room, when my blood pressure was up so high, the doctor gave me pills just to ease the pain, and I started calling Jesus' name and my pressure started to go down. He said all he could tell me was it was good that I knew the man. It's funny when I think about it: my daughter-in-law used "Jesus" for my grandson's middle name, since she is of Spanish descent.

I know the enemy wanted to take me out; since the love triangle didn't work, my body was attacked. Since my first book was published in 2001, it's been a struggle to get God's word out. I was even out of work for six months due to surgeries; no, I don't want to give Satan any Glory but I do my own typing, and the enemy tried to discourage me. I felt like giving up; there's a difference between riding in a car and traveling on a bike. It just wasn't happening; the motivation wasn't there when the pain from the nerve damage set in. It took a supernatural healing, but I was taught I still had to look up in order to receive His promises.

I then had two more surgeries on my hands. I was upset because writing on the computer was my life. God allowed me to come out of both surgeries; they frightened even me. Just before I went in to the first one, a test came back and the doctor said they found a spot on my lung. When I asked about it, for some unknown reason, it had dried up and gone away; he said the finding only delayed the surgery; he then said even though he couldn't explain how it dried up, the x-ray itself would always be a record of the damage and that something occurred. The same doctor told me that when he cut my stomach open, he found a bowel full of tumors but none of them were cancerous. There are many more supernatural interventions than these. God must be given the Glory.

Witnessing Domestic Violence: God's Miracle

Another time, I witnessed a supernatural miracle showing His protection. I took a friend to see his children. This was a few years before my husband and I began to have problems of our own. Phil was stationed in Germany with us on our second tour, and I would baby-sit their children. His wife was very nice to me. His brother George was my children's father's best friend

I was put in harm's way when Phil and I were standing on the front porch of his wife's apartment; within seconds, his wife's boyfriend came running out of the house and cut Phil's throat from one side to the next. I was standing beside him in total shock. All I can remember was my head began to spin; I did not know what to do next, because it happened so quickly. I saw Phil grab his neck; blood began shooting out all over the roof of my brand new car. I wanted to call the police; he said there was not enough time so I drove him to the hospital.

I tried to stay calm; I drove through every traffic light I saw as fast as I could, looking both ways and blowing my horn loudly as all traffic began to stop for me (I knew God was protecting me because the courage to save someone else came from a power much higher than me). Somehow, God allowed Phil to stay awake long enough for us to get to the hospital, where he passed out. When I got to the emergency room, my hands and feet began to shake uncontrollably and I began to scream as loud as I could. A man was taking a cigarette break outside of the hospital; he helped Phil into the hospital. I stayed for hours until they finished operating on him.

My husband was at work; my children's Uncle James was

home with our children, and never in our entire marriage had I stayed out at night. I called to tell James what was going on. My ex-husband could think whatever he wanted to because Phil was in the hospital fighting for his life, and I wasn't going to leave him. It happened so fast; I didn't have anyone's phone number with me.

I stayed in the waiting room until the doctor came out and said it had been touch and go but they saved him. The doctor told me a major vein had been cut; he could have died in moments but I had helped save his life. I give all the Glory to God because I had no idea where that hospital was; I was on the other side of town. God Himself kept my friend awake long enough to give me directions. Somehow, I was reliving the attacks in my past, including how it felt to be attacked (no one knew about some of the attacks, but the attacker, God, and me).

Later, I was the only witness at the trial. I didn't want to go to court, but Phil's attorney said they needed me, since there was no police report (he needed to get to the hospital fast; it all happened so quickly). My children's dad went with me for support (or maybe he wanted to hear for himself what really happened that dark day). My statement alone put Phil's wife's boyfriend in jail. I guess the judge saw the horror on my face and heard the pain in my voice. In my own situation, I would call the police when I was scared but I never pressed charges (until my husband's baby mother came into my life, and even then, I allowed them to go free because my children needed the financial support and I just wanted to get through the divorce).

Helping a Woman in Distress

I'm no stranger to domestic violence; one day PJ and I were riding down the street and saw that the girl in the next car was in distress. At every stoplight, she tried to open her car door while yelling for help. The man driving would pull her back in with his right hand, and when the wheels began to move again, he just started punching her while driving down the street; he must have thought she would not take a chance to jump out while the car was in motion.

I told PJ to follow that car. He did, and when they pulled over, she ran into a restaurant. I followed her; others had seen her but did not want to get involved. She had blood all over her clothes and told me her boyfriend was trying to kill her. I begged the manager to hide her in his kitchen. Just second later, the boyfriend ran in, looking for her. Everyone else was afraid; I wasn't because I had just called the police from my cell phone. I didn't want any attention (we had my grandson with us); I just wanted to do what was right, afterwards my son and I drove off.

The police found us in a shopping mall a few blocks away; they took my statement and home information and thanked me. They arrested the guy. Later, the girl called the number I had given to the restaurant owner and thanked me. She said she had told her boyfriend she was going to leave him, and he threatened to kill her. She then said all she knew to do was to bring attention to his car, but no one but me helped. I told her I had been a victim years ago myself, and I was just thankful she was fine. Again I give all the Glory to God. Yes, as you see, He is still the same God as back in the days of old, using His power to set the captives free.

Supernatural Intervention

I got my job in Germany through a touch from the Master's hand. I didn't even realize how blessed I was until I walked down the stairs and saw the application, reflecting God's Glory. I feel I was given the job by a power that intervened and interceded on my behalf; there were many others, who could have filled the position, but the manager called while we were on vacation in the United States and held the job for me; I ran his store. Many others were more qualified but I got the job. You see that was God's Glory in my life. I was in a foreign country, with a two-year associate's degree, and the job required a master's degree. That was God's favor shining on my life; the lady at the personnel office at the bank even told me I had been given the manager's job because of what I had accomplished in Germany. You see, someone might be in a battered woman's shelter; she may have two small children (like I did) and lost hope, looking for a sense of direction; she may not feel worthy or qualified to do a job. She may think to herself, why fill out the application? The odds are against me, but a little small voice call divine intervention tells her, "Yes, you can." This book is about His power, not mine. It tells how I received the job even when I was left to fend for myself, when the love of my life left me for another woman.

I soon realized the war was in my mind, not in a courtroom. Soon after I met Trotter and my ex fought me to take away my spousal support, he lost his post office job. You see God had blessed him to keep the job for ten years to support me. People understand God will bless you to be a blessing. The Bible speaks of stewardship over God's people. After I realized it was him and not the women who were robbing me of my peace, I was able to let go.

Every tear was the hurt, pain, and betrayal I felt; how could a husband of twenty-four years hold me down on the floor and allow me, the mother of his two children, to get beaten repeatedly, showing no mercy? All I could think was this is betrayal at its highest level. Whenever my ex-husband hit me in the past, I never cried, and I didn't cry on October 20 when the event first took; everything was all over when the officers arrived; they didn't know whom to arrest. I just made it easy on them; they didn't need any handcuffs for me, I just got into the police car myself. I broke my silence after I arrived at the station and cried for the first time; when I told my side of the story, I refused to show fear. Reliving the events of October 20, 1991, is hard on me. All I thought about was my promise to God. If he allowed me to get out of that small holding cell, I would serve Him until I die.

After I met Trotter, Ms. C, my worst nightmare, stopped harassing me. Trotter not only encouraged me to move on, he took me as his wife, he gave me his name, and his children became mine. Even before he married me, he took me to work, picked me up for lunch, and picked me up from work; he's done this for the last fourteen years. Trotter was determined; no one else would harm me. God was fulfilling a promise when He gave me Trotter: I asked for peace, and I got it with Trotter. I asked for a man who would not ever cheat; I got it with Trotter. I asked for someone who would always stand beside me, protect me, and keep me out of harm's way; I got it with Trotter. I asked for a man who would love my children as much as I do; I got it with Trotter. I asked for a man who would join me in the ministry so we could be of one accord; I got it with Trotter. Yes, God did fulfill His promise to me; Trotter was God sent.

When I tell my life story, it will be somewhere between hell and Glory! This intervention saved my life. Trotter and I needed each other; he needed help with his three teenage children, and I needed help with someone stalking me and making my life a living hell. It took me years to tell Trotter the full story; I did not want to scare him away. My brother told me Trotter was the one because he had been a Marine; there was something about Trotter that stood out; others would know just by looking at him not to bother him.

I attempted to write about God's supernatural miracles after they first happened; I found some of the old writings I had in the attic. You would not have understood them because they look like the writings of a mad man; most people don't understand, when you first go through a traumatic experience, it's very hard to sit down and get your thoughts together. I stopped thinking about what had been done to me and decided to help free others by allowing the Lord to use me. Then I began to write and let the words flow!

Modern-Day Miracles and Blessings

God reveals His promises just to show you He is the same God who set others free. When He began to intercede in my life and show divine favor and divine healing, I was set free from myself.

Yes, I was in captivity and didn't realize it, until God told Satan to let me go!

I was no longer bound; I no longer lived in a glass house or a prison with no bars. No longer did the devil have the keys to my heart, my dreams, and my home. God was a doctor in the hospital, a lawyer in the courtroom.

You can always recognize His power when it begins to shine. Anyone can write a check to pay the bills and get things done, but when there's no money in the bank, you need a bailout and begin to feel so alone, on the verge of suicide, needing tunnel vision just to see your way out of the storm. I've been there when only a supernatural power can say, "Come forth," and you hear it! That's God's Glory.

Chapter 16

Providing a Way of Escape

2007

"Intervening from on High"

Some say I'm a great woman of God, I say I'm serving a Great God.

So far you have read how my God revealed His promises to me. You read how He spoke to me and provided a way of escape and told me what to say to help my family and myself.

Just last night, I had a dream that blew my mind. I then woke up and began to type right away. I was with a friend in a small room that had become a war zone; my enemies were all around me. I was surrounded!

In my vision, I wore a headband and held weapons in both hands, with extra weapons on the side of the wall. I thought I was armed and dangerous.

The enemy then shot down my only friend, who was helping me. I was on my own. An angel came through the window while the bullets were flying back and forth. I could feel intervention and anointing all through the room. In the line of fire and heat of battle, I looked up, and the angel began to talk to me in the same voice that came to me in my dreams.

The angel asked me one question: "What is your escape route?"

I said I had a secret plan.

He said, "Show me."

I pointed to a window in the corner I thought my enemy didn't know about. I had a clear view to see him at a different angle.

I was going to use it to aim my gun in the right location to take my enemy out with a snapper shot. I was so excited; my weapon would be aimed directly at him and he didn't know about that small window. The angel then went over and threw a small rock in that window just to see if my plan was solid. Seconds after the rock went through the window; a blast of bullets overpowered the room.

The angel looked at me and said, "Was that your way of escape?"

The angel gave me some great advice: Never underestimate your opponent's next move, because they are watching you all the time.

He said, "If you had used it, you would have been destroyed and overpowered. Their weapons would have taken you down in seconds. Your enemy is just waiting for his opportunity to attack after you take your best shot. Your enemies were watching you all along. You see, while you were trying to outsmart and outthink him on your own without supernatural interception, the enemy's weapons immediately overtook the room."

There were bullet holes on every wall; the angel looked at me again and said, "Was that all you had? Now what's your next plan? I was rescued from the enemies camp when, I realized the battle was not mine and a voice immediately said stand still and see the salvation of the Lord. God divinely gave me another escape route through His word.

Ephesians 6:12
12 For we wrestle not against flesh and blood, but against principalities, against powers, against the rulers of the darkness of this world, against spiritual wickedness in high places.

When I look back over my life, I see God's miracles, divinely intervening. My bishop's name is Willie; let me tell you about another Willie God put in my life. Just last night, I was celebrating our church anniversary; lo and behold, who walks in the door but my good friend Willie Moody. I was typing the last few chapters of this book when a full revelation took form. He reminded me, a few years ago, when I started off, I needed my friend to help edit my book. He told me he was busy getting his master's degree. I went back to my desk. God began to reveal his full cycle of Glory to me.

I told Willie, "God chose you to help me edit the book I am working on."

Willie then said he had to obey God's instructions. He later handed me the finished project.

Then one day he told me the doctor just gave him some bad news. He had cancer.

I began to pray and reminded God how obedient Willie was. Three months later, he was cancer free! He said the doctor had never seen such a case; after treatment, he still had a full head of hair. We just wanted to give God the Glory! To others, it was just a church service; to us, it was how He showed His power years earlier.

I had to stop the car while driving down the road just to write what He said to type later. Yes, I waited to tell you about how His Glory unfolded; it's the mist after the storm. I no longer feel the pain of despair. All hurt is gone; what it took to get me to this point; you see most books leave out the piece of the puzzle that you really need to shine in your life; you always seem to leave with the book was good but something was missing!

This book talks about spiritual victory. I realized now I was on a divine mission. God led me supernaturally. He gave me a divine direction. He allowed me to escape the enemy's camp. Yes, God's voice speaking to me set me free. This book was about bad decisions and bad choices I made only to keep peace. I just was determined that he would take care of his children until they were old enough to take care of themselves; it almost worked until his last lover forced my hand. Job 16:20 says, "My friends scorn me: but mine eye poureth out tears unto God."

That's what my writings are all about; even after you go through the fire, you can still look victorious. Why wonder about a situation you can't control anyway? When my son was sixteen, he said, "We don't care anymore, do we?"

From that moment on, after my son noticed I was starting to give up, I got myself together. I just wasn't having that; I quickly got back on track. What is divine intervention? A voice from heaven stopping disaster, stopping destruction, stopping the breakup of marriages, stopping rebellious children, stopping the demonic takeover of churches, stopping you from losing your job. If you don't need God in those areas, you are blessed and my assignment with you is over; be blessed and tell others of His goodness. Again, if you were like me, struggling to find the light at the end of the tunnel, read on. It's the same situation, but this book shows a different way to solve the problem.

Years earlier, when my nightmare first started, I was going to church in Germany; my ex even started to get crazy and would come and sit in the back of the church, just to see if the children and I were really there.

After church, the pastor would tell me he saw him sitting in the back. When I was having problems with my ex and he was unfaithful on our last tour in Germany (and after the general denied his request to re-enlist with only five years to go), I asked God to give him his club manager's job back. The pastor called me to his side and gave me some advice; he said, "Every Sunday you pray for the same thing. Your husband is working at the Officer's Club, and maybe God doesn't want him there; maybe God had to take it away and get him away from that devil's den, but you are trying to tell God what to do." He said to start praying, "Let thy will be done."

I did, and he didn't get the job back, but instead he moved back to the United States. My ex-mother-in-law told me years later, after I divorced him, that he lived with his lover in one of our rental properties, without my knowledge, until I moved back to the States. I know that's why God Himself shut my ex down. I was still overseas with the children praying for him but God was watching him disrespect me. Your enemies seem to trample all over you; even your closest friend doesn't understand your journey. After

I gained strength, righteous wings began to carry me to safety. God's voice will give you direction, insight, and ways to overthrow your enemies.

You should have learned before this chapter, your enemies couldn't overpower you or stop your dreams. Hopefully, you have discovered the inner strength you didn't know you had. Know that your enemies might knock you down, but they can't knock you out; a supernatural power is watching! After hearing God's voice, I stopped worrying about anything; yes, I stopped worrying! I just tell my enemies, "You might think you are bigger and stronger than me, but when it comes to defeating them, I know a man that can!"

This morning, my grandson Daivon Nelson said he wanted to be a writer. I told him he could be whatever he wants to be. I then smiled and said to myself; *Look at the next generation of warriors*.

Believe you have more power than your adversaries; believe that no devil in hell can overpower your thoughts. We can't be made in His image and act like the devil child; sorry, light and darkness can't deal in the same place. You can't look like an angel and act like a devil! To get blessings, you must be worthy of the inheritance. This book has revealed the secret of the royal priesthood. Attacks and abuse are real; turn on the TV or the radio; read your newspaper; it's time to take a stand for peace. Yes, God speaks of love but He also speaks of treating your brother and sister right. When I was young, I was told, "Do unto others as you would have them do unto you." Help me stop the cycle of deceit and violence by sharing what you read to someone you know is going through the same thing.

Chapter 17

A Warrior's Mentality

2008

"Lose that Slavery Mentality"

In order to be blessed we must first lose that slavery mentality; having low self-esteem is the opposite of being a warrior. No matter what race you are, if you have no sense of direction, are unstable and double minded, and have no ambition, how can God use you if you are afraid to advance forward for a cause you believe in? By working hard and becoming successful in anything you set your mind to do. It's time to become a hero in your child's eyes; begin to put the broken pieces backs together; break away from drama. Warriors advance forward, looking danger in the eye, taking no prisoners, and making plans to get away from an abusive relationship. Warriors can see the victory line before it appears; through faith, warriors feel and smell the success of victory before it happens. Warriors think about their escape while their body is still bound; their mind is always clear to plan an escape from their abuser; warriors have mastered how to smile when they feel like crying. Warriors seize the moment to help themselves and others before the opportunity comes. These are qualities and traits only a warrior can possess.

The enemy can use you without you even realizing it; you react so quickly, without thinking. This book was to make you think about it before it happens; mothers, train your children from birth to respect others and teach them not to raise their hands up against the very ones who love them; there are no excuses. Nothing can justify putting anyone in harm's way. You can be in control, be determined, be defiant by not giving in, be willing to stand and talk back to the enemy when he talks to you; it takes more courage not to raise your hand up and bring it down on your victim. Winners take on fear of the unknown, conquer lions, and bring down giants; does this remind you of someone? Yes, David knew that he just had to follow God's instructions to free his people.

> David said moreover, "The LORD that delivered me out of the paw of the lion, and out of the paw of the bear, he will deliver me out of the hand of this Philistine." And Saul said unto David, "Go, and the LORD be with thee." (1 Samuel 17:37)

Winners Do What Losers Will Never Do!

In the past, I almost gave up writing, but I decided to work overtime on my job to get my books out. I know my warrior's mentality has gotten me this far, and favor played a big part. I also found out if others had helped me in the past, they would have gotten the Glory; now that my work is established, God got the Glory!

I had to make a move so God could intercede to touch everything I put my hands on. I know everything is in God's appointed time

If a man die, shall he live again? All the days of my appointed time will I wait, till my change come." (Job 14:14)

That's why I will never give up trying to get my story to the ones who really need to hear it, even after I'm gone (I'm hoping someone will pick up the torch and run with it). Some soldiers stop and look back to see who's following them, which makes them lose ground. Warriors just keep running because they know they are blessed and highly favored. They know it by the way others look at them, the way others believe in them. Warriors don't hold onto the past because they know they have been delivered. They know if they don't release their minds to new and uncharted territory, they will stay in bondage. Warriors are chosen out of their mother's womb; man gives them a piece of paper. Walk and act just like them; warriors are not dying; they just keep multiplying. My hairdresser said Daivon was a chosen warrior; she said one day he will be a lawyer, at that time my grandson was only four years old; she said he likes to talk and when he walks in the room, he gets everybody's attention.

My assignment as a warrior is to help position workers on the battlefield who have been uprooted when the enemy tricked and beat them down; yes, my role is to restore the war-torn soldier, the ones who gave up, didn't think they had enough power to give them hope. Warriors are rewarded for their long-suffering. God told me a long time ago He would speak through me, and His people would receive me.

In order to have that diehard attitude to be set free, you must begin to believe in yourself, have the ability to survive, and have a desire to overcome the flesh and stay in the spirit at all times, even when you are provoked.

Warriors know how to protect themselves and keep others out of harm's way. Most importantly, you must possess the power to bring down the giants of oppression and despair in the lives of others. A warrior recognizes the enemy's strategy along with his plans and operation. A sign of strength is rebuilding and restoring hope!

Winners Don't Quit! The jaws of victory are strong. I tried to bring you forward with my writings, but it's up to you to move forward in the battlefield of your mind; when you begin to mentally win, I know you have thought about it, but we first think victory before we begin to walk into it. Most soldiers are trained to say, "Go! Go! Go!" No room to think, just move forward in battle.

Even if you lose a loved one, tell that enemy, "You might have taken my smile but you will never take my joy!" After the enemy came in and stole my first marriage, I developed a higher tolerance level. Getting into God's purpose wasn't easy; I had to get my mind right (first, stop blaming others). I quickly found out my goal and my purpose: being free to develop crazy faith. Sometimes we have to gain humility to fulfill His purpose. You know it was God who restored Glory and hope; God, not Satan. If you are at a light and a robber wants to force himself into your car, hit the gas; warriors are survivors, not ones to give into an enemy that means them no good. If the enemy takes your dream, it's because you gave it to him.

Endurance builds patience; suffering builds compassion and sensitivity. I was tired of sitting back and doing nothing. That's why I decided to get this labor of love together. I realized it was time to give back to the God who gave so much to me. When you hit rock bottom and the world has beaten you up, the first step to freedom is learning to believe in yourself. I had to learn to put my emotions under subjection to my spirit man. I knew in order to fulfill my children's dreams; I had to empower my thoughts with ways to escape the traps set by my adversaries. The healing process was to repair and restore broken dreams. It really works; they can't argue by themselves for a long period of time. Sometimes not doing anything at all confuses your enemy. You can program your mind for good or evil; program peace gives you peace, program love gives you love, program hate breaths hate. Just because you have a history of domestic violence doesn't mean you can't change; you have the power to get out of your situation. If you think you are down, you will be; if you think your abuser has power over you, he does. It's time to turn your weakness to bravery. You hold the key; stop letting the robber and thief overpower you in your own home.

Did you think your spouse would betray you when you said, "I do"? Did you think that beautiful baby would grow up and curse you? Did you think after giving your all, your church members would vote you out the door for a younger pastor? Did you think your dream job you went to school for and fought so hard to get would make you lose sleep and make you think about everything but going to work? If all your answers are no, then stop putting others down; I never thought I would lose it all; however, through divine intervention, I got it all back and more. To overcome, you must have a warrior's mentality, meaning stand and deal with the problem, stop looking for someone else to solve it for you, stop looking for a man to fix your problem. Stop thinking selling drugs or stealing is your way out; it's your way into something that started out as an answer but became a short-term fix and took you places you wouldn't want your worst enemy to go. There's nothing wrong in getting rich quick, just do it the right way: go to school, work hard, treat others fairly when you do make it to the top. Warriors win, losers lose their self-respect; you have no outside friends when they lock you up; worse still is when you lock yourself up in a prison with no bars! I will take nothing for my freedom.

Yes, man is trying to break you, but every day, make sure you take some of that power back! Your destiny will not be determined by your past; yes, your past was challenging but you possess the power to change your life.

Say to yourself, my season of pain is over; God has written a new chapter in my life! At times, I felt so alone I felt God had turned His back on me.

Don't let anyone make you feel guilty for trying to keep your family together; just know how to leave if you feel endangered. When they say you are wrong; just lift your head up and say I was wronged!

A weak-minded soldier will fall; you must renew your thinking. Say to yourself, *I was knocked down but my enemies can't knock me out!* Don't self-destruct; take your life back by taking the Kingdom by force. Yes, I hear your cries; I see your faces in my dreams and wake up with nightmares. Whatever you do, never go into retreat, God can't use a weak soldier. Stop hiding; go tell someone if your spouse hit or disrespected you; tell someone close to you: his mom, the pastor, his brother, and ask him to stay for a while and talk about it, if necessary call the authorities. Yes, he will be mad but I'd rather him be mad for a moment than live in fear. In some cases it makes a difference if the cover is pulled off the wolf the pastor thought was a sheep; you stay out of it; let the pastor and your spouse do all the talking unless you are asked something, because you still have to live there after the pastor leaves. The key to enduring: you must motivate yourself, you must have the mind-set you can do it safely! Yes, they talk about you but live your dream anyway. Most of my greatest achievements come from someone telling me I couldn't do it. Prove the haters wrong! Do not bow down to them in defeat. I found out if two people love each other, no devil in hell can break them up; what has always kept me faithful was knowing I didn't make a vow to a man; he might let me down and that requires revenge, but I made a vow to the God that has been there for me. I also kept in mind that I would never jeopardize what I already had. A warrior and hero both endure but a warrior enhances what they have. Add a kind word to get your point across. God told me the reason I came out in my right mind and didn't lose faith was because I trusted in Him and stood strong; that's why I can easily say, "Daughters, be strong." My ministry is different; I live what I preach. Anyone can give you a word but his or her house is all messed up.

I have spoken about my assignment all through this book. One thing you must understand: the devil was given an assignment to bring you down by any means necessary. I was given a gift money can't buy: peace. Remember, Jesus Himself was tested! He gave his enemy the word. He responded with, "It is written." That's why I write: it gives me comfort. I feel so strongly about this book. I thought I had it all in Germany, but when all hell broke loose in my home years ago, I needed His protection, and He delivered and saved me from the hands of my enemies. I turned my life around, stopped running from my calling, a gift from my mother's womb as she passed away the same day I was born. When others try to cut your dreams short, they will leave you alone when they realize they are no matches for divine intervention. Your dreams are promises you haven't even begun to live yet.

You are defeated when you entertain enemies; the hedge around you will keep you out of harm's way! Put your war clothes on; never fight half dressed; get ready for battle. Tell the devil he's evicted; he doesn't pay rent. So many people have asked me what my secret is. I simply say I learned to focus on what I have more than what I don't have. I will end this chapter with some encouraging words: "Daughters and sons, stay strong. Yesterday was your challenge; today is your assignment; tomorrow is your victory."

I know I could never have gone through the pages of my life without divine intervention.

Chapter 18

Conclusion

2009
"Eighteen Years Later"

You have read my life story, from 1953 to 2009.

I revealed it in full detail to help others. I became your spiritual adviser by writing this book. I confirmed to my son-in-law Malik the assignment I was given he said that my gift was special when I expressed to him the different ways God had interceded in my children and my life with a hedge of protection. God's voice kept us out of harm's way after the enemy attacked my home on October 20, 1991. You have read my struggles; my faith in myself was the driving force that kept me sane. I did my best to keep my marriage together but I still went through abuse and betrayal. (As my Bible says, give a bill of divorce in case of adultery.) My ministry and blessings were around the corner and I didn't even know it!

Before I went into the ministry, my mind was in disarray. My thoughts were jarred, and I asked myself, *Why me, God?* I grew up in the church but didn't know the power of God, and when faced with attacks, I wondered what happened. I had done all I knew to be a good mother and wife, and my world was destroyed. I started obeying God's instructions and stopped taking matters in my own hands; I started listening and, for the first time, allowing His voice to intervene with divine instructions. "I will instruct thee and teach thee in the way which thou shalt go: I will guide thee with mine eye." (Psalm 32:8)

I found out that listening provided a way of escape, being set free from every trap, test, circumstance my enemies had set up for my demise. As a former victim, I want you to know the first step to being healed is to stop blaming yourself.

You did nothing wrong. It's a sickness; it is a disease; it's a generational curse, and the abuser is being used (sometimes they are not even aware of it unless you bring it to their attention). You must stop thinking the other woman had the upper hand by being better looking, being smaller, or having more intelligence. In the past, I would go to work with my head up, with my suit on, always trying to look my best in my heels; I was well groomed no matter what happened at home.

It was divine intervention: I worked and retired at the same bank where I had sat on the sidewalk to wait for the bus when I was in high school; I wished that when I grew up, I could wear suits and high heels like those white ladies (back in the sixties, black managers were unheard of at a bank). Years later, I couldn't fool my supervisor at the bank; I will never forget she gave me a picture of a lady's arm holding a can with some pencils with a raggedy torn sweater; to my surprise the arm was white, letting me know even though I made it to the top of my dream world and the corporate ladder, I still had to pass the world of change and equality in a man's world that had no color; we were all treated badly.

The picture said "Tough Times Don't Last But Tough People Do." My boss saw bruises on my arms and legs, which was one of the reasons she gave me the picture along with a phone number to a therapist; this was the beginning of my end; my therapist made me think when she said I must love my ex more than myself because I allowed him to hurt me. She said when he hurt me; I had a low self-esteem and needed to believe more in myself. She made me realize I had a good job and two beautiful children. I told her I never wanted to be on government assistance; that's why I worked so hard to get to the top. She then said, "So why not take advantage of the blessing and let the abuser go?" And I did.

I dedicate this chapter to my former boss, Janice Wilson;

I kept her picture on the same wall with my family pictures. I always loved and respected her because she never saw color, just someone in need; she would invite me to some events at her home; I remember once I rang the door bell and her son came to the door; he said, "You must have the wrong house," but she came behind him and said, "No, she was invited; let her in."

It seems the devil was on my heels because while I was getting help for my marriage, he must have told his lover because that's when she decided to get pregnant to add salt to the wound. She called me and told me she was pregnant; I couldn't wait until my next visit to the therapist to ask her what she thought. I was waiting for a response (she always gave me something long), but this time was different. She only said, "I think you already know the answer."

I spoke to my attorney and that was my last visit; I decided to close the last chapter of the drama myself. I came out of bondage by getting my mind out of bondage first! I filed for divorce for the first time.

Yes, you went through the pages of my life; some of you read straight through, some flipped pages; however, you did it. I hope you learned something to help you endure. I'm hoping to help put an end to domestic violence. I didn't write my life story for fame or notoriety; it took me years to come to grips and put the full story into print. I wanted to leave a legacy with the next generation to let them know the mission will live on. The efforts will never die, and someone will always be handed the torch to carry and encourage others, as my vision to set the captives free stays alive in this nation. I wanted this book to show all of God's Glory and to show what an awesome God He really is.

My assignment is to tell you that you can overcome also; if you have to read this book three times, do it! So many women are looking for answers; they have been through so much pain and abuse, no longer is the label given to just the poor, but the rich and famous have taken over the spotlight. As I wrote, no one knew I was a victim; that's why it's hard to recognize one unless you begin to listen as victims reveal their darkest secret.

Victims of Abuse

Victims say, "You don't know what I've been through"; they begin to just give up on themselves. They might say they don't care to talk to any minister; they just want to give up, just like I almost did. They think, "I don't want to read your book or listen to you preach." Why? Too many preachers have given religion a bad name by not practicing what they preach. I just want to encourage them by saying, "Yes, I do know how you feel; yes, I've been there and felt your pain and cried your tears in the midnight hours; I experienced your fears of uncertainty and lived through the abusive years!"

It was hurtful to write a tell-all book; I admit I liked hiding behind my poems and short stories. After listening to the media, I knew I had answers to questions victims were asking after years of abuse. Those who have never been in the fire could never tell you how it feels to be burned. If I never felt pain, how could I tell you about hurt? If I had never been betrayed, how could I tell you how to trust in someone else? The smile tells my enemies they don't have any idea that they are messing with God's child!

My book tells how a supernatural power interceded and took over my life. My family and fans call all the time to get spiritual guidance. Throughout my book, I told you of God's mercy and grace and how He saved and delivered me.

While I was going through my abuse, my tears were never seen; my cries were never heard. I hid my dark secret to make sure nothing would blemish the appearance of what I had fought so hard to keep a secret.

We were the model family for others but they couldn't see behind the closed doors.

God showed His Glory when He gave me another family after I married Trotter: stepchildren and grandchildren, the love of church families, and a wonderful mother-in-law who anyone would envy; she is God's gift to me. I love you, Francela Trotter! Your son was and is my bridge over troubled waters.

Behind the Glory is a story. God had blessed me beyond what I had prayed for. He had given me the desires of my heart. Eighteen years later, this is the eighteenth chapter of my book; I have relived my life story in detail, with the absence of pain at the end showing His Glory! I wrote one chapter for each year that followed the attack.

When everything first happened, all I wanted to do was crawl in a corner and hide; my perfect world wasn't so perfect after all. This chapter is to show how God intervened to show his Glory. Sometimes God puts us through trials just to see if we trust him, not money. Money is conditional; God's love is unconditional. My mother passed at birth; however, I never made any excuses; I went to school, went to college, did well on jobs, and taught my children to do the same. That's why it hurt so badly when the one I trusted and loved betrayed me. I began to forgive him when I realized he was being used by the devil; I know God would never hurt me so bad. I decided to go on with my life and live for God. I want to help others understand that they must stop blaming themselves. A cheater is just that: a cheater. If he betrays you, he'll usually betray someone else. Just like he smooth-talked you, he smooth-talked someone else into believing they were the best thing that ever happened to him.

You will always fall into that trap of deception and the web of deceit until you realize loving yourself is more important than holding on to broken dreams and living in denial and a false sense of security. My own son said, "Mom, you didn't do anything wrong, your only crime against Dad was you were just too nice, and he took advantage of it."

Their lust drives them wild, causes them to abandon you when you need them the most; their lover needs them more until you leave them and the vicious cycle goes around again! Their loyalty to your vows is gone; they blame you for their infidelity. On special occasions, your partner leaves when the guests arrive. They all bring back memories of sorrow when they find excuses to not be there: Christmas, Thanksgiving, and birthdays—they choose to be at their lover's house. Abusers, you know the game; it's played well. Your lover thinks you are home with your family; that's why she can't call and check up on you, giving you more time to be with another lover. They better not say anything when you return; you will punch them, hit them in the face, spit and kick and knock them down to the floor; they are too afraid to scream too loud because a neighbor might hear and call the police, who would take away the bread winner, which cuts off the money supply. You have read how God shut up all the lying tongues that falsely accused me. The violence stopped; He gave me an elder for a husband. He showed me awesome favor.

He gave me beautiful grandchildren and favor you can't buy, you can't steal, you can't win; you must earn it. Yes, I was a wounded and broken soldier, but God needed someone who would not throw a pity party but would stand and fight. I've been attacked in all areas; I've been beat down and spit on; glass cups and plates have hit my head and caused damage to my legs, arms, and body; I was bruised and swollen many times; as if hurting my body wasn't good enough, he destroyed my clothes, cut up my passport and ID, and broke things in the house just to terrify me. After cutting up my clothes, he would place them in a pile just to instill fear in me. I've been lied to and talked about by his many lovers; yes, I was an unlikely soldier, one of the chosen ones to lead God's people. I still carry the battle scars after the wounds have healed. After eighteen years on this eighteenth chapter, I finally found the courage to write about what happened that dark day in October 1991.

God took this broken person and put all the pieces back together again.

My son said I kept him going when he would remember the saying "blessed and highly favored." I've left the past behind me now that I revealed the pain, which was healing to me; also, you have read of my history of pain but you must never forget the history of my deliverance, which outweighs the pain. To defeat the enemy, we must study the nature of the beast. You have read the pages of my life; hold on to your dream, it will take you through. You must have tunnel vision to see your way out of darkness.

I'm hoping my writings will make a difference in your life. Always remember, all victims have a story. Their names might not be well known or in the history books; they might not drive fine cars or live in fine homes or know famous people; those are the ones in shelters, whose spirits are broken. They are ones with a story but nobody wanted to listen to them. I want to be there for them.

Our founding fathers stood for our freedom and our religious beliefs; Mr. Benjamin Rush was one of them. The war and battlefield are in our streets and backyards; it seems we can't agree on anything. That's why the streets are killing more than the wars, and they are still killing each other after they are locked up. No one has any answers, just going from generation to generation with hate and no answers. When the hurricane hit New Orleans a few years ago, the line for ice and food didn't have one section for colored and one section for whites; there was not one line for rich and another one for poor.

It ended when his lover testified in court how they gave their child our family name; the judge then found him guilty of adultery beyond the shadow of a doubt; it is on my final decree for all to see. "Thou shalt not commit adultery." (Exodus 20:14) As I said, there is a story behind the Glory!

God's Glory: My Children's Weddings

Let's talk about God's Glory after I went into the enemy's camp and took my joy and peace back! My daughter is very happy; she got married five years ago, and it was a dream wedding; she and her husband rode in a Rolls Royce. My ex brought his new wife; when it was time to take pictures, I noticed she was still upstairs. I asked her to come down and take pictures with the family; she said, "Are you sure?" I said yes (she had nothing to do with our breakup).

My son's bride told me about their wedding a few months in advance, and I panicked, thinking, *So much to do, and so little time*. But it all went well. The wedding was huge. The reception at the Officer's Club was my gift to my son.

The moment that stood out in my mind was when my future daughter-in-law and I went to reserve the room on base for the reception. When I saw a picture of the manager's family on his desk, I smiled and told him he had a lovely family; however, it brought back memories of sadder times. I told the manager that it always saddened me when my ex was managing the Officer's Club and I begged him to put a picture of our family on his desk, and he always refused.

Just before we signed the contract for the reception, the manager said to wait. We both looked at each other and then he said, "I can give you the ballroom."

I said that the ballroom, including the food, would cost in the thousands; he said he knew. He added, "My ballroom reservations are always full; it is impossible to schedule anything less than three months in advance. Most people sign up a year in advance, but for some reason, that date—April 12—is vacant; it is the only weekend open for that year, and since your son's picture wasn't on his father's desk, I'll give you the ballroom!"

His new bride was very happy. I know his wedding was blessed because I saw signs and wonders.

That was the same date that Trotter went into the Marine Corps. When my son got married, the lady who made his wedding cake had the same name as the woman who broke my marriage up. But this Ms. C gave me a good feeling.

Only God could have intervened and turned that situation around.

Were these modern-day miracles or divine interventions?

In the past, the devil tried to curse me by making me feel broken; I was told my children's half brother was born on my father-in-law's birthday; with 365 days in a year, what are the chances of that happening? An evil sign turned around for God's Glory because now I know it was all in God's plan for me to help heal others who are brokenhearted. Yes, at the time I had a divine purpose and didn't know it. I was chosen to do good work.

"God also bearing them witness, both with signs and wonders, and with divers miracles, and gifts." (Hebrews 2:4)

My ex and his new wife were also there at my son's wedding, but did not attend the reception. Again I went over and greeted her and thanked her for coming, just as I did for my daughter's wedding, because again she had nothing to do with the breakup (he started dating her after our divorce). I had gone on with my life; I had a new family that loved me dearly and I love them as well. Everyone thought it would rain that day, but there was another intervention (God's hand was all over that day). It was an outdoor wedding, and God held the rain until the cameraman announced, "This is the last shot." When the DJ read the program, my children's father wasn't there. Yes, he came to the wedding but didn't show up for the reception; it seemed he still had commitment issues. His table was reserved; I even put him and his wife on the program, but he didn't show up.

When the cameraman took the shot of Mom and Dad, at the next table his chair was empty, with only a Reserved sign in front of their seats. No one knows why. Was it because I seemed so happy or was it because Trotter's family had come from out of town to show support? His sisters and their husbands were at the table representing him. I saw him once in a store after my daughter's wedding years earlier; however, because of how I felt he disappointed me by not showing up at the reception, I haven't spoken to him or seen him since PJ's wedding on April 12, 2008; there was no excuse for that. My husband Trotter is a man after God's own heart; he said I could still speak to him on the phone, but I chose not too. I'll just keep him in prayer.

Since then, he has tried to make up for it by helping my son to do some remodeling around his house. He's around but it's always on his terms; anyone—I mean anyone—who calls his house has to leave a message. I believe it's because he had a child by a crazy woman who made his life a nightmare.

God's Glory began to shine in my life; after my children left home, I began to go on book signings and sold my books on Web sites and in bookstores, and provided them to libraries. I went into the local library a few years ago and asked for one of my books; they asked whom the author was and I said, "Henrietta Trotter." Later on in the week, my grandson and I went into Barnes & Noble in the mall and I picked up a hardback copy of one of my books. My grandson said, "We are famous, aren't we?"

I know it was God because before I went though my hell on earth, I wasn't thinking of writing. Just look at God's Glory. Once I did a signing in Florida at one of the largest churches in that area; as we hit the state line on our way into town, I heard the announcement on the radio that an author by the name of Henrietta Trotter was coming to town. The timing was great; I also picked up a local newspaper and there I was. Trotter has always been very supportive.

The true answer is written within yourself when you realize you have power!

Even if you never believed in God, something has to come over you after reading my life story; something supernatural took place, something intervened and made a change, something made a difference so that my enemies fell and fell hard. No one has a right to put his or her hands on anyone; help me stop domestic violence. I've always said when I was working; I've never been in a popularity contest. It's not about me, it's about what I represent! Living in His image, a door of favor began to open in my life, one door after another.

Before I found God again, I wanted to give up; all hope was gone. I began to ask, "Where were you, God?" God's voice intervened and said, "I was there all the time, you left me; I didn't leave you." He then said, "I just wanted to know if I could trust you with my inheritance."

One day on my way to work, the visions and dreams began to come as I was driving down the street. I then began to get flashbacks showing more blessings than I had room to receive. I began to get flashbacks, one right behind the other, thinking of God's divine interventions!

I drove down the same road I had driven for twenty-four years;

an eerie, strange feeling came over me as I began to get awesome visions; it was like something out of an old movie; it was as if I was put in a trance. Songs came on the radio; the flashbacks came of all the hell he put me through, one after another.

- I drove past the library; a voice said, "Look to the left; your books are in all the local libraries."
- I drove past the mall and began to see myself at book signings.
- I drove farther and passed some new homes; it reminded me of how my home was once in foreclosure but God intervened, had my bank take it over, and showed me the paid-in-full stamp on the deed.
- I drove farther and passed a graveyard. I could have been there.
- I passed my lawyer's office; I saw myself sitting outside his door.
- My hands began to shake at the wheel; I saw the courthouse, which is on the same street as my job.
- I passed the tall building that seemed so cold after being freed of all the many charges I was falsely accused of.

Flashbacks from the Past

During the divorce hearings, which lasted three years, I took a second look; I had to pull over to the side of the road because my feet and hands began to shake more.

I was passing the same courthouse and jail; my lunch had been taken away. The next day I was released but I will never forget that day I was held on false charges! My picture was taken; I was fingerprinted, thrown in a cell like a nameless person, and given prison clothes to wear for the trial the next day.

- I was denied the legal right to talk to the magistrate.
- I was put in a cell and denied bail.

- I remember the sound of the prison doors when a new inmate came in.
- The smell of those hard-boiled eggs will haunt me until the day I die.

I get some relief when the thoughts of God's Glory set in; I saw the two guards running over to me after the judge dismissed all charges, and they hugged me and gave me words of encouragement, which helped me endure what most people would have lost their minds over, since I had already been through so much in Germany and Fort Story with other women.

That next morning, after I had a dream and began to speak to my husband while I was sitting on the side of the bed combing my hair. I then went downstairs and took a shower, where most of my writings came from; all kinds of flashback came to me. The voice said, "It was exactly eighteen years from today's date, October 20, 1991, that you were attacked by a woman who wanted your husband after she gave birth to his child."

What brought chills down my spine was realizing my daughter was born October 18 (think about it, eighteen years ago today, my daughter was born on the eighteenth). I could see the steam from the shower going up in the air; it was if it was a sign that the later rain would be greater than the first, meaning after I allowed God to order my footsteps and use me to help others.

The past is finally behind me, and my blessings in my ministry will overflow, I just know it!

Then I Remembered His Glory!

Later that day, I remembered how He touched my life, beginning with how He gave favor to my daughter. Her school counselor had told her to pick another career when she said she wanted to be an officer, and she received her master's in law and graduated from the Air Force Academy. My son was set up but all charges were dropped and now he is making more than me working at the shipyard, and God dropped the charges from my stepson's case. God put my books in libraries, bookstores, and newspapers; He helped me publish books and CDs; I am on all major Web sites, and I have TV commercials, a radio ministry, and a nursing home ministry; and I am a guest/motivational speaker licensed to perform weddings in the State of Virginia.

I pressed on to a higher calling and refused to let my setbacks determine my future.

You are defeated when you entertain your enemy's thoughts and give in to the enemy's tricks. Just yesterday my sister-in-law, Valerie Trotter, and I spent the day together; for some odd reason, she asked me questions that were never asked before. I've known her fifteen years and she didn't know about the things I wrote in this book. I have always been a private person, and I know now writing this book was a healing process for me. As I began answering her questions, as we were riding down the street together, I realized I finally found closure. Yes, in the past I wrote but for the first time someone in Trotter's family asked me questions.

Since she was driving, I asked her to turn the corner; without question she honored my request. I showed her a large Victorian-style house on the waterfront and told her that used to be one of my rentals; I owned it for eight years. It's funny because just yesterday I showed Trotter some other houses we used to rent out when I was a landlady. I also told her how the enemy tried to steal my land, which my children's grandmother signed the deed in her own handwriting. This chapter brings the words "Touch not my anointed" alive. God and the judge said, "Not so."

I told her how I was able to go into the attic just last week and clean out my ex-husband's things he left behind. I told her after eighteen years I gave my son PJ trophies and plaques and awards his dad received while he was in the military to give to his father. My son said at first his dad started to complain that I kept them for so long, but in a moment of silence he grabbed them and my son said he could tell it made his day.

My story tells you how God will intercede and give you a way of escape. I know I could have never gone through the pages of my life without divine intervention. That's the reason I'm writing; on the last few pages of this book, *Behind the Glory* is a story.

Never forget, your blessings are around the corner. It takes courage to chase a God-size dream. Victory depends on your disposition to make a change yourself.

We must oppose or resist the influence of those who show a contemptuous disregard of authority. So many authors write about what they went through; I was told to resist but no one ever told me how to resist. I needed some clearly defined directions. When your enemy comes against you, just began to walk in your blessing. Alternately, abusers must want to change unacceptable behavior themselves. When you see signs, seek help or run! You might laugh and say, "Who does she think she is?" Others have written books on abuse in the home, and the media is still having a field day. I say others have fought wars and lost. The enemy destroyed my home, but couldn't take my dreams or break my spirit. After leaning upon faith, I soon saw a beacon light: it's the shore.

God throws the last blow.

I thought my story would end with Trotter and myself riding off on our Harley-Davidson in the sunset.

I also thought it would end with the pain of me riding in a police car, when my trouble first began in October 1991. Or I thought it would end with Trotter and myself riding through the tunnel as a long line of family and friends lined up in front of my house, following us to my son's wedding.

The puzzle and her innocent child (and my grandson), which is her son's nephew, were locked into a web of deception. My grandson is eleven years old; he only understands he loves his uncle and his uncle loves him.

A mixture of hate and love consumes my entire story; the children represent purity, which reveals the moral to the story must be the ending; however, it was a wakeup call to me (a fact based on reality); just to test it out, I told the story to my dental assistant (who I've known for years); she really liked it. She asked, "What movie was that?" I said it was a true story; I then told her the ending wasn't made up; it was as real as the book itself. She said, "No way, get out of here; are you for real?" I said yes, it was my story.

PJ told me he has just paid off his second truck; I was so proud of him. He then said his dad asked him to bring his brother home before his brother went into the military. I immediately thought, *This is not the way this story was supposed to end*. I never thought in a million years that PJ would be driving his Navigator, which I helped him get for his own happiness, would have his brother in it. I almost lost my mind at the very thought of my son being anywhere near the same house where I was attacked eighteen years ago, where PJ witnessed his own father walk out of that same house eighteen years ago. He was only sixteen years old then; feeling helpless, he only said, "Mom, let's go home," as his father left the scene.

Eighteen years later, PJ took his eighteen-year-old brother home to that same house. I had chills down my back just thinking about him being anywhere near that home wrecker's house. I could only tell this story after healing took place. That day, all I could think of was, could hell be worse? Yes, in the end I began to have positive thoughts to help others. They say time heals all wounds. I know now my children's brother was just an ignorant victim of a love triangle, in a family where his name was always blotted out of the family album; only very close family even know his name. It reminded me of Sarah and the bondwoman in the Bible; she just had to go away but the son was still Sarah's son's brother.

The only question I asked was, did his mother come to the door?

My son said he didn't see her (his brother had his own key). I didn't ask any more questions.

The story ends with my son PJ driving his brother home. His brother smiled while he was waving good-bye to my son as he drove away.

This morning, a divine voice came to me and said, "In the past, you saw what you wanted to see and didn't see what you didn't want to see." I wrote these words of hope to encourage others. Help me break the cycle of domestic abuse forever.

The morale to this story: "Hate don't love and love don't hate." Have you read my #1 best seller yet? There will be a test!

Peace.